For Kathy and [illegible]

from Dad

Languages in Conflict

Languages in Conflict

Linguistic Acculturation on the Great Plains

EDITED BY PAUL SCHACH

Published by the
UNIVERSITY OF NEBRASKA PRESS • Lincoln and London
for the
CENTER FOR GREAT PLAINS STUDIES University of Nebraska–Lincoln

Library of Congress Cataloging in Publication Data
Main entry under title:

Languages in conflict.

1. Languages in contact—Great Plains—Addresses, essays, lectures. 2. Language and culture—Addresses, essays, lectures. I. Schach, Paul. II. University of Nebraska—Lincoln. Center for Great Plains Studies.
P130.52.U5L3 401′.9 80–12710
ISBN 0–8032–2106–1

Manufactured in the United States of America

Contents

Introduction

PAUL SCHACH

This book, which is the first in a planned series of studies dealing with ethnic cultures on the Great Plains, includes investigations of one native American tongue, three Scandinavian languages, Czech, Spanish, and four dialects of German. Most of the languages and dialects treated here are moribund; they are doomed to extinction early in the coming century, as are most other native and immigrant tongues still spoken in the Great Plains states. In a sense the research on which these papers are based is part of a last-minute salvage action designed to preserve for posterity as much as possible of the linguistic richness and variety that once characterized the Great Plains from Manitoba to Texas. Field work with bilinguals in this area will soon be a thing of the past, but the records that have been made—and will continue to be made as long as possible—will provide future generations of linguists, humanists, and social scientists with challenging materials to analyze and evaluate.

As the title of the book indicates, major emphasis is on the process of linguistic acculturation, which in turn elucidates and reflects the social assimilation of the various ethnic groups. Immigrants to the Great Plains usually tried to settle among people of their own language or dialect. Under such circumstances, the adult settlers remained monolingual or at best acquired a smattering of English as a necessary *Hilfssprache*. In 1890, for example, one-fourth of the foreign-born in the United States could not speak English, and the foreign-born made up almost 15 percent of the total population of the country. In the Great Plains and midwestern states the concentration of immigrants was higher than the national average. In Nebraska, for example, the foreign stock (immigrants and children of immigrants) in that year comprised almost 43 percent of the total population of about one million inhabitants.

Even for the monolingual, linguistic acculturation in the form of English influence began immediately, since changed and changing conditions required a corresponding linguistic accommodation, which could be effected most readily by means of diffusion (borrowing from English) or by various types of loanshifts in the native vocabulary (semantic extension, loanshift creations, and so forth). The second generation was usually bilingual, using the inherited language for home and neighborhood communication and frequently also for worship, and English for school and for professional purposes. Although the process of acculturation accelerated greatly because of the incessant, constantly increasing pressure of English, this kind of bilingualism, in which differential use is made of the several languages, can theoretically become stable. Indeed, such a form of stable bilingualism has existed for about ten generations among the Pennsylvania Germans. Usually, however, the imported language disappears with the passing of the third generation. Many third-generation Americans are bilingual, but for most of them English is the dominant language. Fourth-generation speakers of immigrant tongues are rare indeed.

The first paper deals not with language per se but with certain social and political forces that heightened the tension between speakers of English and foreigners and thus hastened the demise of non-English languages on the Great Plains. During the last two decades of the nineteenth and the first two decades of the twentieth century there was widespread fear in this country that the amalgamation of immigrants was proceeding too slowly. The distrust and resentment of foreigners was whipped into hysteria by the incredibly vicious anti-German propaganda generated during World War I. Throughout the Great Plains region the public use of foreign languages was forbidden—first through extralegal means and, ironically, in 1919, through the enactment of repressive legislation that remained in effect until declared unconstitutional in 1923. During these years many American families—especially pacifist Hutterites and Mennonites—fled to Canada to escape persecution at the hand of superpatriots. Other Americans abandoned their native languages—especially German—and refused to let their children speak them. Among the many prominent Nebraskans who switched from German to English during childhood are Governor Charles Thone and Professor Bernice Slote, editor of the *Prairie Schooner*. Professor Elaine Jahner was not even permitted to learn the German dialect of her parents. Many Danes discontinued the use of their native tongue for fear of being mistaken for Germans by English-speaking neighbors.

In 1940 the American Council of Learned Societies sponsored a meeting of linguists at Ann Arbor, Michigan to encourage and to plan the recording and analysis of the surviving non-English languages in the United States and Canada. The response to this challenge has been gratifying, as a glance at the footnotes to the articles in this anthology will reveal. Those studies include three University of Nebraska doctoral dissertations dealing with four German dialects.[1] The Great Plains still provide a marvelous opportunity for such linguistic studies—especially for the observation of the interaction between living languages. Much remains to be done—for the dialectologist, the sociolinguist, the psycholinguist. Much has been written about the history of the Great Plains; more needs to be written about the *people* of the Great Plains. And this means studying the languages of all the ethnic groups, native and immigrant; for the social and cultural assimilation of these people was effected through the acculturation, through the americanization, of their languages. But time is of the essence. Most bilingual speakers in the Great Plains region are in their seventies or older.

In contrast to the other immigrant languages discussed here, Spanish has good chances to survive for generations to come. Despite the large number of defectors, there is a high degree of family and language loyalty among Mexican Americans, which is fortified by continuing immigration from and frequent visits to Mexico. As long as there are monolingual speakers of ethnic languages in a family, younger members will need to use that language and thus preserve it. Then, too, because of the importance of Spanish for government and industry, the desirability of extending bilingual education to more Spanish-American communities will eventually become evident to school authorities.

Two essays address themselves to the acculturation of the Lakota language. One analyzes the subtle semantic changes brought about by the transition from a free nomadic life to reservation existence. The other one studies the impact of English on Lakota and the strategies of Lakota speakers to preserve their language from extinction. Having been dispossessed of all else, many Lakota want desperately to hold on to what is left of their cultural heritage—their language. How successful they will be in retaining their linguistic, and thus their cultural, identity remains to be seen.

But linguistic diffusion does not proceed only from the dominant language to the submerged one. Long after the ethnic languages have been displaced by English, influence from the immigrant tongues remains. Pennsylvania-German English fairly bristles with loanwords, semantic borrowings, and idioms translated literally from the rapidly disappearing dialect.[2] In many communities throughout the Midwest and the Great Plains the intonation patterns of the local varieties of American English reflect the speech of the original Czech, German, and Scandinavian settlers, even though these languages are no longer spoken by more than a few elderly persons. It is not unusual to read in the sports pages of newspapers that a basketball player "dunked" the ball, or that team A "put the hex on" team B. Although there is a tendency among some linguists to minimize the importance of substratum influence, I feel certain that many English teachers would agree that such relics of submerged ethnic languages deserve the attention of scholars for very practical, as well as for scientific, reasons. For this reason one paper dealing with the influence of German on the English of central Texas has been included in this volume.

Perhaps these papers will suggest approaches to the further investigation of those languages that are still available for observation. It may even still be possible to create a sociolinguistic atlas of the Great Plains on historical principles that will be of value to future scholars in the humanities and social sciences.

Although the chief emphasis of this book is on the people and languages on the Great Plains, it is not possible to remain completely within these geographic confines. The reason for this is that most Scandinavian and several German communities in this area are extensions of settlements and colonies in midwestern states. This is true, for example, of a Low German dialect spoken in Omaha, speakers of which are more numerous in Aurora, Illinois, in Toronto, Ontario, and especially in Milwaukee, Wisconsin. In some cases, too, it is informative to compare or to contrast attitudes toward foreign languages on the Great Plains with those in more cosmopolitan regions elsewhere.

Let me conclude this introduction by quoting a statement by Einar Haugen that may well have been the inspiration for the title of this collection of studies:

> The immigrant could not be expected to reshape his speech overnight, for habits of speech are rooted more deeply in man's emotional and intellectual life than is generally realized. One's language cannot be tossed aside like last year's bonnet. From his first day in the new land a tug of war between his old and his new self was going on in the immigrant, and nowhere was the struggle more vividly reflected than in his successive linguistic adaptations. It is by slow, incessant attrition that each foreigner has been turned into an American, idea by idea, and word by word. Every language spoken by the American immigrant bears the marks of this conflict, and only by recording and analyzing this evidence can we fully understand the processes of immigration. Only through this highly sensitive index can we reach some of the subtlest and most significant aspects of the immigrant's psychological and cultural development. . . . Each language has been forced to adapt itself to new conditions, and thereby gives us a vivid picture of the immigrant's struggle for a position within the new nation and his gradual accommodation to its demands.[3]

Each study in this collection illustrates aspects of the language conflict that confronted all immigrants and many of their descendants: conflict between "high" and "low" forms of the ancestral tongue, conflict between dialects of high and low prestige, and especially conflict between the imported tongue and the dominant language. The language conflict of speakers of Indian languages was basically no different. The speech of native Americans too had to be americanized.

NOTES

1. Jan E. Bender, ''Die getrennte Entwicklung gleichen niederdeutschen Sprachgutes in Deutschland und Nebraska'' (Ph.D. diss., University of Nebraska, 1970); Andreas Gommermann, ''Oberhessische Siedlungsmundart in Milwaukee, Wisconsin, USA: Tochtermundart einer in Musci (Ungarn) gesprochenen fuldischen Siedlungsmundart'' (Ph.D. diss., University of Nebraska, 1975); and Robert H. Buchheit, ''Mennonite 'Plautdietsch': A Phonological and Morphological Description of a Settlement Dialect in York and Hamilton Counties, Nebraska'' (Ph.D., diss., University of Nebraska, 1978).

2. On Pennsylvania-German English, see Paul Schach, ''The Pennsylvania-German Contribution to the American Vocabulary,'' *Historical Review of Berks County* 19 (1953): 2–8; ''Comments on Some Pennsylvania-German Words in the *Dictionary of Americanisms,*'' *American Speech* 29 (1954): 45–54; and ''Pfälzische Entlehnungen in der amerikanischen Umgangssprache,'' *Rheinische Vierteljahrsblätter* 20 (1955): 223–36.

3. Einar Haugen, ''Language and Immigration,'' in *The Ecology of Language: Essays by Einer Haugen*, sel. and introd. Anwar S. Dil (Stanford, Calif.: Stanford University Press, 1971), pp. 1–2; reprinted from *Norwegian-American Studies and Records* 10 (1938): 1–43.

Legal Restrictions on Foreign Languages in the Great Plains States, 1917–1923

FREDERICK C. LUEBKE

A major effect of World War I on American social history was that it focused attention on the nation's apparent difficulty in assimilating the millions of immigrants and their children who had streamed to the United States during the preceding two decades. The national mood, darkened by fears and resentments of long standing and deepened by systematic wartime propaganda, favored the adoption of stringent laws limiting the use of foreign languages, especially in the schools. During the war itself, restrictions were usually extralegal and often the consequences of intense social pressure recklessly applied. After the war, however, many state legislatures enacted measures that were highly restrictive. The denouement of the movement came in 1923 when the United States Supreme Court declared one of these laws, Nebraska's Siman Act, to be unconsitutional.

Laws regulating the use of languages in the United States evolved in the latter half of the nineteenth century. Before then English was so preponderant in usage that its official adoption seemed superfluous in most states. Louisiana, which became a state in 1812, was an early exception because of its large French-speaking population. After the Civil War, when the number of non-English-speaking immigrants increased greatly, many states passed laws regulating the publication of legal notices in languages other than English. These were generally permissive rather than restrictive. Similarly, a few states legalized the practice of conducting public school in languages other than English. Such laws usually legitimized what was happening informally. When the population of a school district was solidly German, which was often the case in those years, the locally elected school board was likely to hire a German teacher who would instruct the children in the German language, or in both German and English, irrespective of what the statutory provision might have been. Thus, a Kansas law of 1867 permitted instruction in the German language when "freeholders representing fifty pupils" demanded it. Although German was specified in some laws, the provisions usually applied to all foreign tongues, even though German Americans were nearly always responsible for the enactments and were their chief beneficiary.[1]

The mere passage of such laws invigorated opposition among guardians of Anglo-American traditions who insisted that English be the language of instruction in the public schools. California was the first to shift to this ground. Kansas followed in 1876, and three years later the Dakota territorial legislature directed that English be used exclusively in its schools. By 1890 the language issue dominated political debate in Wisconsin, where the famous Bennett law of 1889 made attendance in public or private schools compulsory for children and defined a school as one in which the common subjects were taught in the English language. Similar legislation was enacted in Illinois. Opposition in Catholic and German Lutheran quarters was massive and effective; in both states the restrictive laws were repealed in the early 1890s. Nevertheless, the trend continued elsewhere. In 1897 an Iowa law provided that all instruction in the public schools was to be in English, except in the teaching of foreign languages, and Louisiana specified in its constitution of 1898 that English was to be the language of its schools, save in its French districts.[2]

A fairly consistent pattern of legislation emerged during the decade before World War I, as European immigration reached its highest levels in the nation's history. At least seven states, including Texas (1905), Montana (1907), and Colorado (1908), obliged teachers to use English exclusively in their instruction. When Oklahoma and New Mexico were admitted as states in 1907 and 1912, English-language provisions were written into their constitutions, although in the latter case the needs of the large Spanish-speaking population were recognized. Other states again tied instruction in English to compulsory attendance and to textbook laws. None of these measures prohibited the teaching of foreign languages as subjects, since they were aimed primarily at the use of foreign languages as media of instruction.[3]

Support for laws specifying English as the language of instruction in the public schools often came from persons who lacked confidence in the nation's assimilative powers. They were eager to support any number of programs that promised to Americanize the immigrant. Too many immigrants had come in too short a time, they thought. In 1910, when the total population of the United States was 92 million, 23 percent of the nearly 13 million foreign-born persons ten years of age and over were unable to speak English.

Additional support for restriction came from champions of public school education who saw private and parochial schools as obstacles to their improvement programs. Parents who objected to reform measures, they argued, could always withdraw their children and enroll them in private church schools.

One-room parochial schools with pastors as teachers and with much instruction in a foreign language were not uncommon in the Great Plains states during the prewar years. Of all the ethnoreligious groups, the German Lutherans were most deeply committed to this kind of education and were therefore most frequently criticized for the inadequacies, such as they were, of their schools. Naturally, they felt threatened by the movement to specify English as the language of instruction, believing that laws restricting their own schools were next on the agenda, as they had been in Wisconsin and Illinois in 1889. They feared similar legislation in North Dakota, where in 1910 and 1920 bills were introduced to restrict instruction to English in all schools, public and private, and in all subjects except religion. Determined opposition from immigrant churches contributed to the defeat of both these bills. In Wisconsin in 1912 another bill, denounced as a "second Bennett law," which aimed to improve the quality of education in parochial schools, was also defeated.[5]

While the movement for restriction seemed to be the dominant theme during this period, counterpoint of a different spirit could also be heard. Several states enacted laws that specifically authorized public school instruction in a non-English tongue, usually at the behest of well-organized ethnic associations of nonreligious character. For example, Colorado in 1908 permitted German or Spanish to be taught when requested by the parents or guardians of twenty or more pupils. Similarly, a Nebraska statute of 1913 required the request by parents of fifty or more pupils for instruction to be given in any modern European language for one hour per day above the fourth grade. Unlike the Colorado measure, which served the needs of pupils deficient in English-language skills, the Nebraska law was partly intended to provide English-speaking pupils with an opportunity to study a foreign language. More importantly, however, it enabled a minority of German-American citizens in a given school district to secure formal instruction for their children in the mother tongue. Known as the Mockett Law, this measure had been lobbied through the state legislature by the Nebraska branch of the National German-American Alliance. No friend of ethnic parochial schools, the alliance aggressively sought to broaden the influence of German language and culture in the public school system.[6]

Thus, by the time World War I broke out in 1914, several separate trends in the regulation of foreign languages could be discerned. First, there were laws that provided a legal basis for instruction in foreign languages as a practical measure in communities dominated by non-English-speaking people; second, there was an opposite trend that favored laws to establish English as the language of the schools; and third, some states passed laws that made foreign-language instruction possible for English-speaking pupils.

The war in Europe placed severe strains on America's heterogeneous society during the period of United States neutrality, which extended from

August 1914 to March 1917. There was a natural tendency for persons of Anglo-American heritage to sympathize with Britain and her allies, just as citizens with German antecedents often felt an emotional bond with their ancestral homeland. Inevitably the events of the war intensified loyalties and diminished tolerance for cultural diversity.[7]

Many German-American citizens, especially those who advocated programs of ethnic cultural maintenance, were tempted to indulge in extravagant partisanship for Germany. They staged rallies and bazaars for the German Red Cross; they bombarded their representatives in Washington with strongly worded letters and telegrams; German-language newpapers published intemperate editorials attacking the president for what were perceived as pro-Allied policies. While the opinions of these more vocal groups were not necessarily representative of the masses of German Americans, they were believed to be by dominant Anglo-American elements of the society. In the German-American view, it was in the interest of the United States to stay out of the conflict completely. That meant no loans to belligerents on either side, no shipments of war materiel, and no travel by American citizens on the ships of nations at war. In President Wilson's opinion, such policies would ultimately work to the advantage of Germany and therefore were unneutral and un-American. In a series of public statements, Wilson questioned the patriotism of German-American leaders whose understanding of the American interest differed from his own, though he never specified them by name or even by ethnicity.

Meanwhile, British propaganda had begun to portray Germany as a land of barbarians at war against western civilizatiion, Kaiser Wilhelm as a merciless, grasping tyrant, and his soldiers as butchers of innocent women and children. By 1915 a hate-Germany campaign was well under way in the United States. German Americans became resentful and fearful as their language and culture were disparaged and things German became objects of hatred.

When the United States declared war on Germany in April 1917, President Wilson emphasized that the enemy was the imperial government of Germany, not the German people, their language, or their culture. But in the frantic effort to mobilize the country's resources for war, such distinctions were lost to many minds. Rumors of German-American subversion flitted about, and many Americans succumbed to the fear that the country was swarming with spies.

A variety of government agencies and private organizations contributed to the growing anti-German hysteria. The Committee of Public Information created a national mood of aggressive patriotism as it attacked dissent as disloyalty, extolled British culture, and fostered hatred for Germany. Meanwhile, the American Protective League organized a massive program to search out domestic espionage. The National Security League and its offshoot, the American Defense League, spread a virulent strain of superpatriotism and intensified the anti-German hysteria through indiscriminate attacks on

German-American churches, schools, societies, and newspapers, describing them as inhibitors of assimilation and as agents of a worldwide Teutonic conspiracy.

Both organizations made special war on the German language. By eliminating German-language instruction from the elementary and secondary schools, the American Defense League proclaimed, the nation could destroy the means by which the Kaiser and his henchmen were seeking to pervert American youth. One of its pamphlets, "Throw Out the German Language and All Disloyal Teachers," illustrates the logic of superpatriotism: "Any language which produces a people of ruthless conquestadors [sic] such as now exists in Germany, is not a fit language to teach clean and pure American boys and girls." The Germans, according to this tract, were "the most treacherous, brutal and loathsome nation on earth. . . . The sound of the German language . . . reminds us of the murder of a million helpless old men, unarmed men, women, and children; [and] the driving of about 100,000 young French, Belgian, and Polish women into compulsory prostitution."[8] The American Defense League also encouraged the public burning of German-language books.

Superpatriotic politicians and newspaper editors joined in the cry. In Lincoln, Nebraska a newspaper began a campaign, ultimately successful, to remove a thousand German-language books from the collection of the State Library Commission. Richard Metcalf, a political lieutenant of William Jennings Bryan, broadcast unconfirmed tales, soon repeated across the nation, about teachers in German Lutheran schools in Nebraska who whipped pupils who dared to speak English during recess periods.[9]

Many educators lent their authority to the war on German-language instruction in the schools. The most moderate argued that foreign-language instruction had to end because the heterogeneous mass of American society could be welded together only by means of English as the common national tongue.[10] In an address delivered to the National Education Association, the dean of the University of Minnesota College of Education asserted that subversive Germans expected to achieve their nefarious goals "by having German teachers teaching German ideals through the German language" in American schools.[11] Another educator announed that the German language was "lacking in euphony" and therefore "savors of the animalistic and does not induce a certain polish and refinement essential to civilized people." There should be no place for the German language in our schools, he insisted, because it upholds a philosophy that "prides itself in its inhumanity [that] murders children, rapes women, and mutilates the bodies of innocent men."[12] With comparable logic, a retired United States admiral insisted that German-language instruction be dropped because the textbooks glorify German things and German men who have shown themselves to be "arrogant, domineering, treacherous, dishonest, mendacious, scheming, unscrupulous, without honor, cruel, and murderous."[13]

The National Education Association also supported the campaign. Through one of its commissions the NEA condemned "the practice of giving instruction in a foreign tongue" as "un-American and unpatriotic." Although it was silent on classes in which students were taught to speak a foreign language, the NEA urged that "every legitimate means, both state and federal, be used" to make English the language of instruction in all public and private schools.[14]

The clamor was in fact very much ado about very little. The campaign was directed chiefly against German-language instruction in the first eight grades. Yet few school systems offered instruction in any foreign language at that level. The United States Bureau of Education compiled statistics in autumn 1917 on the question. The data revealed that in only 19 of 163 cities of twenty-five thousand plus were such classes offered.[15]

In secondary schools, however, relatively few German-language classes had been dropped, though enrollments had decreased significantly. A *Literary Digest* poll of school superintendents conducted early in 1918 showed that only 149 of 1,017 respondents reported discontinuation of German-language classes. Many individual comments were published in the article, and most reflect the closed-mindedness and intolerance fostered by war propaganda. A superintendent in Grafton, North Dakota offered a minority view when he replied that "to drop German as a language-study because we are at war with Germany would be indicative of that sort of stupidity and lack of vision that we believe is native in the Prussian intellectual atmosphere." Few of the educators quoted agreed with the calm assessment of Philander P. Claxton, the United States commissioner of education, who opposed the elimination of German-language instruction on the secondary school level. The United States is not at war with the German language, he wrote in a widely publicized letter, and "the fewer hatreds and antagonisms that get themselves embedded in our institutions and policies, the better it will be for us when the days of peace return."[16]

State councils of defense also shared in the fight to eliminate "the enemy language" from the public schools. Shortly after war had been declared, President Wilson urged each state government to form a commission to coordinate food and fuel production and conservation, mobilization of labor, sanitation, Americanization programs, and other aspects of the war effort on the state and local level. All states eventually complied, although the councils varied greatly in name, structure, and authority. Subordinate county councils of defense were also created and the various functions farmed out to committees of unpaid civilian appointees. In some states, especially in the West, state councils of defense were granted sweeping powers, sometimes of doubtful constitutionality. Public attention was most often attracted to the zealous manner in which some councils performed their duties relative to patriotism, Americanization, or disloyalty.

The councils of defense for the several Great Plains states each joined in the anti-German campaign. Most issued orders or requests in 1918 to eliminate German-language instruction in the schools. But in some states the councils of defense went much further, banning the use of the German language in church services, parochial schools, public meetings of all kinds, and even on the telephone. German-language newspapers were also attacked. The principal argument for suppressing the language was that the country, for the sake of unity, had to Americanize its foreign-born citizens and that continued use of the German language kept the immigrant "subservient to the Hohenzollern autocracy."[17]

The Nebraska State Council of Defense was one of the most active and influential of the several commissions established in the plains states. Its activities were guided by men who were thoroughly imbued with superpatriotic sentiments; it had the consistent support of influential newspapers, most notably the *Lincoln Star*, whose publisher himself became a member of the council. Bothered by the alleged failure of Nebraskans to support the war effort with appropriate enthusiasm, the state council in July 1917 conducted an investigation into the loyalty of the strong German element in the state. Leaders of the several German Lutheran synods were singled out for special attention and were broadly accused of disloyal behavior. Subsequent meetings of the council with Lutheran church officials moderated the antagonism a little, yet it is clear that the council deliberately sought to focus public indignation on the German Lutherans and their continued strong attachment to their ancestral language and culture.[18]

The Nebraska council took several steps in the development of its policy to curb foreign languages in the churches. On 12 December 1917 the council, relying on the force of public opinion rather than law, banned the teaching or use of foreign languages in all private and denominational schools of the state. Church services in foreign languages, however, continued to be seen as a problem, and on 8 June 1918 the council issued a proclamation requesting that the ban on German be extended to all means of communication to the fullest possible extent. "All sermons and public speeches should be exclusively in the English language," the council ordered, "but where there are old people who cannot understand the English language and it is deemed necessary to give instruction in a foreign tongue, all publicity should be avoided in such instruction." Two months later the council clarified its ruling regarding religious instruction in German. Sunday schools were to be conducted in English, the council decreed, as should all religious services. The old people who could not understand English, according to this directive, could have the sermon briefly summarized for them in the foreign language shortly before or after the regular services. The regulation, still without force of law, applied equally to religious meetings in Swedish, Danish, Czech, and other languages in use in Nebraska, as well as German.[19]

The records of the Nebraska council reveal that very few clergymen were willing to risk the wrath of adverse public opinion, which had been so effectively marshalled by the council. The Reverend John Gerike, a pastor of a rural Missouri Synod Lutheran congregation near Crete, Nebraska, was a courageous exception. He coolly informed the council that his congregation had voted to continue German services "until a law is passed forbidding the use of it."[20] But most church leaders, while objecting to the action as illegal and unfair, urged a willing conformance for the sake of harmonious public relations.

Other state councils pursued similar courses with similar results. In Montana, where the use of the German language in the pulpit was also forbidden, a few congregations fearfully suspended all public worship. In South Dakota, where the state council was empowered to act in any way "not inconsistent with the constitution and laws of South Dakota . . . which are necessary and proper for public safety," the ethnic conflict was as sharp as in Nebraska. On 22 February 1918, even before it had statutory authority to do so, the South Dakota council ordered the first statewide ban in the nation on German-language instruction in all public schools from the elementary grades through the universities. Its Order No. 4, which went into effect on 1 June 1918, prohibited the use of the German language at all public gatherings, including church meetings, and the ban on German-language instruction was extended to private and church-related schools. A subsequent order "prohibited the use of the enemy's language in public conversation except in cases of extreme emergency."[21]

In Kansas the state council acted with moderation and understanding, compared to its counterparts in most other Great Plains states. Although the Kansas council was thoroughly committed to its program to make the English language "universally understood and habitually used by all citizens," it carefully avoided the harsh and autocratic methods employed in neighboring states. This was due largely to the efforts of Martin Graebner, a clergyman and professor at Saint John's College, a Lutheran institution in Winfield, who had been placed in charge of the foreign-language problem in the state. A sensitive and knowledgeable man, Graebner successfully enlisted the voluntary support and cooperation of German-speaking organizations and communities in the state.[22]

On the local level, however, county councils of defense were often less circumspect than the state councils and tended to ignore the complexities of their tasks. A county council, for example, dictated in one instance which members of a German Lutheran church could attend German-language services and which could not. In Oklahoma, the Major County Council of Defense brusquely asserted that since "God Almighty understands the American language, address Him only in that tongue.'' In Nebraska, the Dixon County Council of Defense resolved on 10 May 1918 that all persons should abstain from the use of the German language at all times and in all places, including church and home, and ''that the reading of German-language papers should immediately be discontinued by all who are to be considered loyal Americans.'' Two weeks later the Hall County, Nebraska council resolved ''that in this hour of our nation's greatest peril brought upon us by the murderous and ruthless Hun,'' all instruction in German in every school in the county, public and parochial, should stop and that all German school books be removed from every school. It requested further that the *Anzeiger-Herold* (Grand Island) cease publication at once; that the Liederkranz and the Plattdeutscher Vereen, two social organizations, change their names to English, rewrite their constitutions in English, and conduct all organizational activities in English; and that ''the use of the German language in public and private conversation . . . be discontinued.'' The resolution was larded with such pornographic phrases as ''brutal hordes of German ravishers and murderers.'' The council also declared its belief that Germany had ''forfeited all claims to be classed among the civilized nations of the world.''[23]

In their zeal to promote ''a true spirit of patriotism,'' county councils of defense fostered disrespect for law. In South Dakota, when church officials protested an interpretation of the state council's Order No. 4, the Douglas County Council of Defense replied that it did not care what the state council or the state or federal judiciary had said; it simply would not tolerate preaching in the German language.[24]

A mob spirit took over in some communities. German Americans were subjected to threats, intimidations, beatings, tar-and-featherings, flag-kissing ceremonies, and star chamber proceedings in council of defense meetings. Their homes and buildings received liberal applications of yellow paint as a symbol of disloyalty.[25] In Texas a German Lutheran pastor was whipped after he allegedly continued to preach in German after having been requested not to by the Nueces County Council of Defense. In South Dakota a county council of defense itself became the object of mob threats when it met to consider the question of granting permits to pastors of German churches to give synopses of their sermons in German at the close of English-language services. In Nebraska a German Lutheran pastor of a church in Papillion was beaten by a mob; in Riverdale another was hanged in effigy and given three days to leave town. Schools and churches were ransacked for German-language books.[26] In South Dakota, Yankton high school students were praised for having dumped their German-language textbooks into the Missouri River as they sang the ''Star-Spangled Banner.'' The burning of German-language books as parts of super-patriotic exercises occurred in Oakland, Hooper, and Grand Island, Nebraska. In Boulder, Colorado a German-book-burning rally was sponsored by the

University of Colorado preparatory school. Early in September 1918, the Lutheran parochial school in Herington, Kansas was destroyed by fire by superpatriots.[27]

In both Kansas and South Dakota German-speaking Mennonite and Hutterite pacifists suffered grievous persecution. Superpatriots condemned them not merely because of their tenacious retention of the language, but also because of their refusal on religious grounds to accept military service or to buy war bonds. In Collinsville, Oklahoma a Mennonite named Henry Reimer was strung up by a mob on 19 April 1918. Police persuaded the would-be executioners to cut him down before he died, on the promise that he would be given a trial by the county council of defense the next day. In Kansas vigilantes besieged rural families at night, firing pistol shots into the air and scattering written threats and warnings about the yard. In Newton a mob intimidated the students of the Mennonite Bethel College and displayed a sign that read, "Germans: speak the language of a civilized nation. The Hun language will be barred even in Hell." By the summer of 1918 some of the most conservative Mennonites of the Great Plains states decided that their status within the United States had become intolerable, and well over fifteen hundred persons resettled in the Canadian prairie provinces of Alberta, Saskatchewan, and Manitoba. The largest numbers came from Oklahoma and South Dakota, although others fled from Kansas, Nebraska, and Minnesota.[28] Many Hutterites from South Dakota also emigrated, starting in 1918. Within a few years all but one of their agricultural colonies in the state had been abandoned.

Most of the restrictions placed upon the usage of foreign languages during the war were extralegal. Even though the council of defense pronouncements were widely heeded, they were not legally binding. They were supported by the force of public opinion and by the threat of mob action. Some local governments passed city ordinances against speaking German in public places. Though unenforceable, such local measures were not often challenged. The attorney general of Nebraska gave it as his opinion that a proposed ordinance to forbid the speaking of a foreign language on the streets of Campbell, Nebraska would be invalid because the legislature had never granted villages of the state such authority. He also implied that the ordinance would be unnecessary since "prudence and public policy" would soon prompt immigrants to desist from the use of the native tongue.[29] Had state legislatures generally been in session in 1918, many restrictive laws would have been passed. As it was, the governors of several states called special sessions to consider such legislation.

The most extreme of the wartime measures was enacted by the Louisiana legislature, which made it unlawful for any teacher or professor in any public or private institution at any level to teach the German language to any pupil or class.[30] A more moderate restriction was enacted in South Dakota. In this case the legislature forbade instruction by means of any foreign language in the public elementary schools of the state; it applied the same restrictions to public secondary schools and colleges, except for foreign languages as subjects; and finally, in the private schools and colleges of the state, the restrictions also applied, "except for foreign and ancient languages and religious subjects." In other words, South Dakota legislators, in contrast to the state's council of defense, made an explicit accommodation to its ethnoreligious minorities.[31]

In Nebraska the governor called a special session of the legislature to enact a sedition law and to repeal the Mockett language law of 1913, which he now denounced as "vicious, undemocratic, and un-American." By its repeal, the legislature removed the provision that school districts had to offer foreign-language instruction upon the request of the parents of fifty pupils. The legislature then approved the request by the Nebraska State Council of Defense that no foreign languages be taught in the elementary grades.[32] It also enacted a sedition law that enhanced the power of the state council of defense by requiring publishers of all materials in any foreign language to file copies with the council, along with English translations, as required by the federal Espionage Act. More significantly, enemy aliens were forbidden from acting "as lecturer, priest, preacher, minister, teacher, editor, publisher, or educator" without first filing an application and obtaining a permit from the Nebraska State Council of Defense. One senator courageously but ineffectively denounced the act as "an insidious attack on the right of free speech and religious liberty." He was outraged by the provision that, as he said, made "our lawful and constitutional authorities subservient and subordinate to the council of defense, whose members are not elected, nor answerable to the people."[33]

The signing of the armistice on 11 November 1918 ended the war against Germany, but the war against German language and culture in the United States continued with scarcely any diminution. Just days before the fighting ceased, the voters elected new legislatures, which went into session in January 1919. Many of the new lawmakers were more determined than ever to impose linguistic uniformity upon the American people. Certain journalists and politicians continued to exploit popular fears. Gustavus Ohlinger, for example, continued to attack German-language instruction in American schools as he had during the war. In his view it was the keystone of subversion, just as the German-language press was the archenemy of Americanization. Before long twenty-one states enacted new laws relating to foreign languages in the elementary schools. Among them were the Great Plains states of Colorado, Kansas, Nebraska, New Mexico, Oklahoma, and South Dakota. All enactments specified English as the medium of instruction, and all except the New Mexico measure applied to all schools, public, private, and parochial.[34]

The passage of these new restrictive laws of 1919 was also due in part to proposed federal legislation known as the Smith-Towner bill, introduced in Congress in October 1918. One section of this bill specified that no state was to share in the apportionment of federal funds unless it "shall have enacted and enforced laws requiring that the basic language of instruction in the common-school branches in all schools, public and private, shall be the English language only." Yet many legislatures went beyond the requirement of the still-pending Smith-Towner bill and prohibited entirely the teaching of foreign language up to and including the eighth grade.[35]

The Kansas measure was forthright and unyielding: "All elementary schools in this state, whether public, private or parochial, shall use the English language exclusively as the medium of instruction." Oklahoma's law was nearly as blunt. South Dakota enacted a new law that listed the subjects that had to be taught in English; religion was not listed and therefore could be taught in German in parochial schools. Colorado used a similarly devious method to make English the language of instruction without touching religious education. New Mexico managed to specify English as the language of instruction in its public elementary schools, but made Spanish reading a mandatory subject for Spanish-speaking pupils.[36]

It was Nebraska's language law, however, that gained broader significance because it was ultimately declared unconstitutional by the United States Supreme Court in 1923. Sponsored by Senator Harry Siman, it was one of several bills introduced early in the 1919 session to restrict the use of foreign languages in the state. Sentiment in favor of restriction was especially strong because of publicity given the recommendations of Nebraska's Americanization Committee, which had been appointed by Governor Keith Neville to take the language issue out of the hands of the Nebraska State Council of Defense. Neville, in his address to the legislature as outgoing governor, had also called for a ban on foreign-language instruction in order, as he put it, to guarantee that Nebraska would be American in language, thought, and ideals. But Neville also favored a provision that would have specifically exempted religious instruction from the ban.[37]

By 1919 the ethnic churches, principally the body known today as the Lutheran Church—Missouri Synod, no longer objected to legislation requiring English in their schools, so long as the directive did not apply to religious instruction. Their acquiescence was partly an acceptance of political reality, but it was also a matter-of-fact recognition that in most parochial schools English was commonly used except in religion classes. The language laws of several neighboring states, including Iowa, South Dakota, and Colorado, explicitly applied to secular subjects only. Several lawmakers with Lutheran and Catholic connections tried in committee to amend the Siman bill similarly, but Siman and the majority were adamant despite editorials in leading state newspapers urging moderation.[38] One lawmaker's response distills the intolerance of the time:

> If these people are Americans, let them speak our language. If they don't know it,

> let them learn it. If they don't like it, let them move. It is a good thing to learn. I would be ashamed to face my boy, when he returns from France, if I voted for this amendment [to authorize specifically the use of foreign languages for religious instruction in parochial schools] and had to tell him that I had done nothing to crush Kaiserism in this country.[39]

Other supporters of the Siman bill favored the closing of all parochial schools in the state. Some were motivated by a deeply rooted religious prejudice. For them the language bill was a ready and popular preliminary step toward the diminution of Catholic power in the United States. That the Siman bill would also work contrary to the interests of the German Lutheran synods was merely an unfortunate but unavoidable consequence of their commitment to parochial schools.[40]

Governor Samuel McKelvie signed the Siman bill into law on 9 April 1919. Overwhelmingly approved in both houses of the legislature, the measure made it a misdemeanor "to teach any subject to any person in any language other than the English language . . . in any private, denominational, parochial or public school." The restriction applied only to the first eight grades.[41]

Shortly after the passage of the Siman law, officials of the Nebraska District of the Lutheran Church—Missouri Synod sought an injunction against the enforcement of the act on the ground that it was an unconstitutional infringement upon religious liberty. This action was guided by Arthur Mullen, a prominent Irish Catholic lawyer of Omaha, who arranged to have a Polish Catholic parish of South Omaha join the Lutherans as petitioner. The district court judge issued the injuction, but the attorney general immediately appealed to the Nebraska State Supreme Court.[42]

After much controversy and public debate, the Nebraska Supreme Court on 26 December 1919 denied the injunction and upheld the Siman Act.This tribunal understood the measure, not as an unconstitutional interference with religious liberty, but as an effort within the police power of the state to treat the language problem that had developed in the country because of the World War. Fearful perhaps of constitutional objections, the court added that the law did not prevent instruction of or in foreign languages outside regular school hours.[43]

This ruling by no means settled the matter. Some parochial schools, acting on the cue from the judiciary, arranged their daily schedules so that courses taught in foreign languages, chiefly religion, were offered before or after regular school hours.[44] Inevitably such steps were perceived as evasions of the law by the superpatriotic advocates of language uniformity and champions of public-school education; during the next two years they continued to push hard for new restrictive laws.

It was not until 1921 that state legislatures were again in session and able to respond to the continued agitation for language restriction. Five states, including South Dakota and Nebraska, thereupon enacted new laws. In Nebraska the

Siman Act was replaced by the even more stringent Reed-Norval Act, signed into law on 14 April 1921. This measure forbade all instruction in foreign languages in public and private schools at all times, thereby closing the loophole noted earlier by the Nebraska Supreme Court. Ironically, the bill was originally introduced by Senator Richard Norval of Seward to weaken the restrictions of the Siman Act. But in committee other senators, acting under strong pressure from the American Legion, wrote additional restrictions into the bill, leaving Norval no alternative but to disavow the legislation that bore his name.[45]

Shortly after the passage of the Reed-Norval Act, officials of the Lutheran Church—Missouri Synod sought an injuction against its enforcement just as they had in the case of the Siman Act. This suit was quickly appealed to the Nebraska Supreme Court, which on 19 April 1922 again upheld the constitutionality of the law forbidding the use of foreign languages in elementary schools.[46]

Meanwhile the famous *Meyer* v. *Nebraska* case was on its way to the United States Supreme Court. This litigation involved the teacher of a one-room parochial school maintained by Zion Lutheran Church of rural Hampton, in Hamilton County, the pastor of which was Carl F. Brommer, the president of the Nebraska District of the Lutheran Church—Missouri Synod. In January 1920, shortly after the Nebraska Supreme Court had observed in its decision of 26 December 1919 that the Siman Act did not prohibit foreign-language instruction outside regular school hours, Zion congregation declared its official schools hours to be from 9:00 to 12:00 in the morning and from 1:30 to 4:00 in the afternoon. It further directed the teacher, Robert Meyer, to conduct a class in religion in the German language from 1:00 to 1:30 P.M. each afternoon. Attendance was technically voluntary. On 25 May 1920 the county attorney appeared at the school while Raymond Parpart, a youngster in the fourth grade, was reading aloud in German the Old Testament story of Jacob's Ladder. Several days later Meyer was charged in the Hamilton County Court with having violated the Siman language law.[47]

Meyer's trial was conducted on 13 December 1920. The transcript reveals that the county attorney tried to blur the distinction between religious instruction in the German language and language instruction in which pedagogical materials happened to be religious. Meyer unquestionably was engaged in the former, but the jury was more likely to convict if the latter were the case. Further, the prosecution succeeded in convincing the jury that the announced starting time of 1:30 P.M., rather than 1:00 P.M. was a subterfuge to circumvent the law. Meyer was thereupon convicted and fined twenty-five dollars. With the support of church officials, he refused to pay and began his appeal.[48]

The Nebraska Supreme Court heard the case more than a year later, in

February 1922. In the meantime the legislature had replaced the Siman Act with the Reed-Norval Act, although this did not alter the judicial proceedings. By a four-to-two vote the court decided against Meyer and upheld the constitutionality of the language law. Writing for the majority, Justice Leonard Flansburg asserted that permitting resident foreigners to educate their children in the language of their native land was inimical to the safety of the state. Justice Charles B. Letton, in a dissenting opinion, called the Siman Act a product of crowd psychology. He declared that foreign-language instruction was not harmful to the state and that the Siman Act was an arbitrary exercise of police power that interfered with the fundamental right of parents to control the education of their children.[49]

Another year passed before the United States Supreme Court heard the Meyer case. The Lutheran Church—Missouri Synod had decided to couple its suit (*Evangelical Lutheran Synod* v. *McKelvie*) with Meyer's and to place them both in the hands of Arthur Mullen. Meanwhile other litigation over Iowa and Ohio language laws (*Iowa* v. *Bartels* and *Pohl* v. *Ohio*), each of which involved teachers in Lutheran parochial schools, had been appealed to the Supreme Court and were heard during the fall session of 1922.[50]

Mullen's reading of legal precedent convinced him that to base his case on the First Amendment would be fruitless, since it applied to the federal government, but not to state governments. He decided instead to argue that the Fourteenth Amendment embraces religious liberty also when it prohibits state government from abridging privileges of United States citizens or depriving them of life, liberty, or property without due process of law. Mullen submitted a brief to the court in October 1922 and presented oral arguments in February 1923.[51]

The United States Supreme Court delivered its decision on 4 June 1923. The majority opinion, written by Justice James McReynolds, declared the Siman Act to be unconstitutional interference with Meyer's right "to teach and the right of parents to engage him so to instruct their children." Moreover, the court observed that no emergency had "arisen which renders knowledge by a child of some language other than English so clearly harmful as to justify its inhibition with the consequent infringement of rights long freely enjoyed." The Iowa and Ohio rulings were, of course, also reversed.[52]

Although the Meyer decision ended restrictive language laws among the states, the related issue of private and parochial school education continued until 1925, when the United States Supreme Court struck down an Oregon law requiring all children between the ages of eight and sixteen to attend public school. This act, championed by an alliance of the Ku Klux Klan and several Masonic bodies, was overturned in the *Pierce v. Society of Sisters of the Holy Names of Jesus and Mary* decision. Both the suit and the judicial ruling drew upon the precedents of the Meyer case.[53]

Thus the Supreme Court of the United States brought the movement to impose legal restrictions on the use of foreign languages to an end. Although the trend had originated in the prewar period, it had been strengthened greatly by war-born fears of German subversion in America and anxiety over the nation's capacity to absorb its millions of foreign-born citizens. The climax of the movement came in 1919 during the six months following the armistice. Drawing support from diverse elements in the population—superpatriots, xenophobes, champions of public-school education, and later such organizations as the American Legion and Masonic orders—the advocates of language restriction were especially strong in the states of the Great Plains. Every legislature in this region enacted some sort of restriction on foreign languages from 1918 to 1921. Ethnic churches, whose interests were most directly and most adversely affected by the movement, immediately turned to the courts for redress. Although state tribunals were unresponsive to their constitutional arguments, the federal judiciary ruled in their favor and thereby clarified and enlarged American freedom.

Notes

The author acknowledges with gratitude the assistance of a fellowship in state and community history from the Newberry Library, Chicago, which enabled him to use its exceptional resources in the research and writing of this essay.

1. Heinz Kloss, "German-American Language Maintenance Efforts," in *Language Loyalty in the United States: The Maintenance and Perpetuation of Non-English Mother Tongues by American Ethnic and Religious Groups*, ed. Joshua A. Fishman, Vladimir C. Nahirny, John E. Hoffman, and Robert G. Hayden, Janua Linguarum, series maior, no. 21 (The Hague: Mouton, 1966), pp. 233–35.

2. Ibid.; Cleata B. Thorpe, "Education in South Dakota, 1861–1961," *South Dakota Historical Collections* 34 (1972): 224; Paul Kleppner, *The Cross of Culture* (New York: Free Press, 1970), p. 158; Richard Jensen, *The Winning of the Midwest* (Chicago: University of Chicago Press, 1971), pp. 123, 134, 219; J. C. Ruppenthal, "The Legal Status of the English Language in the American School System," *School and Society* 10 (6 December 1919): 658–60.

3. Ruppenthal, "Legal Status of the English Language," pp. 659–60.

4. I. N. Edwards, "The Legal Status of Foreign Languages in the Schools," *Elementary School Journal* 24 (8 December 1923): 270; U.S., Bureau of the Census, *Thirteenth Census of the United States: 1910*, 1:1266–67; Edward G. Hartmann, *The Movement to Americanize the Immigrant* (New York: Columbia University Press, 1948).

5. Walter H. Beck, *Lutheran Elementary Schools in the United States*, 2d ed. (Saint Louis, Mo.: Concordia Publishing House, 1965), pp. 318–19.

6. Ruppenthal, "Legal Status of the English Language," p. 660; Frederick C.

Luebke, "The German-American Alliance in Nebraska, 1910–1917," *Nebraska History* 49 (Summer 1968): 165–85.

7. This and following several paragraphs are summarized from my book *Bonds of Loyalty: German Americans and World War I* (De Kalb: Northern Illinois University Press, 1974).

8. Quoted in Wallace Henry Moore, "The Conflict Concerning the German Language and German Propaganda in the Public Secondary Schools of the United States" (Ph.D. diss., Stanford University, 1937), pp. 33–34.

9. Robert N. Manley, "The Nebraska State Council of Defense: Loyalty Programs and Policies during World War I" (Master's thesis, University of Nebraska, 1959), pp. 125–27; Luebke, "German-American Alliance," p. 183.

10. "German Language," *School Review* 25 (October 1917): 598–600.

11. L. D. Coffman, "Competent Teachers for American Children," *National Education Association: Proceedings and Addresses* (1918), p. 63. Coffman further charged that the National German-American Alliance was "responsible for the existence of 491 evangelical schools in this country, some of which were supported by state funds, in which German was the only language taught." In fact, the alliance did not favor parochial schools, and none of them was supported by state funds. Moreover, German was usually not the sole language of instruction in them by the time of World War I.

12. H. Miles Gordy, "German Language in Our Schools," *Educational Review* 56 (October 1918): 257–63.

13. Caspar F. Goodrich, "Shall We Teach German in Our Public Schools," *Outlook* 119 (29 May 1918): 192.

14. *Journal of Education* 87 (9 May 1918): 514.

15. "Foreign Languages in the Elementary School," *School and Society* 6 (17 November 1917): 583–84; *New York Times*, 3 February 1918.

16. "American Students Boycotting German," *Literary Digest* 56 (30 March 1918): 29–31, 44–74; *New Republic* 14 (2 March 1918): 146; *School and Society* 7 (30 March 1918); *New York Times*, 20 March 1918.

17. Frank W. Blackmar, ed., *History of the Kansas State Council of Defense* (Topeka, Kans.: State Printer, 1921), pp. 31, 68–74; *Report of South Dakota State Council of Defense* (n.p., n.d.), pp. 43, 51–52, 74, 110; "Record of Proceedings of the State Council of Defense," manuscript, Nebraska State Historical Society, Lincoln.

18. Robert N. Manley, "Language, Loyalty and Liberty: The Nebraska State Council of Defense and the Lutheran Churches, 1917–1918," *Concordia Historical Institute Quarterly* 37 (April 1964): 12–13.

19. Unidentified newspaper clipping, scrapbook, Werkmeister Collection, Nebraska State Historical Society, Lincoln; *Lutheran Witness* 37 (28 May 1918): 185; Jack W. Rodgers, "The Foreign Language Issue in Nebraska, 1918–1923," *Nebraska History* 39 (March 1958): 7.

20. John Gerike to Nebraska State Council of Defense, Crete, Nebraska, 12 March 1918, Papers of the Nebraska State Council of Defense, Nebraska State Historical Society.

21. *Proceedings of the Thirteenth Convention of the Montana District of the Lutheran Church—Missouri Synod* (Glendive, Mont., 24–26 August 1964), p. 69;

Lutheran Witness 37 (28 May 1918): 164, and (11 June 1918): 187. See also *School Review* 26 (June 1918): 458–59; *Report of the South Dakota Council of Defense*, p. 71; *New York Times*, 23 February 1918.

22. Blackmar, *Kansas State Council of Defense*, pp. 70–71.

23. Alan N. Graebner, "The Acculturation of an Immigrant Lutheran Church: The Lutheran Church—Missouri Synod, 1917–1929" (Ph.D. diss., Columbia University, 1965), p. 27; Edda Bilger, "The 'Oklahoma Vorwärts': The Voice of German-Americans in Oklahoma during World War I," *Chronicles of Oklahoma* 54 (Summer 1976): 255; *Lutheran Witness* 37 (28 May 1918): 164; unidentified newspaper clipping, Werkmeister Scrapbook, Nebraska State Historical Society.

24. Graebner, "Acculturation of an Immigrant Church," p. 29.

25. Luebke, *Bonds of Loyalty*, pp. 1–24, 244–59; Luebke, "Superpatriotism in World War I: The Experience of a Lutheran Pastor," *Concordia Historical Institute Quarterly* 41 (February 1968): 3–11; unidentified newspaper clippings, Werkmeister Scrapbook, Nebraska State Historical Society.

26. *Lutheran Witness* 37 (10 December 1918): 393; *Delmont* (S.D.) *Record*, reprinted in ibid., p. 392; Manley, "Language, Loyalty and Liberty," p. 7; Clifford L. Nelson, *German-American Political Behavior in Nebraska and Wisconsin, 1916–1920*, University of Nebraska–Lincoln Publication no. 217 (Lincoln, 1972), p. 31.

27. *Sioux Falls Argus Leader*, 9 May 1918; *Hooper* (Nebr.) *Sentinel*, 18 July 1918; Lyle W. Dorsett, "The Ordeal of Colorado's Germans during World War I," *Colorado Magazine* 51 (Fall 1974): 287; *Wichita Eagle*, 6 September 1918.

28. Arlyn John Parish, *Kansas Mennonites During World War I*, Fort Hays (Kansas State College) Studies, History Series, n.s. no. 4 (Hays, Kans., 1968), pp. 51–54; James C. Juhnke, *A People of Two Kingdoms: The Political Acculturation of the Kansas Mennonites* (Newton, Kansas: Faith and Life Press, 1975), pp. 95–110; Norman Thomas, "The Hutterian Brethren," *South Dakota Historical Collections* 25 (1951): 276–80; *Report of South Dakota State Council of Defense*, pp. 62–67; Allan Teichroew, "World War I and the Mennonite Migration to Canada to Avoid the Draft," *Mennonite Quarterly Review* 45 (July 1971): 219–49.

29. *Report of the Attorney General of Nebraska, 1918*, pp. 220–21.

30. *Compilation of War Laws of the Various States and Insular Possessions* (Washington, D.C.: Government Printing Office 1919), p. 47.

31. *South Dakota Session Laws, 1918*, chs. 41, 42, pp. 47–48.

32. *Senate and House Journals, Special Session*, 1918, pp. 38, 91, 180.

33. *Laws and Resolutions Passed by the* [Nebraska] *Legislature at the 36th (Extraordinary) Session, 1918*, ch. 9, pp. 50–51; unidentified newspaper clipping, Werkmeister Scrapbook, Nebraska State Historical Society.

34. Gustavus Ohlinger, *The German Conspiracy in American Education* (New York: Doran, 1919); Edwards, "Legal Status of Foreign Languages," p. 272.

35. Moore, "Conflict Concerning the German Language," p. 91.

36. *Kansas Session Laws*, 1919, ch. 257, p. 352; *Oklahoma Session Laws*, 1919, ch. 141, p. 201; *South Dakota Session Laws, 1919*, ch. 168; *Colorado Session Laws, 1919*, ch. 179, p. 599; *New Mexico Session Laws*, 1919, ch. 146. p. 300.

37. Unidentified newspaper clipping, Werkmeister Scrapbook, Nebraska State Historical Society.

38. *Lutheran Witness* 38 (4 February 1919): 35; Edwards, "Legal Status of Foreign Languages," p. 274; *Senate Journal* (37th session) *1919*: p. 1046; *House Journal* (37th session) *1919*: pp. 1007–8; unidentified newspaper clipping, Werkmeister Scrapbook, Nebraska State Historical Society.

39. *Omaha World Herald*, 25 February 1919, quoted in Rodgers, "Foreign Language Issue," p. 13.

40. William H. Werkmeister, "Der Kampf um den Deutschunterricht in den öffentlichen Schulen Nebraskas," manuscript, Werkmeister Collection, Nebraska State Historical Society; Arthur Mullen, *Western Democrat* (New York: Wilfred Funk, 1940), pp. 208, 212.

41. *Nebraska Session Laws, 1919*, ch. 249, p. 1019.

42. Werkmeister, "Der Kampf um den Deutschunterricht;" Mullen, *Western Democrat*, p. 215.

43. *Nebraska District of Evangelical Lutheran Synod* v. *McKelvie, Reports of Cases in the Nebraska Supreme Court* 104 (1919): 93.

44. Beck, *Lutheran Elementary Schools*, p. 331.

45. Edwards, "Legal Status of Foreign Languages," p. 272; *Nebraska Session Laws, 1921*, ch. 21, pp. 244–45; Beck, *Lutheran Elementary Schools*, p. 332; Werkmeister, "Der Kampf um den Deutschunterricht"; Mullen, *Western Democrat*, p. 219.

46. Mullen, *Western Democrat*, p. 219.

47. *State of Nebraska* v. *Robert T. Meyer*, Transcript of Testimony, District Court, Hamilton County, Nebraska, copy in the possession of the author. In his testimony Parpart incorrectly identified the Bible story as "Joseph's Ladder."

48. Ibid.

49. *Meyer* v. *Nebraska, Reports of Cases in the Nebraska Supreme Court* 107 (1922): 657.

50. Beck, *Lutheran Elementary schools*, p. 333.

51. Mullen, *Western Democrat*, pp. 220–26. Some account of Mullen's thinking is summarized in Thomas Hanley, "A Western Democrat's Quarrel with the Language Laws," *Nebraska History* 50 (Summer 1969): 151–71.

52. *Meyer* v. *Nebraska, U.S. Supreme Court Reports* 262 (1923): 390.

53. The *Society of Sisters* case is conveniently introduced in Lloyd P. Jorgenson, "The Oregon School of Law of 1922: Passage and Sequel," *Catholic Historical Review* 54 (October 1968): 455–66.

Frontier Norwegian in South Dakota

EINAR HAUGEN

South Dakota was still a battleground between the Sioux Indians and the United States government when the first Norwegian settlers arrived. A treaty of 1859 had opened the land to white settlers, and in 1861 Dakota Territory was created by Congress. The bloody Sioux War of 1862 in Minnesota led to the removal of the Minnesota Sioux to the Missouri River in 1863. Beginning in 1855, the government had established a series of forts on the Missouri, which performed the dual function of protecting white settlers and feeding the displaced Indians. The accompanying map shows where the major forts were located in relation to the cities which eventually grew up in the area.[1] Through 1872 Sioux City, Iowa was the terminus of the railroad; it was little more than a collection of stores and homes on the river bottoms near the confluence of the Sioux River with the Missouri. Its growth coincided with the coming to America of large numbers of Norwegian immigrants, who found that land was already taken in the older settlements of Illinois, Wisconsin, Iowa, and Minnesota.[2] So they wended their way out to the open prairies of the new Dakota Territory. Many of them found employment in Sioux City and formed the nucleus of a long-enduring urban community in that city. Others spread into the nearby area in South Dakota, made their land claims, and developed solidly Norwegian rural communities in the eastern strip, especially in the southeastern corner, of what was to become the state of South Dakota.[3] But before they could build proper homes and become the prosperous farmers of a later age, most of them needed to earn the cash they could get only by manual labor for American employers. In the 1870s the chief employer in this wilderness was the United States government, which needed blacksmiths, lumberjacks, and carpenters, as well as just common labor to sustain the forts.

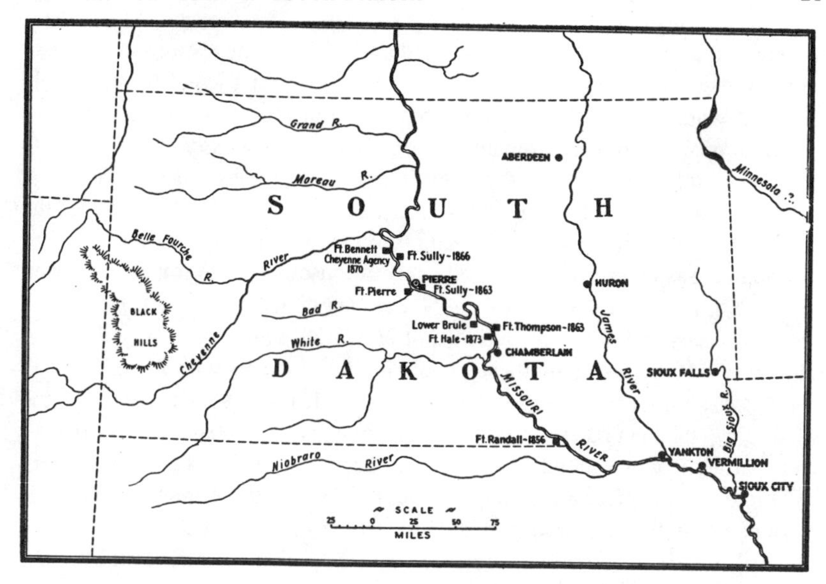

Missouri River Forts in the Seventies

This was the area in which it became my good fortune to do my first field work on the Norwegian language in America. The field work was entirely incidental to the historical research which my mother, Kristine Haugen, was performing as editor of an annual publication known as *Opdalslagets aarbok*. This annual, which she edited from 1928 to 1935, was the organ of an old settlers' organization of the type known as *bygdelag,* studied in a volume by Odd Sverre Lovoll.[4] Opdalslaget, as the name suggests, consisted of people from (or associated with people from) the community of Oppdal (as it is written today) in the county of Sør Trøndelag, in Norway. Group emigration from this community began in the late 1860s, as part of the post–Civil War migration wave. This secluded inland mountain valley was not among the first to send out emigrants to America. For this reason their first group settlement was in the Sioux City–South Dakota area which I have described. The first known group to arrive came to Sioux City on 16 May 1869 and duly combined a celebration of their safe arrival with a commemoration of Norwegian independence day, 17 May. Others followed shortly, until one could speak of an Oppdal community in the farming area between Yankton and Sioux Falls, particularly by the small towns that sprang up later with the names of Volin and Irene. The community stretched northward to Viborg, where it met a settlement of Danes from Jutland.[5]

The contents of the annual devoted to Opdalslaget were in my mother's time primarily of a historical-biographical nature. By letter and by personal interviews she gathered data on people from Oppdal, chiefly the living earliest settlers, but also on those who had passed away. The results were written up in standard Norwegian and printed as biographies or obituaries of the grand old men and women of the community. My share in this, aside from acting as chauffeur on these totally unsubsidized safaris (it was all a labor of love), was to record as best I could the words that fell from the lips of these ancient narrators. The experience was enthralling to a young man who already had discovered the study of Scandinavian dialects and languages as the central interest of his life. The language as I heard it was a wholly unself-conscious (with some exceptions tions I shall note) example of a local Norwegian dialect (my own), laced with bits and pieces of book Norwegian, but above all with remarkably distorted English words picked up by these people in their contacts with Americans. In many cases the form showed that they were learned at a time when the Norwegian speakers had not yet mastered any form of English. *Fort Sully* (as I later learned it was spelled) was regularly pronounced [fort ʃā'le], while *the government* was [guvvamenten], no doubt reflecting the common American [gəvəmənt], with the Norwegian definite article hooked on the end.[6]

There were of course no recording devices available in 1929, the summer when I did most of my scribal work, taking down from dictation the narratives which my mother would use. For her purposes it was adequate if I got the content, since she would rewrite it into proper Norwegian for publication. But I already had a year of graduate work and a great deal of reading in phonetics behind me, and I did my best to render the words as I heard them. The results were not adequate for a phonetic transcription, but they reflect in a broad way the variations from dialect to standard to English of our speakers. The English was all in the loanwords and loanshifts, however; I cannot recall that we spoke English with a single one of our informants. Norwegian in its Oppdal dialect form was still the dominant language throughout the community, including the towns of Volin and Irene, where we often went shopping evenings. Even before this summer I had myself visited the area, spending parts of summers there with cousins of my mother and their descendants, who formed our base of operations. There were also the annual meetings of the society itself, usually held in Canton, South Dakota in the assembly hall of Augustana Academy, later merged with Augustana College in Sioux Falls.[7] The young people of my own age were completely bilingual, speaking Norwegian at home and English at school and to outsiders. We were not outsiders.

The results of our joint research were published in *Opdalslagets aarbok,* and it is regrettable that they are not available in English for the benefit of the descendants of those whose lives are here portrayed. The contents are often humdrum, but the first settlers had much to tell about inhumanly harsh conditions, particularly before there were roads and adequate means of transportation or living. It was rough country, dominated by cowboys and soldiers, often in conflict with Indians and entrepreneurs of the saloonkeeper type, who made their living by providing for the social needs of men on the edge of the wilderness. We were fully aware that we were treading in the footsteps of our great countryman and friend, my teacher O. E. Rølvaag, whose novel *Giants in the Earth* had become a sensation in 1927. But even in his great epic there are aspects of life among the Norwegians of South Dakota that are missing: some of the rough edges that we heard about from our saga narrators.

The preceding is by way of prelude to some notes and comments on the American-Norwegian contact dialect which I recorded in that summer of 1929. I still have all my original notes, but they could hardly be published as authentic linguistic texts in view of their imperfections.[8] One of them I have in two versions, evidently told on two different occasions. I shall present these exactly as recorded and discuss the differences. They throw light on problems of language contact, while providing a key to the sociocultural landscape in which these Norwegian farm youths had to orient themselves.

The narrator, Halvor O. Aune (1846–1932), emigrated to America in 1869, followed by his brother Ole Lie in 1870.[9] They had difficulty in finding work in Sioux City, so together with a number of other Norwegians they made their way into the wilderness of South Dakota and found employment at one or another of the government forts. Aune dictated a very long narrative (it took some ten hours to get it all down), full of lively anecdotes, amusing but occasionally less than plausible. They gave a remarkable picture of the Wild West as seen by a group of Norwegian greenhorns. The following text is one short sample. In the first formulation it is part of the long, dictated narrative. In the second it is told freely, in a form much closer to his natural speech. Loanwords are italicized, loanshifts starred.

Text 1

[Halvor and his brother Ole returned from Fort Sully to Yankton in the spring of 1871 because there was no more work.] Så fikk vi brev fra basen at vi skulle komo opp igjen, men kun e o Ola, oss villa 'n ha. Så skulle vi spare penger, vi skulle gå tri hundrede mil* tefoss. Og så ble vi sårføtte. Så kom vi te et *rensj* en aften, en fransmann som ha ei *skvå*. Hann ha *salon,* og de kosta fem og tjug *sent* glase, du mått betal før du fekk fengra i glase, de va itt no kreditt å fo der. Så mått vi stoppe over natten* der. Så si franskmann, vask deres fødder godt, her er såpe, skur dem godt. Da vi va færdi med de, kom hann me en stor vaskebolle*, hann to vist en par *gallona,* full me viski. No ska du vask føtn me de derre. Så sa e te Ole, de bli en kostbar vask. De ikke non ann rå, de får berre skure, vi må *rønne resken.* Vi vaska oss, vi låg der og kvilte godt og bena blev *all rait*. Så sier e te Ola, gad vite om hann slo vekk den viskien. Vi så efter, og hann slo den ikke vekk. Hann fyllte den vist i flasken igjen, og nogen fekk dyrt betaɫe vasken vor. Vi betalte om morgenen for *brækfest* og seng og *søppeɫ,* en daler* og en halv på kvar. Så spurte jeg hva viskien skull kost. Inginteng, sa'n.[10]

("Then we got a letter from the boss that we should come back up, but only

Ole and I, he wanted to have us. So we were going to save money, we would walk three hundred miles on foot. And then we got sore feet. So we came to a ranch one evening, a Frenchman who had a squaw. He had a saloon, and it cost twenty-five cents a glass, you had to pay before you got your fingers on the glass, there was no credit to be had there. So we had to stop over night there. Then the Frenchman says, 'Wash your feet well, here's soap, scour them well.' When we were through with that, he brought a big wash bowl, it took at least a couple of gallons, full of whisky: 'Now you wash your feet in this here.' Then I said to Ole, 'This is going to be an expensive washing. But there's no other way, it'll have to do, we have to run the risk.' We washed, we slept there and rested well, and our feet were all right. Then I said to Ole, 'I wonder if he poured that whisky out.' We watched, and he did not pour it out. He probably filled it back in the bottle, and someone had to pay through the nose for our washing. In the morning we paid for breakfast and bed and supper, a dollar and a half each. Then I asked what the whisky would cost. 'Nothing.' he said.")

Text 2

Hann Ola bror min og e, oss gjekk fir honnder mil*. Så va de en dag oss vart så sårføtt, oss ha vel *kjippe* sko, au. Så kom oss åt en *rench*. Den ranchmanden* ha ord for ikke at være mors beste barn. Hann ha no ei *skva*, kanske fler. Så sa'n oss skull ta tå oss sko'n, og så fann 'n ti et tå sæ sto'r kvi't vaskarfatom som dem enno bruke og fyllt med viski. Så sa'n oss skull vask føtn ti di. Minn da vesst oss itt ka oss skull gjårrå. Dæ kjem te å kost oss nå, ditte her, Ola, sa e. For ett lite glas kosta fem og tjug *sent*, og de gjekk mange slike glas ti di fate. Da oss ha vaska oss, tømt hann det på ei krokk, og sia sælt hann det vist. Om morgon skull oss beta'l for oss. De var femti sent for losji og femti sent for mat. Men kva skull viskien kost, spurt oss. Inginn teng, svara'n. Menn da tøkt e de tok oss rekti godt. . . . Og bena vart go. Sia ha e godt for den mann, sjøl om hann ha ord for itt å vårå tå di bǣ'st.

("My brother Ola and I, we walked four hundred miles. Then it happened one day that our feet got very sore, I suppose we had cheap shoes, too. Then we came to a ranch. The rancher there had the reputation of not being of the best kind. He had a squaw, perhaps several. Then he told us to take off our shoes, and he brought out one of those big white washbowls that they still use and filled it with whisky. Then he told us to wash our feet in it. But then we didn't know what we should do. 'This is going to cost us something, this here, Ola,' I said. For one little glass cost twenty-five cents, and it took many glasses to fill that bowl. When we had washed, he poured it back into a jug, and later on I guess he sold it. In the morning we went to pay up. It was fifty cents for lodging and fifty cents for food. But what did the whisky cost, we asked. 'Nothing' he replied. But then I felt real good about it [notes unclear here] . . . And our feet were healed. After that I had a good feeling about this man, even though he had the reputation of not being of the best sort.")

Neither transcription shows such phonetic details as the palatalization of *ll, nn, tt,* or the retroflex flapped *l* (used once also in the word *supper*, written ł). With a little editing Text 1 could pass as standard Dano-Norwegian of the nineteenth century, with some highly bookish forms, reflecting unfamiliarity with urban spoken standards: for example *vask deres fødder* 'wash your feet' (for *vask føttene*, [compare the dialect form *vask føtn* a few lines down]), *kun* 'only' (for *bare*), *morgenen* 'the morning' (for *mornen*), *nogen* 'someone' (for *noen*), and so forth. On the other hand the dialect substratum clearly shows through in forms like *komo* 'come' (for *komme*), *tri* 'three' (for *tre*), *tefoss* 'on foot' (for *til fots*), *ha* 'had' (for *hadde*), *kosta* 'cost' (preterite for *kostet*), apocope in *mått betal* 'had to pay' (for *måtte betale*), and *skull kost* 'should cost' (for *skulle koste*). There are alternations between dialect and standard: for example: *fekk / fikk* 'got', *skull / skulle* 'should', *Ole / Ola, itt / ikke* 'not', *e / jeg* 'I', *si* (should be *sie*) / *sier* 'say' (present). Of nineteen instances where the dialect apocopates *-e,* our speaker has it in thirteen but drops it in six. Of the latter, three are infinitives after modals (*betal, kost, vask*), three preterite modals (*mått* [2], *skull*). While these lapses are understandable, they are not consistent. Weak preterites keep the dialect *-a* (*villa, vaska*), but not nouns (*fengra* 'the fingers', *bena* 'the feet' versus *natten* 'the night', *flasken* 'the bottle'). Two consistent deviations from the dialect are the use of *vi* 'we' as subject instead of *oss* and the suppression of the dative case.

More examples could be given of the curious range of forms from rural basilect to literary acrolect. What language can one describe as underlying this text? Aside from the loanwords, it is unmistakably Norwegian. But within that framework there is a norm conflict between his written and spoken codes. Here it does not help to count items. One must ask what the speaker's intent was. That this was to speak literary (standard) Norwegian is clear from the fact that he is known to have written this account down. He was in effect reading it from memory as he dictated. He intended it to be in a form appropriate to the presence of literate persons who were busy writing down what he had to say. But his modest educational opportunities and his life as primarily a manual laborer made his diglossia imperfect.

Text 2 reveals an entirely different picture of his language. Here the *oss* 'we' and the dative case are not suppressed, and apocope is regular, as well as the circumflex accent here marked with an apostrophe (*sto'r kvi't* 'big white' for *store kvite*). While there are minor deviations from correct dialect, no doubt due to his association with Norwegians speaking other dialects (for example, *men* 'but' for *minn, var* 'was' for *va, ta* 'take' for *tå, spurt* 'asked' for *spor*), there is only one intrusive passage in literary style: (*ha ord for*) *ikke at være mors beste barn* '(had the reputation) of not being one of mother's best children', that is, of being a scoundrel. This is interpretable as a quotation, a switch to the literary code.

The English loans appear to be of virtually the same order in both texts, with perhaps a slight increase in his "high" style in Text 1. They show some minor variation in form (*rench / rensh / ranch-, skvå / skva*) which may be due to imperfect transcription; note also *en* versus *et ranch*, the former being the usual form.[11] Note that Norwegians have difficulty distinguishing *ranch* from *wrench*; the final cluster is nonexistent and usually simplified, while there is no short æ sound in this position. Other phonetic adaptations are apparent in the ø of *rønne* 'run' and *søppeł* 'supper', the *e* of resken 'the risk' (in the dialect *fisk* 'fish' is *fesk*). *Salon* 'saloon' and *gallona* 'gallons' both have stress on the first syllable and long *o,* reflecting familiarity with the spelling; these are essentially spelling pronunciations. But the gemination of the consonants in *gallona, rønne, søppeł,* and *kjippe* 'cheap' reflect preceding short vowel in the Norwegian system, with medial consonant lengthening. Grammatical adaptation is complete in *rønne resken* (*run* plus infinitive *-e, risk* plus masculine article*-en*), *kjippe* (*cheap* plus plural adjective *-e*), *gallona (gallon* plus masculine plural *-a*). *Squaw* gets the correct feminine indefinite article *ei*, regular for females.

Only the more obvious loanshifts are noted: the Norwegian *daler* came to mean "dollar," *mil* the American mile; loanshift creations are *over natten* 'over night' (for *natten over*), *vaskebolle* 'wash bowl' (note the correct word in Text 2: *vaskarfat*), *ranchmanden* 'the ranch man' (that is, "rancher").

Most of the loans are key terms in the new landscape: land measured in *miles*, liquids in *gallons*, payments reckoned in *dollars* and *cents*, meals known as *breakfast* and *supper*, ranches where the ranchers were Frenchmen with *squaws*, who ran *saloons*. It was a perilous country where you had to *run risks* and could only hope that things would come out *all right*. An especially interesting loan is *cheap* shoes: back home shoes were still made on the farms by itinerant shoemakers from hides furnished by the farmers. In America one had the choice, and if one were poor, the necessity, of buying *cheap* ones. Although *bas* 'boss' and *viski* 'whisky' may have been learned in America, they are attested far enough back in Norwegian not to be considered loans here.

The narrative quality is also rather different in the two texts. Text 1 is more circumstantial and probably more accurate (at least the distance from Yankton to Fort Sully is more like three than four hundred miles). Text 1 makes it clear that the two wanderers were first asked to wash their feet in soap and water before soaking them in whisky. But Text 2 has a narrative directness and cohesion that is far superior: it establishes the rancher-saloonkeeper as a man with a heart beneath his crude exterior and dubious mode of life. The unorthodox foot bath becomes a small study in character, an encounter between two cultures, a true frontier exemplum.

Aune commented occasionally on the problems which these newcomers faced in learning English. Of his brother Ole Lie he said: "I could talk a little, but he didn't know anything. He was such a stick-in-the-mud [*tørpinne*] that he was here for two years before he tried to say a word. But then his tongue loosened." On their first trip into the Dakota wilderness, they were accompanied by another, earlier settler from Oppdal, Iver Furunes. "He had studied English in school in Norway, but I was much better in English than he. I could get along, and I hadn't gone to any English school.'' Aune's pride in his English was matched by his skill as narrator; but in the race for worldly goods he fell far short of his ''stick-in-the-mud'' brother.

The small samples here presented from a much larger body of materials collected of frontier Norwegian show first of all that Norwegians did take part in the winning even of the wild west. They offer illuminating evidence of how radically the speech situation can alter a speaker's language, inducing a virtual diglossia that can inhibit even a practiced and skillful narrator when he believes he must elevate his language. Finally, they show how a living language is quite naturally reshaped to meet new situations in one's life and how speakers follow the general norms for bilingual behavior both in the kinds of words adopted and in the manner of their adaptation.[12]

NOTES

1. The map was drawn for my article ''Norwegians at the Indian Forts on the Missouri River During the Seventies,'' *Norwegian-American Studies and Records* 6:(1931): 89–121. For further details see this article.

2. On Norwegian settlement in South Dakota, see Carlton C. Qualey, *Norwegian Settlement in the United States* (Northfield, Minn: Norwegian-American Historical Association, 1938), pp. 130–48. It should perhaps be explained that Sioux City was my birthplace and for many years the home of my parents.

3. In 1900 the Norwegian element included 51,455, or 12.8 percent of the total population of South Dakota (ibid., p.134).

4. Einar Haugen, *The Norwegian Language in America : A Study in Bilingual Behavior* (Philadelphia: University of Pennsylvania Press, 1953; 2d ed. Bloomington: Indiana Universiy Press, 1969) includes references to this work on pp. 552–55 (a sample text) and p. 615.

5. For a full account of the issues of the yearbook, see my ''A Case of Grass-roots Historiography: Opdalslaget and its Yearbooks'' in *Norwegian Influence on the Upper Midwest: Proceedings of an International Conference at University of Minnesota-Duluth, May 22–24, 1975,* ed. Harald S. Næss (Duluth: University of Minnesota–Duluth, 1976), pp. 42–49.

6. Odd Sverre Lovoll, *A Folk Epic: The Bygdelag in America* (Boston: Twayne Publishers, for the Norwegian-American Historical Association, 1975).

5. Although Opdalslaget was founded in Seattle, where many people from Oppdal had settled, nearly half of its members (46.7 percent in 1929) lived in South Dakota.

6. For detailed discussion of the adaptation of English loanwords to Norwegian phonological and grammatical patterns, see my *Norwegian Language in America,* chaps. 16–18.

7. This was the same academy at which O. E. Rølvaag had gotten his first American education, when it was known as Augustana College; but the college section had been moved to Sioux Falls in 1918 (O. M. Norlie, *History of the Norwegian People in America* [Minneapolis, Minn.: Augsburg, 1925], pp. 281–82). For a detailed study

of the Oppdal dialect see my *Oppdalsmålet: innføring i et sørtrøndsk fjellbygdmål* (forthcoming). On a recent quick trip to the South Dakota community I found no one able to speak Norwegian.

8. They include extensive notes on Halvor O. Aune and shorter interviews with Jørund Dørum, Goro Bøe, Jens Hoxeng, Ole Lie (Lee), Sivert Mellem (specimen in *Norwegian Language in America,* pp. 552–55). The writer hopes eventually to publish them for content, if not for language.

9. For obituaries see *Opdalslagets aarbok: 1936–38,* p. 59; also my article cited above, note 1. The difference in last names between brothers was not uncommon; for discussion see *Norwegian Language in America,* p. 200.

10. A slightly edited version of this text was printed in my *Norsk i Amerika* (Oslo: Cappelen, 1939), p. 119; 2d ed., (1975), p. 111.

11. Of twelve informants recorded in *Norwegian Language in America* (p. 590), nine made it masculine (*en*), one feminine (*ei*), two neuter (*et*), one of the latter being our speaker; but as appears here, masculine is probably his normal form as well. The neuter may be induced by an underlying *hus* 'house', or *hotell* 'hotel', both neuters.

12. For further discussion of the last-named problem, see my ''Norm and Deviation in Bilingual Communities'' in *Bilingualism: Psychological, Social, and Educational Implications,* ed. Peter A. Hornby (New York: Academic Press, 1977), pp. 91–102.

Swedish Dialects in the Midwest: Notes from Field Research

Folke Hedblom

Early Swedish Colonization in the Midwestern States

Swedish immigration to the Midwest began in the 1840s and 1850s. The best known of the first settlers is the Uppsala student Gustaf Unonius, who settled in the wilderness west of Milwaukee in 1841.[1] Most important by far was the group immigration of the Erik Jansonist sect to Illinois in the fall of 1846, when about one thousand persons arrived at the same time with about five hundred more following during the next few years. They founded a religious-collectivistic colony called Bishop Hill in northwestern Illinois. Even before the Civil War several Swedes and their families settled in Iowa, Minnesota, Kansas, and Nebraska, but the bulk of them arrived in the years 1865–80. After the Homestead Act had been passed, the war was ended, and severe crop failures had stricken Sweden in the years 1867 and 1868, emigration from Sweden increased considerably. By 1930 about 1.2 million Swedes had immigrated to the United States.

To a considerable degree these immigrants could retain their Swedish mother tongue as their everyday speech and pass it on to their children. As late as 1930 the United States census recorded over six hundred thousand Americans whose mother tongue was Swedish.[2] This is a significant number—almost 10 percent of all Swedish speakers in the entire world at that time. The majority of the immigrants settled in the midwestern and Great Plains states. In 1880 no less than 76.54 percent of all Swedish-born in the United States were living in this area, among them more than 21 percent in Illinois, 20 percent in Minnesota, 9 percent in Iowa, 5 percent in Kansas, 5 percent in Nebraska, 4 percent in Michigan, and 4 percent in Wisconsin.[3] The proportions remained relatively unchanged in 1900, although the percentage of Swedish-born had decreased, especially in Kansas.

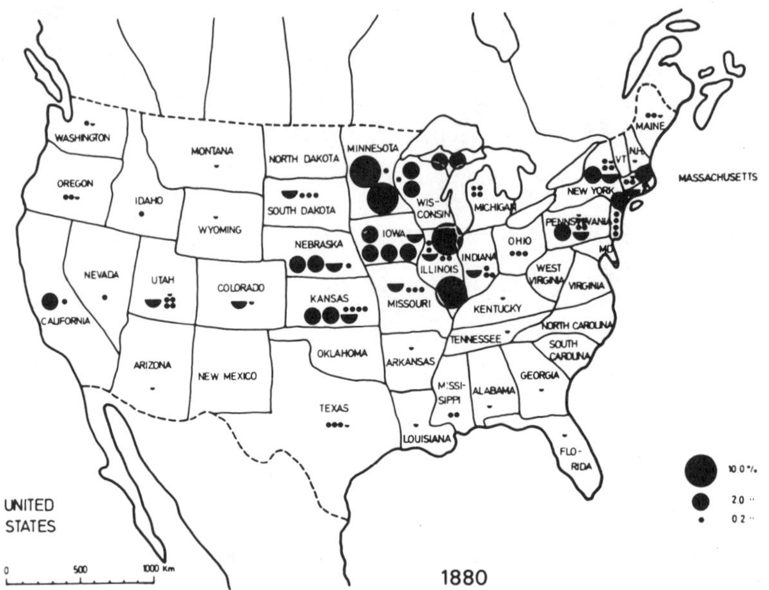

THE DISTRIBUTION OF THE SWEDISH-BORN POPULATION IN THE U.S. 1880
Sources U.S. Census 1880, Part I; H. Norman (1974), pp. 218f.

These early immigrants were for the most part farmers, sons of farmers, crofters, and farm hands. They came to America in the hope of acquiring land of their own on the fertile plains and in the adjoining woodland. Whether they traveled in large groups, as families, or as individuals, they remained in contact with people from their native districts in Sweden and bought land near to one another. Very often they had a relative or a neighbor who had gone on ahead to find a suitable place on which to settle.[4] In this way relatively closed colonies were established, in which the large majority consisted of people from the same native village or parish. Here they retained as long as possible the good old customs and way of life brought from Sweden, which had been handed down from generation to generation.

In no part of Swedish America have Swedish dialects been preserved as well as in the midwestern states, especially in Minnesota, but also in Wisconsin, Illinois, and Kansas. Here they have continued to live on as a second language among the immigrants' grandchildren—that is, in the third generation—down to the 1970s. Most of the immigrants spoke only dialect. At the time of emigration their school education had been slight, and some of the oldest ones were probably illiterate.

Beginning with the 1870s, when the mass emigration from Sweden set in, the stream of immigrants turned more and more to the cities. These immigrants found employment primarily as laborers in industry, in the mines, in lumber camps, and in railroad construction. To be sure, people from the same region of the home country tried to remain together in the cities also; but there people from various provinces, whether from the country or from the city, mingled with each other at their places of work, in social organizations, in churches, and in similar places. The speech development followed the usual pattern for Swedish America: the most striking and distinctive dialect features were sloughed off rather early, within the first generation. Among their children, the second generation, who were bilingual and attended American schools, the position of Swedish was quickly weakened, even as the daily language of the home. And by the third generation Swedish had disappeared. Good examples of this are afforded by such cities as Omaha, Chicago, and Minneapolis.

The following presentation is concerned with bilingual Swedish speakers born in America. They will be referred to as second- and third-generation speakers. Immigrants who arrived in America before the age of fifteen will also be regarded as second-generation speakers. These people, who lived their entire lives in the country and belonged to the rural, or farm, population, were in general not affected by the America-Swedish cultural propaganda, which strove for the retention of the Swedish language and a distinct Swedish way of life in America. They represented what Joshua A. Fishman has called "the little tradition level." None of the dialect speakers cited in the following has ever been to Sweden.

The Dialects in the Rural Settlements

It was in the ethnically homogeneous farming communities, more or less isolated from the linguistically foreign environment, that the prerequisites existed that made it possible for the various Swedish dialects to continue to live their own lives, and it was there that they could remain the clearly dominant language far into the twentieth century. In these communities the homogeneity extended not only to Swedish language and traditions in general but also to the traditions and speech of a specific province or even parish in Sweden.

The continuity and strength of tradition in these settlements was often very strong. Even in the 1970s I met various farmers in Isanti and Chisago counties in Minnesota who still lived on the very farms their grandfathers had cleared from the wilderness in the 1850s and 1860s. If there were several sons in an immigrant family, the father often helped them clear the land for their own farms in the vicinity. Thus the family remained in the new community. Marriage outside the community was unusual. Similar conditions prevailed in the adjacent settlements in Burnett and Polk counties in northeastern Wisconsin until 1880, according to the historian Hans Norman. Here too the immigrants remained living for a very long time at the place where they had originally settled. Twenty years later 43–49 percent of them were still there. In that area the Swedes comprised the largest immigrant group.[5]

In these settlements life was lived as long as possible according to the model of the self-contained economic society, which was characteristic for Sweden even during the middle of the nineteenth century. This ancient way of life was now reproduced in America, especially in forest regions, where nature was more similar to that in Sweden. Most of what was needed was produced or created by the people themselves. Money was in extremely short supply. It is surprising that the isolation of these farming communities lasted so long—until well into the twentieth century. It was not until the advent of the automobile that it was broken. In 1962 a farmer in Lindstrom, Chisago County, Minnesota (born there in 1900) discussed this matter in the Småland dialect.

> Still during my childhood, before the time when everybody got his own car, you heard only Swedish, mostly Småland vernacular, here in the streets of Lindstrom. That was the only speech you heard, you couldn't hear an English word in many, many years [sic]. Now it's the other way. If I start talking Swedish, there is not even a third of them who understand me! The other people think I am half mad! You could hear from the language from where the people came. There are great differences between the people down here and those who came from Vibo, north of Center City [just one to two miles distant]. We heard it also when they spoke English, they have a different accent. We seldom saw them. They came into town once or twice a week, that was all. Maybe they came from different provinces in Sweden. We called them Småland people, and Skåne, Öland, Östergötland, Västergötland people. But what those places [in Sweden] were like we had no idea about. But the Småland people around here, they spoke the same way, all of them.[6]

Thus third-generation Americans identified each other on the basis of their Swedish dialects. The biblical shibboleth was in working order in the Småland settlement!

This permanence of settlement, or high "persistence level" of the inhabitants of the old Swedish farming communities, was the first prerequisite for the preservation of the dialect.[7] The second was the circumstance that people lived in extended families, in which grandmother and grandfather lived their entire lives with their children and grandchildren—there were, after all, no old peoples' homes in those days. Since the grandparents spoke no other language than their native dialect, the grandchildren had to learn it in order to be able to communicate with them. In this way many families preserved the ability to speak Swedish even after English had otherwise become the language of everyday communication. When the old people died, the dialect fell into disuse. The third condition that contributed to the preservation of the dialect was the fact that the community was constantly supplied with new immigrants who came from the same dialect area in Sweden. If, on the other hand, such newcomers had lived in America for a considerable length of time among

Swedes who spoke other dialects, their native dialect had usually undergone a certain degree of leveling. This, in turn, contributed to a weakening of the position of the original settlement dialect. And when the stream of new immigrants from Sweden was almost completely cut off around the turn of the century, the position of Swedish on the whole was attenuated.

The Dialects of Sweden: Field Investigation in America

The Swedish language is split up into many different dialects. For almost a thousand years Sweden has been divided into twenty-five provinces (*landskap*) and more than two thousand state-church parishes (*socknar*). In many of these parishes dialects are spoken that are quite distinct from those of neighboring parishes. Certain parish dialects, particularly in Dalarna, differ so greatly from standard Swedish that outsiders find it difficult to decide whether they are actually Swedish. Many dialects are still in use as the everyday speech within the family or the village, though they have undergone change through the constantly increasing influence of standard Swedish.

What happened to these dialects during the second half of the nineteenth century, when they were uprooted from their native soil and transplanted in a new environment side by side with a dominant foreign language and with other Swedish dialects that were also strange to them?

Until 1962 practically nothing was known in Sweden about the Swedish language in America. In that year the first research expedition was sent out from the Institute of Dialect and Folklore Research of Uppsala. It was followed by new expeditions in 1964 and 1966. It was natural that in these expeditions emphasis should be put on the dialects and on dialect-colored American-Swedish colloquial speech. Soon the program was broadened, however, to include American standard Swedish. From the beginning it was clear that the undertaking was a salvage operation. It was essential to collect quickly the most varied and comprehensive material possible.

All in all over five hundred voices were recorded with a combined recording time of almost three hundred hours. Technically the recordings were made on a professional level with an experienced accoustical engineer as technician and driver of the specially equipped microbus that was brought along. The recordings were made in situations as natural as possible: sometimes several persons were recorded in informal conversation, sometimes without the speakers' knowledge. It would have been desirable (as was done with similar recordings in Sweden) to have an interviewer who spoke the same (or similar) dialect as the informants, but this, of course, was not possible. To a certain extent this drawback was compensated for by the fact that the leader of the expedition had had direct experience for about thirty years with dialect speakers and environments in all of Sweden's provinces.

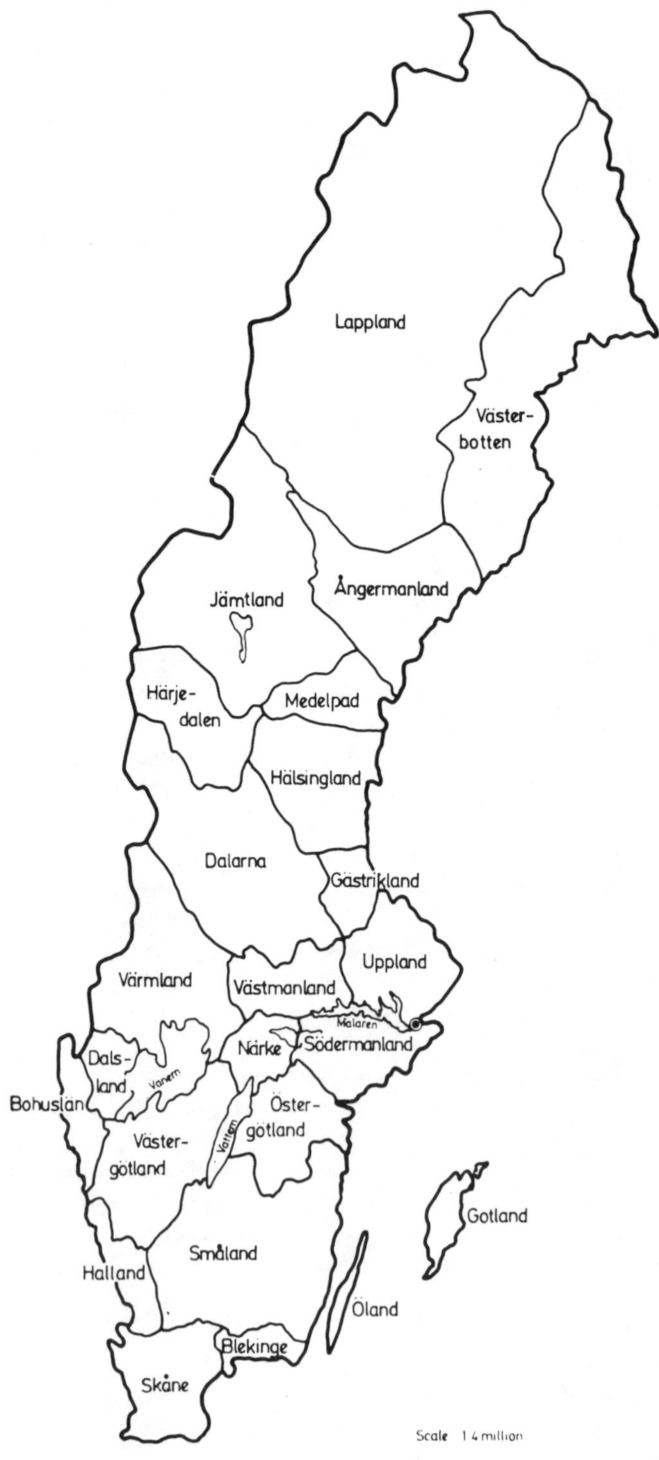

SWEDEN. PROVINCIAL BOUNDARIES *(landskap)*

The purpose of the expeditions was not exclusively linguistic. We had to use these opportunities to try to arrive at a broad, objective documentation of the speakers' life environment, that is, the actual connection between the language and the life of the people in the Swedish settlements.[8] The author made supplementary investigations in Illinois and Minnesota in 1973 and 1976.

SOME OF THE MAIN PLACES IN THE MIDWEST STATES WHERE TAPE RECORDINGS OF SWEDISH DIALECTS WERE MADE, 1962–66

Surviving Swedish Dialects in Homogenous Settlements: Two Examples

A good example of an American-Swedish dialect that is very much alive in the third generation is the Hälsingland speech of Bishop Hill, Illinois. I reproduce here a short excerpt from a conversation I recorded there in 1973. I conversed with a woman, born in 1906, about life on the farm on which she and her sister had grown up.[9] Her mother had also been born in Bishop Hill as the daughter of a woman who had immigrated with the Erik Jansonists in 1850. Her father had immigrated at the age of ten with his parents from a neighboring parish in Hälsingland. In their parents' home she and her sister always spoke the Swedish dialect, the only form of Swedish they knew. In school they learned English, the language they used in speaking with their schoolmates, who liked to poke fun at their funny Swedish. The sisters themselves call their dialect "Bishop Hill Swedish," and they are aware of the fact that it is not *fin*, correct Swedish. Nowadays they use Swedish only when speaking with each other and with a few old friends—especially when the conversation turns to the old days—and in speaking to visitors from Sweden. Otherwise English has long been their everyday speech, even when speaking with their husbands and children. The children do not know any Swedish at all. Around 1935 all religious services in Swedish ceased in the only church in town (Methodist).

In the following she tells about helping their parents shock oats:

> Dåm sjacka [*shocked*] havra . . . å vi följde mä förståss. Iblann så sätte vi åpp en sjack [*shock*] å då skulle vi sätta en tåpp [*top*] på den å så sa vi: "Ja, nu skulle vi marka [*mark*] den så vi visste åm den stog åpp tell dom tröska." Moster Liva bruka säja "Dä var mejntingen [*the main thing*], dä." Dä var mejntingen åm han stog åpp tell dåm tröska. Åm sjacken stog . . . när ä regna . . . å åm dä blåsste hårt så blåsste den bundeln [*the bundle*] såm dåm sätte åppå, blåsste åv.

> ("They shocked oats and we accompanied them, of course. Sometimes we put up a shock and then we had to put a top on it and so we said, 'Now we should mark it so we can know if it will be standing till they start the threshing.' Aunt Liva usually said, 'That is the main thing.' The main thing was that it remained standing until they threshed. If the shock was standing . . . where it rained . . . and if the wind was hard, the bundle on top blew down.").

The dialect is easy to identify as that of the parish Hanebo in southern Hälsingland close to the border of Gästrikland—the parish from which her grandmother emigrated in 1850. The dialect is close to the one I spoke as a child. Elderly people in southern Hälsingland who listened to these tape recordings were astonished at the genuine intonation of the dialect as well as at its old-fashioned authenticity on the whole. The English and standard Swedish elements do not disturb the general impression. The standard Swedish words and phrases she knows were probably learned in church, where she and her sister were very active.

The foreign elements are quite modest in number. As even this short specimen shows, the English loanwords (in brackets) are not numerous. The phonology, prosody, accents, vowels, and consonants are essentially those of the dialect. There is no English brogue. Only sporadically do such English phonemes as /r/, /l/, and /o/ intrude into Swedish words. In morphology the declensional and conjugational systems have been retained virtually undisturbed. Even loanwords are adapted to the morphology of the dialect. *The main thing* became *mejntingen, the bundle* becomes *bundeln, the shafts* becomes *sjåftene, shocked* becomes *sjacka,* and so forth. In contrast the old three-gender system is in a state of dissolution—a condition to which both standard Swedish and English have contributed. The speaker often vacillates between all three genders. Sometimes the masculine predominates, but more often it is the standard Swedish nonneuter (*utrum*). In her lexicon the speaker has retained many words that have long since become obsolete in the original dialect, a circumstance that contributes strongly to the general impression of archaism. As is usually the case with immigrant tongues in America, a considerable portion of native vocabulary has been lost and replaced with borrowings from English.[10] In the syntax there are various forms of English interference such as are common in American Swedish in general.

This speaker is perfectly bilingual in American English and Hälsingland Swedish. Her English is faultless, and there are few traces of an English substratum in her Swedish.[11] She switches to English when, for example, someone injects a comment in that language into the conversation. When her Swedish vocabulary is inadequate, she resorts to an English word in unchanged form. The English loanwords of the ordinary American-Swedish type that have been integrated into her Swedish in the great majority of cases follow the rules of the dialect in regard to phonology and morphology—as, for instance, in words like *fence, field, porch, shock, store, stove*.[12]

It should be noted, however, that the individual differences among conservative dialect speakers are significant. This becomes apparent when we compare this woman with another Hälsingland dialect speaker, from Isanti County, Minnesota. He also belongs to the third generation and is of the same age, having been born in 1903. He grew up on a farm in a settlement in which most of the families came from the same parish in northern Hälsingland, many as early as the 1860s. He too attended English-speaking schools and uses English for most of the day's situations, even when speaking to his wife, but his English reveals distinct traces of the phonology of his Swedish dialect. But his command of his dialect is substantially more certain and consistent than that of the Bishop Hill speaker. Phonology and morphology are well preserved, and even the three-gender system functions as it did in the original dialect. His dialect is the only kind of Swedish he knows, and standard Swedish levelings are insignificant. The state of his dialect is so stable and dominant that he makes use of English terminology when his Swedish vocabulary is inadequate—for example, in speaking about technical matters. But he does not switch to English. The English words (with certain phonetically difficult exceptions) conform to the phonological, morphological, and syntactic patterns of the dialect. The following short example is taken from a conversation dealing with a picture of an old steam engine used for threshing in his younger days:

> Då du *starter injårn* . . . å drar på-n-här *levvern,* då *engedjer* n-här *klöttjn*. . . . Du *revösjer rotesjn* på jule hänne. . . . Å sö ä en annan *revösjlevver* då, söm du *tjentjer tajmninga* hänne.[13]

> ("When you start the engine and pull this lever, then this clutch engages. You reverse the rotation of this wheel. And then there is another reverse lever by which you change the timing here.")

Only one noun (*hjul* 'wheel') and one verb (*draga* 'pull') are Swedish. For the rest, only pronouns, auxiliary verbs, and adverbs are taken from the Swedish. As for the word *tajmninga* 'the timing', pronunciation, word formation, gender, and inflectional suffix are those of the dialect. The text shows how the speaker ingeniously makes maximal use of the English store of technical terms with minimal infringement upon the phonetic and morphologic patterns of his Hälsingland dialect. His appropriation of English words is clearly different from the immigrant's desultory mixing. For such a transfer of words the speaker must be bilingual; but he is, as has been shown, a bilingual of a type quite different from the woman in Bishop Hill.

The truly dialect-homogeneous settlements, in which a single parish dialect is completely dominant as in the above two cases, are, naturally enough, in the minority. Of all of the recorded material, homogeneous dialects comprise about five to ten percent. In the two cases here discussed the prerequisites for the retention of the Hälsingland dialect are especially favorable. The families from Hälsingland were numerous among the Erik Jansonists, and they had arrived early. This put them into a socially advanced position. In regard to the Swedish settlements in Wisconsin Hans Norman has demonstrated that it was those groups of immigrants who on the one hand arrived first and on the other hand were large in number who achieved a socially dominant position in the community.[14]

These settlements in northeastern Wisconsin along the Saint Croix River constitute a continuation of the Swedish colonization area on the western side of the river in Chisago and Isanti counties in Minnesota. These two counties on the Chisago lake system northeast of Minneapolis make up the largest cohesive rural area in all of Swedish America. Nearly every farm on an area of 2,237 square kilometers was cleared and cultivated by Swedes. The first ones arrived in the 1850s, and as late as 1920 almost one-fourth of the total population were

Swedish born.[15] Here dialects that had existed far apart in the homeland for the first time confronted each other on a rather large scale. Yet they were neither blended nor leveled out, but continued to exist side by side. People from the various provinces settled close together, and the permanence of these province and parish settlements was so strong and persistent that the author as late as the 1970s, when English had become almost exclusively the everyday speech within the family, could trace the dialect boundaries that run through the region between, for example, Småland, Hälsingland, and Dalarna and even between different Swedish parishes within the various provinces. The inscriptions on the gravestones of the small burial grounds, which most often were churchyards, show that the first settlers on the surrounding farms came from closely circumscribed areas—parishes and villages—in Sweden. On some farms the dialects still exist, some of them surprisingly conservative, others leveled in the direction of standard Swedish, with the usual influence from English. But the dialects have not become blended with each other. The fact that a large number of them were Baptists contributed to their cohesion, but there were also many Lutherans in the vicinity. I had similar experiences among the still more numerous Småland people in Chisago County and in the adjacent settlements in Wisconsin, on the eastern side of the Saint Croix River, where the majority of the Swedish settlers had come from Västmanland and surrounding provinces.

In the question of the dialect-conservative settlement, the people of the upper parishes of Dalarna occupy a special position. Their dialects, which differ sharply among themselves, must be some of the most conservative in northern Europe. They were completely incomprehensible to Swedish outsiders and could be used only within a very small circle. But just as they had done in Sweden, the American Dalecarlians also spoke a modified standard Swedish. In 1966 we made recordings of the speech of second-generation people whose parents had come from the parish of Älvadalen. The settlement, founded in 1880, is near Mille Lacs Lake, Minnesota. The informants—twelve in number—conversed entirely in dialect. But in Bishop Hill the situation was quite different. Here the Dalecarlians were in the minority. It is reported that they frequently used their dialect as a secret language—for example, on the party telephone line. This aroused suspicion and stamped them as socially inferior, and therefore they gradually abandoned their dialect. Some of them are even said to have denied their Swedish origin.

While editing our recordings of speakers of conservative dialects we became aware of the fact that some of them retain linguistic features that long ago disappeared from the living dialects in Sweden. This holds true for phonetic, morphological, and syntactic features that until then had been known only from older literature. One of the dialects for which this obtains is the old city dialect of Stockholm.[16]

Swedish Dialects in Heterogeneous Rural Settlements

In the large majority of cases no one dialect group was in such a strong position in its settlement that it could maintain its speech outside the family in a more or less unchanged form—aside from the usual English loans. This holds true especially for speakers of the second and third generation. As a rule the minority leveled out the most divergent features of their dialects in accordance with the speech norms of the majority, which came close to standard Swedish, was perceived as being *finare* and therefore enjoyed higher social prestige. There follow several illustrative examples.

I encountered a case of dialect confrontation that led to a change of dialect in Kimball, Minnesota. A farmer, born on his farm in 1894, and his two sisters told me the following in Swedish:

> Father (born 1852) came from northern Värmland in 1876 and mother (born 1861) from the province of Dalarna. When we were small, we always spoke the Dalarna dialect, mother's and her mother's language. Later on the family moved to this place, and we began school here, where all the children came from Värmland families. They laughed at us because we spoke Dalecarlian. So we turned to speaking the Värmland dialect like father, even within the family. But to grandma we always spoke Dalecarlian, the only language she understood. So we could speak three languages, Värmland, Dalarna, and English. It was easy for us to change language.[17]

The brother, who had remained on the farm, now spoke only his Värmland dialect and English. A Värmland dialect expert has assured me that this man's dialect is a pure, archaic north Värmland vernacular with no traces of other dialects except for the usual English loans. The sisters, who had been living in different Swedish-speaking areas in America, now spoke standard American Swedish. They remember only individual words and phrases from their mother's Dalecarlian.

Such a change of dialect, of course, can take place only in childhood. This example sheds light on the question whether it is the father's or mother's dialect that prevails in the family. This usually depends on which dialect is spoken by the majority in the community and which enjoys higher social prestige. In those cases where the difference between the dialect of the minority and that of the majority was so great as to make mutual understanding very difficult, or in cases where the minority was not certain that the dialect of the majority was correct Swedish or that it represented a reliable standard Swedish norm, it lay near at hand to resort to a more radical expedient: one abandoned Swedish in favor of English, the language one had learned in school and whose social status was beyond question. The following case from Kansas is instructive.

In 1964, not far from the city of Enterprise (southeast of Abilene), we visited a Swedish colony that had been founded by immigrants from the province of Gästrikland in the 1860s. Most of them had come directly from Sweden, and they formed a very close-knit community with little intermarriage at first. By now the community had dissolved. Agriculture in the vicinity had been streamlined, and the descendants of the settlers had moved away. But once each year they met at the old church for "clean up day"—to decorate the graves of their relatives—and we met them there just on that day. After we had conversed somewhat haltingly for awhile, the dialect of Gästrikland emerged. But a woman said in Swedish with an accent that betrayed that she did not have the same origin as the others: "Father came from the island of Gotland and mother from Östergötland. Thus they had quite different dialects. When we people spoke, the other people laughed at us. So we went over to English. The north Sweden (Gästrikland) people—they thought they knew how to speak, but we didn't. Theirs was right, but ours was not." The Gästrikland dialect had a higher level of prestige. It was not only the speech of the compact majority, it was also closer to standard Swedish, which has its historical origin in the neighboring provinces around Stockholm.

But settlements of this kind, where there is a majority with a relatively uniform dialect, were, to the best of my knowledge, unusual in the Great Plains states of Kansas and Nebraska and even in Iowa. This is because of the different character of Swedish immigration in these states. Most immigrants did not come here directly from Sweden; rather, they had lived for a longer or shorter period of time in Illinois, especially in Chicago and Galesburg or in other rather large cities, together with people from various parts of Sweden, and there they began to level their dialects. The great majority of the earliest Swedish immigrants to Kansas came in groups organized by colonization companies in Illinois at the close of the 1860s. Even though to a certain degree they remained together according to their places of origin in Sweden and even though relatives and friends from there joined them later, no settlements developed here that were as unified in regard to language as those in Minnesota.

In the largest Swedish concentration in Kansas, in the center of the state, around the little town of Lindsborg, south of Salina, one can observe how children and grandchildren of people from Värmland, Västergötland, Småland, Blekinge, and elsewhere are predominant at this or that place, but no group of them was dominant to such a degree that the preservation of its own dialect was a matter of course. Quite early, too, there seems to have been extensive intermarriage between people whose parents were from different provinces and even marriage with non-Swedes. The speech of most of those we met in the 1960s had undergone leveling. In New Gottland, descendants of immigrants from the provinces of Västergötland and Blekinge were predominant. Various features of the Västergötland dialect have been preserved, but of the Blekinge dialect scarcely more than a few weak traces can be heard in spite of the fact that the immigrants from this province on Sweden's south coast were quite numerous. Among the immigrants themselves this dialect seems to have had low status, even among those who spoke it. Here are several examples. A Mr. and Mrs. Berg were both born in or near New Gottland of parents who immigrated in the 1860s and 1870s from Blekinge. The speech of both is leveled out. Mr. Berg's parents always spoke Blekinge dialect, but he himself said (in Swedish), "I think the Blekinge dialect is one of the worst kinds of speech in Swedish," and he took pains even when young to speak as *fint* as possible. But opinions regarding what was *fint* varied. In the community of Assaria, where the Blekinge people formerly were the dominant group, it was felt that the Småland people spoke *fint*.[18]

In Lindsborg a man whose parents had been among the numerous immigrants from Värmland in 1869 maintained that his wife's speech was ugly (*fult*). "It has too much Blekinge in it," he said in Swedish. "She does not speak Swedish fluently." And he complained about both her pronunciation and her vocabulary, which deviated from his own normal Värmland speech.[19] Sweden's southermost dialects—those of Blekinge, Skåne, and southern Halland—had low status. They differ sharply from standard Swedish and are very close to Danish. Nowhere in Swedish America have I found more than remnants of dialects from Skåne, Blekinge, or southern Småland among second-generation speakers.

In Boone, Iowa, I met a ninety-six-year-old widow who had emigrated from Småland with her parents at the age of two. She had lived her whole life among Swedes in Moigona, Swede Valley, and Fort Dodge. Her speech was still colored somewhat by her native dialect. But she said she had always been ashamed of her Småland speech, especially when she heard *norrlänningar* speak, that is, persons whose dialects are closer to standard Swedish. A similar attitude was expressed by a ninety-year-old Småland immigrant in Wisconsin. He patterned his speech on that of the Våstmanland majority, to which his wife and her parents belonged. The dialects of Våstmanland are very similar to standard Swedish.

In Nebraska, too, we found the same negative attitude toward their native dialects among people of southern Swedish extraction. A ninety-two-year-old woman in Funk, not far from Holdrege, where she was born, related that in her youth she had spoken like her mother and her mother's mother, who had come from Skåne. But after she had married a man from central Sweden, he removed (*plockade bort*) most of the dialect from her speech. Her Swedish was now strongly leveled. And she added that most speakers were now so intermingled (*så blandade*) that they had been forced to level out their speech. Now the family language was predominantly English.

In Nebraska the dialects clearly were in a weak position among Swedish speakers right from the beginning. The Swedes were certainly numerous; in 1900 the Swedish-born and their children numbered about 74,000.[21] The greater number of them were farmers, for the most part concentrated in about ten settlements in the regions around Axtell and Holdrege, Stromsburg and Swede Home, and other places in the eastern half of the state. Many of the immigrants had not come directly from Sweden, but had lived among Swedes in other parts of the United States before settling in Nebraska, whereby their dialects had been leveled out. That Swedish died out so early here in comparison with states such as Minnesota, Kansas, and Texas, was probably due to the fact that immigration directly from Sweden came to an end relatively early, at the beginning of this century.

In regard to Iowa one can observe that the Swedes there were a mobile population, so that that state often served as a transition area for immigrants who continued on to other states. Among the Swedish speakers recorded in 1960 in the old settlements in the vicinity of Boone and Des Moines the dialects had been leveled out. A powerful leveling factor in this connection was no doubt the coal-mining industry, which employed many Swedes from various places in Sweden.

But even in these states, especially in Kansas, we encountered several cases of well-preserved dialects among third-generation speakers in mixed settlements. This was true of families who still lived on the farm that grandfather and grandmother had cleared and where the feeling for family traditions was especially strong and lively.[22]

The second-generation dialect speakers whom we met in the Dakotas had strongly leveled speech. This was what one should expect. Immigration there was, on the whole, of late date and secondary; to a large extent the settlers came from Minnesota and other states.

When dialects from various provinces in Sweden came in contact with each other in such secondary settlements, it was not the present majorities that came to dominate the language. More important were people's attitudes toward the various dialects. People tried to model their speech on the dialects which had the highest social prestige, those which one perceived to be closest to standard Swedish and were spoken by people from central and northern Sweden—for example, from Gästrikland and Västmanland. A third-generation Hälsingland speaker in Chisago County, Minnesota, told us how provoked he was when a Småland speaker from the adjacent settlement, where the Småland people formed a strong majority, addressed him in his dialect, characterized by diphthongs and a uvular *r*. "I answered him in English!" he said. That he should have modified his own dialect was obviously out of the question!

Dialects in America and in Sweden: Swedish Dialects and American English

A mixing or amalgamation of different Swedish dialects in the second and third generation that might have led to the formation of a composite dialect

(*Ausgleichsmundart*) like Pennsylvania German is not to be found in our recordings except in individual cases in a few families. The clearest case of this occurred in Bishop Hill, and I have given a very brief report of it in *Studies for Einar Haugen*.[23] The individual in question is a woman with a Småland and Västergötland background who in the 1920s married into a family from Gästrikland, in which four generations lived together. In order to make herself understood by the oldest generation (great-grandfather and great-grandmother), she had to introduce both words and pronunciation from their dialect into her own speech. But after the death of the old people, she and her husband have very seldom spoken Swedish, and their children do not speak Swedish at all. It seems safe to assume that the children—in case they had taken over their parents' language—would have followed their father's dialect, which is quite similar to standard Swedish rather than their mother's mishmash.

Thus it can be stated without hesitation that the American-Swedish dialects that were not leveled maintained their identity to the end—to their impending annihilation, which will accompany the disappearance of the third generation. (The youngest third-generation speaker recorded by us was born in 1921.) The salient features of grammar and lexicon that make possible an immediate identification of the home province (and sometimes also the parish or even the village) have been preserved by those speakers who were characterized above as conservative. What distinguishes the American-Swedish dialects from the original ones (as we know them from recordings of the late 1800s and the 1900s) is, naturally enough, the strong impact of English, not least of all the syntactic one, together with the loss of significant parts of the vocabulary that became irrelevant in America. When one plays recordings from America for older dialect speakers in the original homelands, the usual reaction is: "Oh, my, it sounds as though grandpa had returned! Only a very old person can speak like that." The English element does not detract from the total impression. It is interesting to observe that the conservative features—primarily lexical and inflectional—that have been preserved in American Swedish are different from those that have been retained by the most old-fashioned among the dialect speakers in the home regions of Sweden. In Sweden it was primarily those words and forms that deviated most markedly from standard Swedish that disappeared and were replaced by correspondences from the standard language. In America such words and forms could be preserved, for here there was no reliable standard spoken Swedish with which the dialects could be compared. Words and forms such as *kräkene* 'the cattle', *skonene* 'the shoes', *blistra* 'to whistle', *skörva* ' pull a person's hair', *dömpa* 'to fall', and the like in Bishop Hill Swedish have been given up in Sweden. In such cases the difference between dialect speech in America and in the places of origin was brought about by the language development in Sweden. Similar observations have been made by several scholars regarding German as spoken in America.[24]

There is another interesting difference between Swedish dialects in the home country and those I have recorded in America. In Sweden many words are common to both the dialects and the standard language—loanwords that have been so completely adapted to the phonology and morphology of the dialects that they seem natural even to older dialect speakers. Many of these words, such as *konstig* 'queer' and *boskap* 'cattle', are unknown to Swedish dialect speakers in America. The reason for this is probably that these words had not gotten a foothold in the dialects at the time of emigration, the 1850s and 60s. The absence of such words from the dialects in America can also be regarded as a kind of conservatism.

This is easily overlooked by people in Sweden when they listen to American Swedish. When the Swedes in America felt the need to express concepts like *konstig* and *boskap* and when the various dialectal terms were felt to be out of fashion or unusable, they simply supplemented their word stock from English with *crazy* and *cattle*.[25] The problem of why one in American Swedish exchanged words that are common and practicable in standard Swedish in Sweden for English loanwords cannot be solved without taking into account the dialects that lie behind the Swedish American's more or less dialect-colored speech. This, of course, holds true especially for the many Swedish-speaking Americans who cannot read Swedish.

In editing the field recordings from America we also discovered that it is often difficult to distinguish between old dialect and English words and phrases as we heard them from the loudspeaker. Often the dialects, especially those from central Sweden, are closer to English than to standard Swedish. This can hold true for phonetic, morphologic, lexical, and syntactic details. Sometimes it is a matter of a chance coincidence, sometimes of features of older language periods that have been preserved on both sides. Examples: dialect *marka* 'to mark' (standard Swedish *märka*), dialect *lika* 'to like' (standard Swedish *tycka om*), dialect *vara bråttom* 'to be in a hurry' (standard Swedish *hava bråttom*), and so forth. Similar observations on German dialects in the United States have been made by Paul Schach.[26]

Circumstances such as these show that a thorough knowledge of the dialects in the homeland is necessary when we endeavor to distinguish in emigrant tongues between changes caused by the impact of the language of the new country and the linguistic heritage that the speaker or his forebears brought from the old country.

The Swedish language that the children and grandchildren of the rural farm immigrants to America spoke in the 1960s and 70s reveals a spectrum of grammar, vocabulary, and modes of expression that extend all the way from a conservative dialect with an essentially unchanged structure and a restricted number of easily identified English elements to a strongly leveled American standard Swedish of the same type that is spoken in cities like Chicago and Minneapolis, a *koine* with shifting dialectal coloring. Both the conserving and the changing factors are to be found above all in social and cultural conditions. These factors are, of course, based also to a significant degree on the speakers' own attitudes toward their dialects; here the personal disposition—rearing and family tradition—plays an important role.

That the Swedish language in America was doomed to die out with the disappearance of the second and third generations was not merely a result of the steady pressure exerted by English and by the prestige-laden culture that sustained that language. It also resulted from the circumstance that the Swedish language was largely split up into many different dialects and from the lack of a recognized Swedish colloquial norm that could constantly make itself felt among those who lived on the plains and in the woodlands outside of Swedish cultural centers like Chicago and Minneapolis and who thus lived on "the little tradition level."

[Translated from the Swedish by Paul Schach]

NOTES

1. Gustaf Unonius, *Minnen från en sjuttonårig vistelse i nordvestra Amerika*, 2 vols. (Uppsala, 1862); English translation, *A Pioneer in Northwest America*, trans. Jonas Oscar Backlund, ed. Nils William Olsson, 2 vols. (Chicago: University of Minnesota Press for the Swedish Pioneer Historical Society, 1950–60).

2. Helge Nelson, *The Swedes and the Swedish Settlements in North America*, 2 vols., Skrifter utgivna av Kungliga humanistiska vetenskapssamfundet i Lund 37 (1943) 1:49.

3. Hans Norman, "Swedes in North America," in *From Sweden to America: A History of the Migration*, ed. Harold Runblom and Hans Norman, Acta Universitatis Upsaliensis, Studia Historica Upsaliensia 74 (1976), p. 242.

4. Ibid., p. 260, regarding Wisconsin.

5. Ibid., p. 269; Hans Norman, *Från Bergslagen till Nordamerika: studier i emigrationsmönster, social rörlighet och demografisk struktur med utgångspunkt från Örebro län 1851–1915*, Acta Universitatis Upsaliensis, Studia Historica Upsaliensia 62 (1974), pp. 294–300.

6. Folke Hedblom, "Svenska dialekter i America: Nagra erfarenheter och problem," in *Kungliga humanistiska vetenskaps-samfundet i Uppsala, Årsbok 1973–74* (Uppsala, 1975), p. 37.

7. On "high persistence level" see Norman, "Swedes in North America," p. 226.

8. A chart of these expeditions is found in Folke Hedblom, "Swedish Speech in an English Setting: Some Observations on and Aspects of Immigrant Environments in America," in *Studies in Honour of Harold Orton on the Occasion of His Seventieth Birthday,* ed. Stanley Ellis, *Leeds Studies in English* 2 (1969): 100.

9. Most of the recording (about one hour) is printed in *En hälsingdialekt i Amerika: Hanebomål från Bishop Hill, Illinois,* text and commentary by Folke Hedblom (Uppsala: A. B. Lundequistska Bokhandeln, 1978) pp. 7–55.

10. Einar Haugen, *The Norwegian Language in America: A Study in Bilingual Behavior,* 2d ed. (Bloomington: University of Indiana Press, 1969) speaks of the "great vocabulary shift" (pp. 74–97).

11. According to Einar Haugen, who listened to a part of the tape in 1977.

12. For additional examples, see Nils Hasselmo, *Amerikasvenska: en bok om språkutvecklingen i Svensk-Amerika* (Stockholm: Esselte Studium, 1974); and Haugen, *The Norwegian Language in America.*

13. The transcription here is very broad. A larger part of this recording is printed in Folke Hedblom, "Amerikasvenska dialektproblem," in *Dialectology and Sociolinguistics: Essays in Honor of Karl-Hampus Dahlstedt, 19 April 1977,* Acta Universitatis Umensis, Umeå Studies in the Humanities 12 (Umeå, 1977), pp. 56–62.

14. Norman, *Från Bergslagen till Nordamerika,* p. 260.

15. Nelson, *The Swedes and the Swedish Settlements,* 1:190.

16. Hedblom, "Svenska dialekter i Amerika," p. 40.

17. Ibid., p. 45.

18. *Am* 194, *Am* 204. (*Am* designates the series of tape recordings from America in the Institute of Dialect and Folklore Research [Dialekt- och folkminnesarkivet], Uppsala, Sweden.)

19. Hedblom, "Svenska dialekter i Amerika," p. 48.

20. *Am* 227, *Am* 242.

21. Nelson, *The Swedes and the Swedish Settlements,* 1:285.

22. Hedblom, "Svenska dialekter i Amerika," p. 49.

23. Folke Hedblom, "Bishop Hill Swedish after a Century," in *Studies for Einar Haugen: Presented by Friends and Colleagues,* ed. Evelyn Scherabon Firchow, Kaaren Grimstad, Nils Hasselmo, and Wayne O'Neil, Janua Linguarum, series maior, no. 59 (The Hague: Mouton, 1972), p. 293.

24. Paul Schach, "Zum Lautwandel im Rheinpfälzischen: die Senkung von kurzem Vokal zu *a* vor *r*-Verbindung," *Zeitschrift für Mundartforschung* 26 (1958–59): 201.

25. More examples can be found in Folke Hedblom, "Amerikasvenska dialekter i fonogram: Hanebomål från Bishop Hill, Illinois," *Svenska landsmål* [Swedish dialects] (1978); also in *En hälsingadilekt i Amerika: Hanebomål från Bishop Hill, Illinois,* pp. 16–55.

26. Paul Schach, "Die Lehnprägungen der pennsylvania-deutschen Mundart," *Zeitschrift für Mundartforschung* 22 (1954–55): 222.

The Linguistic Norm and the Language Shift in Swedish America

NILS HASSELMO

The linguistic development in the Swedish immigrant community in America involved a rather rapid language shift. When the Swedish immigration began, English was strongly dominant in the United States. In spite of the inpouring of several tens of millions of immigrants between 1850 and 1925, English maintained its dominance. It has been estimated that at least 85 percent of the population of the United States had English as its mother tongue even during the height of the foreign influx. At the same time, the competition was split among over forty immigrant languages, of which only German seems ever to have exceeded about 5 percent of the population.

The interpretation of the linguistic development in an immigrant setting that is presented below should be seen against the background of a general language shift among the immigrants and their descendants. The reasons for this shift have been sought in the interaction of a number of factors. The strong dominance of English is certainly one of the most important. In addition, it has been stressed that the immigrants in a very real sense came prepared to start anew; they were to some extent ready to allow themselves to become americanized. The social and economic mobility in American society has furthermore been seen as a reason why the immigrant communities dispersed and the immigrant languages lost their main bastions in the new country. American mass culture has been suggested as a factor in the loss of appeal suffered by the traditional ethnic cultures.[1]

All of these factors are taken for granted in the interpretation that follows. To them are simply added some that have to do more directly with the linguistic situation in Sweden at the time of the great migration and with emigrant Swedish and its relationship to English.[2]

Linguistic Norms and Diglossia

Three types of norms are important to the analysis of the linguistic development in Swedish America: the *codified norm* that governed the Swedish "high" language, that is, Swedish in its official, primarily written, manifestations; *de facto norms* characteristic of the "low" language spoken by the immigrants in their original home communities in Sweden; and *perceived norms* which were assumed by outsiders to govern the verbal behavior of certain reference groups.

The Swedish setting from which the immigrants came was characterized by diglossia.[3] A high language was in use in the church, the schools, the press, and among certain officials, while a low language was in use in the home and the neighborhood. Some persons mastered both varieties, while others had only a very limited ability to manipulate certain linguistic patterns of the prevailing low language in the direction of the perceived norms of the high language.

The Swedish diglossic system, such as it was, was transferred to America with the immigrants. In the early concentrated Swedish settlements, especially in the countryside in the Midwest, the Swedish system probably remained practically intact for several decades: the Swedish high language was used above all in the churches and in the press, while the low language was the normal speech form of the immigrant community. In areas where the settlement followed not only provincial but even parish patterns from the old country (reflecting the Swedish local church district of the *socken* and its subdivision into *rotar*), the local Swedish dialect could of course remain unchanged for a long time. Often, however some mixing of speakers of different dialects led to a certain leveling in the direction of the high language. Among the later immigrants, traces were also found of the linguistic leveling that was going on in Sweden in connection with industrialization and urbanization. But in spite of these tendencies it seems feasible to assume that a Swedish diglossic situation was typical of much of Swedish America during the second half of the nineteenth and the early twentieth centuries.

The system that first arose in Swedish America should perhaps be termed *triglossia*.[4] Beside the Swedish high and low languages, English also become part of the system as an alternative to both the Swedish varieties, conditioned by the domain of interaction. In America the dynamism in the system was to a considerable degree due to the presence of English and to changes in the relationship between it and the immigrant language. The tension between the Swedish high and low languages could be released not only through a leveling between these two language varieties but also through a shift to English.

At the same time, the influence that English exerted on the Swedish low language in America widened the gulf between the two varieties of Swedish in a new dimension. The distinction between high language and low language also became a distinction between "pure" Swedish and so-called *rotvälska* ("lingo," "gibberish").

At a later stage a new diglossic system arose in certain speech communities where English can be said to have functioned as the high language in contrast to a Swedish low language. In these cases a language shift took place earlier at the level of the high language than at that of the low language. On the other hand, the Swedish low language was influenced by English to a considerably greater extent than the Swedish high language.

Language Contact

The Swedish newspaper language in America does not seem to have been much influenced by English. However, a debate concerning the use of English expessions in the written language did take place. Men such as Gustaf Andreen, a philologist by training and for many years president of Augustana College in Rock Island, Illinois, and Vilhelm Berger, a prominent journalist and author of several studies on the Swedish language in America, advocated the adoption of certain English terms. Among them are found administrative terms such as *county* and *township,* designations for officials such as *mayor* and *sheriff,* and measures and weights such as *yard, acre, pint,* and *quart*. But the redoubtable Ernst Skarstedt, journalist and chronicler of Swedish America, objected strenuously to any suggestion that a new language was developing in the immigrant community. He took strong issue with a statement by Adolf Noreen in his multivolume Swedish grammar *Vårt språk* [Our language] to the effect that, beside *rikssvenska* (''standard Swedish'') and Finland Swedish, a new variety of Swedish might in the future have to be recognized in America. Skarstedt maintained that the Swedish high language norm was as valid in Swedish America as ever: ''The fact that one adopts a few foreign words, especially such as do not have any complete equivalents in one's own language, does not turn the language into a new language.''[5]

Other commentators thought that a double standard was being applied in Sweden: ''It is rather strange—just happened to think of it—that the Swedes in America are considered to be lacking in culture because once in a while they mix a little English into their Swedish, when in Sweden it is actually regarded as a sign of culture to be able to use as many English words as possible.'' ''In the works of modern literature in Sweden there even rather often occur swedicized words borrowed from English, which here we regard as anglicisms of a type from which the careful Swedish written language ought to be kept clean. Such words are, for example, *flirta, starta, träna, cykla,* and a number of other sports terms.''[6]

A certain hypersensitivity to criticism from the old homeland is noticeable as the living contact with its high language is slipping. The result is that a perceived norm begins to assert itself, one that demands that the language be kept free not only from Swedish-American anglicisms but also from anglicisms that had begun to gain currency in Sweden itself.

In contrast to the high language, the American-Swedish low language often showed considerable influence from English. As early as 1897 Johan Person, another Swedish newspaperman, maintained that "when the beautiful Swedish and the not so beautiful English language form a union, a misshapen monster is born therefrom. It has no name, but we may call it *rotvälska*." Some commentators were uncertain whether the new variety of language was Swedish or English "since the 'nuisance' is presumably mutual," to quote a teacher at Augustana College. Especially while the newcomers were learning English, a strongly varying language variety seems to have occurred. The *mixing,* as it was called, was often condemned from both a linguistic and a moral point of view. Johan Person described this stage as follows: "This is when *he* loads his speech with *baj gadd,* is interested in *base ball,* and calls his enemy . . . a *sanna förbiss*. This is when *her* entire striving is to *mäka mäss' me' en jänkefeller* ["make a match with a Yankee fellow"]—often of Irish descent. This is when they both answer the Swedish-American newspaper agent that they cannot *rida svid päper*." But according to Person these newcomers eventually return to the fold and adopt, one may assume, a more stabilized American Swedish which was found—and is still to be found—in more homogeneous Swedish settings in America.[7]

This more stabilized American Swedish is represented—together with more idiosyncratic versions—in the rich materials recorded by Folke Hedblom of the Dialect and Folklore Archives at Uppsala in Sweden and in my own recordings and tests.[8] It also appears in a number of sketches by Anna Olson (pen name "Aina") of Rock Island, Illinois and in the five-act play *Härute* [Out here] (1919) and the novel *Charli Johnson, svenskamerikan* (1909) by G. N. Malm of Lindsborg, Kansas.[9] The varieties of American Swedish found in Anna Olson and Malm are characterized by the transfer and copying of English words and phrases and by code-switching. These somewhat idealized versions differ from recorded texts primarily by the relative rarity of mixing due to the so-called trigger effect, that is, switching caused, for example, by loanwords, names, and interlingual homonyms.[10]

In the case of the low language, perceived norms also seem to have played a role. The newcomers heard their countrymen using certain English expressions in their Swedish and copied what they regarded as a prestige norm. But since they did not know the de facto normalization that had occurred, their attempts at anglicization become especially noticeable and were made the special butts of linguistic jokes.

Linguistic Democratization

The democratization of Swedish in America could have taken two different forms. On the one hand it is possible to imagine that the Swedish high language could have followed the democratization of the high language norm in Sweden;

on the other hand it is also possible to imagine that a new American-Swedish high language norm could have developed on the basis of the English-influenced American-Swedish low language. In order to give a direct answer to the question to what extent the Swedish high language in America followed the development of the high language in Sweden, it would be necessary to have studies of a type that is not available. We have to be satisfied, at least for the time being, with a more indirect way of answering the question.

First of all we find that during the early decades of the history of Swedish America the contact with Swedish in the original homeland was maintained simply by the fact that the ministers and journalists who became the main bearers of the high language in Swedish America had received their education in Sweden. They seem also to have maintained a rather close contact with colleagues in the old country. Around the turn of the century, however, something of a crisis makes itself noticed. In 1904, for example, a rather heated debate took place between *Svenska kuriren* and *Hemlandet, det gamla och det nya*, one a liberal, the other a conservative Swedish-American newspaper. *Svenska kuriren* maintained that "there does not exist in this press a single newspaperman who can handle the Swedish language moderately well without having received his education in Sweden."[11]

Even if *Hemlandet* was able to name some Swedish Americans educated in America who, according to the paper, could handle Swedish quite satisfactorily, the debate as well as many other statements of a similar nature indicate both the existence of a problem as well as the nature of the problem. In 1899 Andreen pointed out in a lecture at Uppsala that the Swedish high language was available to most Swedish Americans only via the written language.[12] Among those who have been educated at the Swedish-American colleges, said Noreen, one notices "that the differences among the Swedish dialects have been smoothed out [*afslipats*] through the mixing and that their speech is more grammatical, that is, is closer to the written language, than is the case in Sweden. This is of course no advantage, but it does nevertheless show the nature of the influence under which we find ourselves. Thus, it is not unusual to hear *icke, mig, dig*. . . ." Andreen points out that if in Sweden one would stop using plural verb forms in writing, this would also "among other things present the small advantage that we Swedish Americans, who are so dependent on the *written* word, would not immediately run the risk of revealing our foreignness by speaking more grammatically than the Swedes themselves!"[13]

As early as 1884 *Hemlandet* had stressed the need to adopt the new Swedish Bible translation in the Augustana Synod, the major Swedish religious body in America.[14] But even if the development of the religious language in Sweden did not pass entirely without notice among Swedish Americans, G. N. Malm's criticism of *prestsvenskan* ("ministerial Swedish") suggests that the churh can hardly be regarded as a linguistic innovator. In the play *Hårute,* direktör Bork, Malm's mouthpiece, says to his friend pastor Hallner: "I like your conversational language a good deal better than the stiff grammatical ministerial Swedish that you resort to as soon as you have put on your ministerial collar."[15]

Many comments thus indicate that the high-language tradition in Swedish America had become almost entirely a written-language tradition. There are also comments that indicate that at the same time the native Swedish and the American-Swedish written language were sliding farther apart. A statement by Johan Person from 1912 presents the situation in a nutshell: "It [the American-Swedish written language] is thus rather untouched by the orthographic vagaries of the last decade and has not been much influenced by the contempt of form and the grammatical carelessness of the newest Swedish literature. . . . As concerns the linguistic development in Sweden during the last few years, with its uncertainty, irregularity, and confusion, there are admirers of the earlier, clear, classical style who consider this development as decadence."[16]

The much feared *språkskred* ("language slide"), a sudden erosion of the immigrant language, set in around the time of World War I. In a few years all hope that Swedish would remain the main language of Swedish America was lost. If one may judge from the scathing attacks on Swedish-American writers and speakers for their linguistic barbarisms that were launched during this period, one can only conclude that at the time of the great language shift the American-Swedish high language was characterized by advanced rigor mortis.[17]

How then did one regard the possibility of democratizing the high language by allowing it to become more similar to the English-influenced American-Swedish spoken language, that is, by allowing the codified norm to reflect the new de facto norms that were developing in the Swedish-American communites? The most ambitious, and perhaps the only serious, attempt to introduce American Swedish in literature is Malm's use of it in *Charli Johnson, svenskamerikan* and *Hårute*. The reviewers of *Charli Johnson* were generally rather positive towards Malm's linguistic experimentation, but they stressed the limits of such innovation. *Svenska Amerikanaren* said: "One has wanted to ban this dialect, if it may be so called, but isn't it as justifiable in a description of folklife [*folklivsskildring*] as the different provincial dialects in Sweden?" *Nya Idun* first stated: "On a hasty paging through, one's eye is met here and there by samples of the Swedish-American language confusion we know so well from everyday life." Later the reviewer added: "Perhaps the book's naturalistic photographing [*fotografering*] of the settlement language can make all of you and us in the future guard more carefully against having the *rotvälska* sneak up on us which the author has portrayed so masterfully."[18]

Swedish America found itself between Scylla and Charybdis. If one followed the native Swedish norm in its development, one would in certain cases further increase the distance between the American-Swedish high language norm and the American-Swedish spoken language. If one brought the American-Swedish high language norm closer to the American-Swedish spoken language, one would break the continuity with the native Swedish norm system. It is not possible to tell how in the long run the problem might have been solved. The language shift took place before the question was brought to a head. English eventually replaced both the high and the low language in Swedish America.

There is also another angle to the question of linguistic democratization in Swedish America. Many comments give evidence of the immigrants' awareness of the extent to which certain behavioral patterns brought from Sweden were tied to a certain social class. In his novels Vilhelm Moberg has captured essential features of this problem in the person of Ulrike of Västergöhl, the parish whore who gained respectability in America. The hat and the title of *Mrs.* became important symbols of the liberation from Swedish class society. Language was one of the most strikingly class-bound of the behavioral patterns that the immigrants brought with them. The Swedish visitor Ernst Beckman observed as early as 1883 that "in English they [the children of immigrants] speak as well as anyone else; if they open their mouths for Swedish, they talk peasant language, of which they are ashamed. It is the same way with one of our famous nightingales; when she speaks her mother tongue, she is from Småland, otherwise she is a Parisian."[19] Änni in Malm's novel finds that her use of Swedish complicates her relationship with the educated newcomer Charli: "But it is as if he thought that we are not good enough, it is as if he were high above us. I don't know why he always has to make fun of the language. Look what he does with Lindgren and his brogue. When we talk English, it isn't like that. Then we are more equal."[20] Johan Person finds that women especially are sensitive to the class-boundness of Swedish: "They speak English because this language is spoken in a rather similar way by all social classes. . . . Their Swedish, on the contrary, is a provincial dialect of which they are ashamed when they wear dresses and hats that are just as fine as those of the American ladies."[21]

Even if English of course was not free from class-distinguishing characteristics—as recent American sociolinguistic research has so abundantly demonstrated—it was nevertheless free from many of the class-distinguishing characteristics that clung to the Swedish of the immigrants. At least the social meaning was different, smacked less of peasanthood, was more urban. The result was that the democratization—and the urbanization—of the language above all took the form of a shift to English. And of course it was not only a matter of equality within the Swedish immigrant community; it was a matter of equality in American society—and there the transition to English was a fundamental condition. Thus, before a possible internal democratization of the language could take place in Swedish America, many simply stopped using both the high and the low varieties of the immigrant language.

Linguistic Death

The language shift did not simply involve a change from one living language to another; to some extent it involved a transition from a language already marked for death to one full of life. The language shift of course did not take place because Swedish was structurally incapable of serving as a means of communication in the new land. On the contrary, the development of the American-Swedish spoken language towards a new English-influenced norm showed that the language was a flexible instrument which could very well be adapted to the new conditions.[22] But in America the Swedish-speaking group, as well as other immigrant groups, did not get enough time to solve the problems connected with the internal tension between high and low language before English offered them a simpler solution. The high language rather rapidly became petrified in its isolation both from the changing native Swedish high language norm and from the American-Swedish spoken language. In spite of certain tendencies towards de facto normalization, the low language by and large lacked stability, and above all legitimacy, because it could not be properly tied to a living high language norm. Puristic pedantry contributed to the death of the high language, while ridicule undermined the low language. The former turned into Malm's *prestsvenska*, the latter into the *rotvälska* of popular humour. Only in some Swedish core areas in America can one still hear a type of American Swedish which gives an inkling that, given different social conditions, a viable new language, adapted to American conditions, could have arisen. The generation that speaks this language is now of retirement age, and the language will not survive them.

NOTES

A Swedish version of this paper was presented at the Five Hundredth Anniversary Symposium of The Humanities Faculty of the University of Uppsala, Sweden 6–8 June 1977.

1. Joshua A. Fishman, "The Historical and Social Contexts of an Inquiry into Language Maintenance Efforts," in *Language Loyalty in the United States: The Maintenance and Perpetuation of Non-English Mother Tongues by American Ethnic and*

Religious Groups, ed. Joshua A. Fishman, Vladimir C. Nahirny, John E. Hoffman, and Robert G. Hayden, Janua Linguarum, series maior, no. 21 (The Hague: Mouton, 1966), pp. 29–32.

2. Nils Hasselmo, *Amerikasvenska: En bok om språkutvecklingen i Svensk-Amerika* (Stockholm: Esselte Studium, 1974), pp. 73–78.

3. Charles A. Ferguson, "Diglossia," *Word* 15 (1959): 324–40.

4. In a more detailed account, English should also be described in terms of a high and a low language. The variety of spoken English that the immigrants encountered among their English-speaking neighbors differed from educated spoken English as well as from written English. On the whole, however, the differences between the high and low languages in English were smaller than between the corresponding varieties of Swedish, a fact that was often noted by Swedish-American observers. (See C. F. Peterson, *Sverige i Amerika: kulturhistoriska och biografiska anteckningar* (Chicago: The Royal Star Co., 1898), p. 204; Johan Person, *Svensk-amerikanska studier* (Rock Island, Ill.: Augustana Book Concern, 1912), p. 133.

5. On Swedish newspaper language, see R. Gustafsson Berg, "Svenskan i Amerika: studier i de utvandrades språk," *Språk och stil* 4 (1904): 1–21; Gustaf Andreen, *Det svenska språket i Amerika* (Stockholm: Bonnier, 1900), p. 7; Vilhelm Berger, "Svensk-amerikanska språket," *Nysvenska studier* 15 (1935): 1–37; Adolf Noreen, *Vårt språk* (Lund: Gleerups, 1903), 1:97; Ernst Skarstedt, *Svensk-amerikanska folket i helg ock socken* (Stockholm: Björck & Börjesson, 1917), p. 435. All translations from the Swedish are the author's.

6. Johan Person, "Svenska språket som det skrifves och talas," *Vestkusten* (San Francisco), 5 October 1911; E. A. Zetterstrand, "Engelskans inflytande på det svenska språket i Amerika," *Ungdoms-vännen* (Rock Island, Ill.) 9 (1904): 180.

7. Johan Person, "Svenska språket, "*Svenska tribunen* (Chicago), 5 October 1897; teacher at Augustana: Zetterstrand, "Engelskans inflytande på det svenska språket i America," p. 180; Person, *Svensk-amerikansa studier*, p. 140.

8. Folke Hedblom, "Om svenska folkmål i Amerika: Fran Landsmåls- och Folkminnesarkivets bandinspelningsexpedition 1962," *Svenska landsmål och svenskt folkliv* 86 (1962): 113–57; "Bandinspelningsexpedition till Svensk-Amerika 1964," *Svenska landsmål och svenskt folkliv* 90 (1966): 97–115; "Swedish Speech and Popular Tradition in America: A Report from the Uppsala Tape Recording Expedition 1964,"*The Swedish Pioneer Historical Quarterly,* Fall 1965, 137–54; Hasselmo, *Amerikasvenska*, pp. 170–76.

9. See ibid., pp. 90–93; and Nils Hasselmo, "Language and the Swedish Immigrant Writer: From a Case Study of G. N. Malm," in *Scandinavians and America: Essays Presented to Franklin D. Scott, Swedish Pioneer Historical Quarterly* 25 (1974): 241–53.

10. Michael G. Clyne, *Transferrence and Triggering* (The Hague: Martinus Nijhoff, 1967), pp. 84–90.

11. *Hemlandet, det gamla och det nya*, 14 Sept. 1904.

12. Later published as Andreen, *Det svenska språket i Amerika*.

13. Ibid., pp. 15–16.

14. *Hemlandet*, 5 March 1884.

15. G. N. Malm, *Härute* (Lindsborg, Kans.: Bethany Printing Co., 1919), p. 29.

16. Person, *Svensk-amerikanska studier*, p. 125.

17. E. W. Olson, "Grodor ur svartbäcken," in *Bläckfisken: årsbok av svenska journalistförbundet i Amerika*, 1920, pp. 37–40.

18. *Svenska Amerikanaren*, 13 January 1910; *Nya Idun*, 1910, pp. 112–13.

19. Ernst Beckman, *Amerikanska studier* (Stockholm: Z. Haggströms Förlagsexpedition, 1883), 1:142.

20. "Men dä som han tyckte att vi inte ä fina nog, dä som han vore högt öfver oss. Ja vet inte hvarför han jämt å ständigt ska ha fön ["fun"] mä språket. Se hva han gör utå Lindgren å hans bråg ["brogue"]. När vi talar engelska, är det inte så. Då ä vi mer jämlika." G. N. Malm, *Charli Johnson, svenskamerikan*, (Chicago, Ill.: Engberg-Holmberg Publ. Co., [1909], p. 183.)

21. Person, *Svensk-amerikanska studier*, p. 133.

22. See Einar Haugen, *The Norwegian Language in America: A Study in Bilingual Behavior* (Philadelphia: University of Pennsylavania Press, 1953), pp. 60 ff.

Danes and Danish on the Great Plains: Some Sociolinguistic Aspects

DONALD K. WATKINS

The number of Scandinavians in the upper Midwest in 1850 was insignificant compared to the tens of thousands who arrived annually after the Civil War; but the early settlements, primarily in northern Illinois and eastern Wisconsin, typically served as way stations for the Scandinavians who came later, staying near the Great Lakes for shorter or longer periods of time before moving westward where more favorable conditions beckoned. It is in this connection one finds the nominal beginnings of a Danish presence in the prairie states, the region of the country most favored by the somewhat more than three hundred thousand Danes who immigrated in the half century after 1865. Pre–Civil War settlement by Scandinavians in the Mississippi Valley was dominated by Norwegians and Swedes, with an incidental number of Danes among them. The Scandinavians as a group were at this time a small minority of the white population which pressed hard against the eastern boundaries of the constantly decreasing Indian lands as yet unacquired by the United States government. It had been the seeming uselessness, or at least remoteness, of the trans-Mississippi area in the 1820s which had guided presidents Monroe and Jackson to set this region aside as Indian Territory, but by 1840 the Permanent Indian Frontier had been redefined as the lands west of the ninety-fifth meridian, primarily in present-day Kansas and Oklahoma. As a result of war and treaties in the 1830s, Indian rights to land in southern Wisconsin, eastern Iowa, and southeastern Minnesota had been voided, and very quickly the frontier between white and Indian territory moved from the Mississippi to the Missouri River. By 1840 eastern Iowa had a population estimated at forty-three thousand, and in the following decade the valleys of the Mississippi and Saint Croix rivers in eastern Minnesota became the domain of lumbermen and a constantly growing number of farmers.[1]

In the vanguard settlements of Norwegians in Wisconsin one finds a personality who appropriately symbolizes the onset of Danish colonization on the prairie frontier. Danish-born Claus Lauritsen Clausen, one of the earliest ministers of the Norwegian Evangelical Lutheran Church in America, was instrumental in extending Scandinavian settlement from Wisconsin into northeastern Iowa and southern Minnesota. The early Norwegian immigrant communities of Saint Ansgar, Forest City, Albert Lea, and Blooming Prairie, among others, were created as a result of Clausen's expedition in 1852–53 in search of good farmland which might relieve the population pressure in the growing colonies of eastern Wisconsin. The earlier foundation in 1848 of Denmark, Brown County, Wisconsin, by immigrants from Langeland and Zealand has been attributed in part to Clausen's inviting letters home to kin and friends, and in 1854 many of these Wisconsin Danes joined the Norwegians in the vicinity of newly established Saint Ansgar in Mitchell County, Iowa.[2]

This small group of Danes in the midst of a major Norwegian colony represents one of the earliest rural populations of Danes so far west of the Great Lakes. As a symbol, the Saint Ansgar settlement also rightly suggests that the Danes, even in rural localities, seldom lived apart from other Scandinavians or German-speaking Americans, who were at home in large number in virtually every section of the Midwest. The fact that C. L. Clausen was a churchman also anticipates the important role of the nationally oriented church in the creation of Danish colonies. The Danish Lutheran synods, once established in the last quarter of the century, were a significant organizing and cohesive force within Danish-American communities.[3] Finally, the Wisconsin origin of the Danes in Mitchell County, Iowa, reiterates the prominence of secondary, planned colonization in the growth of *dansk Amerika*.

The boundaries that immigrant groups perceived between each other and the English-speaking population were generally those of language and culture rather than geography. The common cause frequently made by Danes and Norwegians in many areas of organized social life (for example, church membership, the publication of Dano-Norwegian newspapers, periodicals, and books) points out that some boundaries were naturally too weak and gave way to force of practical needs. It was rare that a rural concentration of foreign-born settlers of common stock was not leavened by speakers of English or of yet another language. The use, maintenance, and transmission of the Danish language, in particular, was seldom aided by pure and simple geographic isolation of the *nybygd*, or settlement, as may have been true, for instance, of the rather late Danish colonies in northwestern North Dakota.

While the internal use of Danish by immigrant families was as natural as speech itself, the equally natural and accelerated process of language change in the new multilingual environment alternately amused or alarmed Danish-born observers whose education gave them the conventional view that language purity was a reflection of individual intelligence, if not national virtue. This attitude took a more sophisticated form in the conviction of many Danish Lutheran churchmen and other intellectuals that the preservation of a distinct Danish cultural identity within American society was both desirable and possible, given the proper exertion of will power combined with educational facilities. Many speakers for the cause of bicultural allegiance, *danskhedens sag*, as it was called, eventually accepted the fact that a language shift was taking place. They later separated the question of language from that of Danish cultural values, but before the turn of the century it seemed to be a reasonable belief in this nation with its large and growing population of foreign-born Americans that a stable bilingualism could be maintained, even though other kinds of social assimilation might be welcomed in the adopted country.

My primary purpose here is to sketch the distribution of Danish settlements in the prairie states between 1865 and 1930 and to point to cultural phenomena which mirrored the condition and status of Danish vis-à-vis English. With respect to the latter point, the history of two social institutions provides a great deal of information. These are the Danish Lutheran synods and the Danish-American press. The use of Danish in church-related activities is well documented and rather clearly reflects the language preference of several generations. The growth, viability, and decline of Danish-American newspapers and other publications likewise indicate a good deal about the language loyalty of Danish-Americans. One recognizes, however, that circulation and commercial success in the publishing business depend as much on attractive journalism, sound management, and favorable competition as on the language skills and habits of the potential readership. For a thorough report on Danish-language journalism in America, the reader is referred to the studies by Marion T. Marzolf.[4]

This is not, to be sure, primary linguistic data, nor are there contemporary published studies from those years that objectively describe in linguistic terms Danish-American language usage. Yet there are many vignettes and comments in novels, travelogues, and the press which characterize American Danish in some detail. These contemporary insights by Danes and Danish Americans, often friendly self-portraits and sometimes satirical caricatures by visitors from Denmark, may imply a uniformity of language among the Danish Americans that actually was not present. In fact, the study of Danish-American society and its institutions indicates that all degrees of linguistic self-consciousness were present, together with corresponding levels of concern for proper Danish. Concerning the possible unreliability of the portrayal in fiction of American-Scandinavian speech, one takes warning from the sins committed by the realistic writer Vilhelm Moberg in his immigrant tetralogy. His misrepresentation of important facets of American Swedish underscores the fact that writers more often use speech differences to typify a group than to document a dialect or an idiolect.[5]

In the case of Danish-American fiction—written, of course, by highly literate immigrants and exceptional individuals—one is far more likely to find that the typing of characters through language is achieved by the use of a limited number of quite predictable Danish dialect shibboleths rather than by the depiction of American-Danish speech as a coherent linguistic system. Yet even the use of dialect forms is rare when measured against the bulk of Danish-American fiction, virtually all of which is written in the contemporary standard language of a nation where for centuries the written and spoken Danish of Copenhagen had been the norm of educated usage. Education, of one sort or another, was something all Danish-American authors shared, and as writers they had little inclination to demonstrate the linguistic realities of Danish speech in America. One feels the problem was practical. The major Danish settlement in Shelby County, Iowa, for example, was settled in the period 1865–70 primarily by natives of the three islands Fyn, Møn, and Ærø. This diversity of origins was later increased when other Danes arrived from western Iowa, Wisconsin, Illinois, and Indiana. The dialectal variety present in this and most Danish-American communities, not to mention the special complications of American Danish, probably dismayed many a realistic writer who considered recording actual speech in his fiction. The standard language offered a neutral and safe haven from the dangers that lay in wait for the writer who would attempt to be too realistic in the portrayal of the American-Danish language.

Nonfictional literature by or about Danish Americans, on the other hand, does contain hints—they cannot be called data—about the language actually spoken by the uneducated majority of working-class Danish Americans. I list here selected examples of loanwords and loanshifts which parallel phenomena recorded by Haugen and Hasselmo in their work with American Norwegian and Swedish, respectively.[6]

Loanwords appear in this order—English model, American-Danish replica, native Danish equivalent: *(street)car 'karen' (sporvognen), casket 'kasketen' (kisten), creek 'krikken' (bækken), lawyer 'løjeren' (sagføreren), mower 'moren' (slåmaskinen), road 'roden' (vejen), (rain)shower 'sjoveren' (regnbygen), pillow 'pilleren' (puden), (barbed)wirefence 'weierfensen' (pigtrådshegnen), to fix 'fixe' (ordne), to husk (corn) 'huske'* ([approximately] *afskalle), to jump 'jumpe' (springe, hoppe), to kill 'kille' (dræbe, myrde), to lose 'lusse' (tabe), to start out 'starte ud' (begynde, tage afsted), to kick 'kigge' (sparke)*. Loanshifts in which the meaning of the Danish morpheme is expanded to include an English meaning, appear in this order—Danish morpheme with translation, example of American-Danish usage with translations and standard Danish: (1) *hjælpe* 'to help': "Jeg kan ikke hjælpe det" ("I can't help it") ("Jeg kan ikke andet"); (2) *gøre* 'to do': "Jeg gør for tiden temmelig godt"

(''I am doing pretty well these days'') (''Jeg har det for tiden temmelig godt''); (3) *se* 'to see': ''Jeg så hende hjem'' (''I saw her home'') (''Jeg fulgte hende hjem''); (4) *miste* 'to lose': ''Så har jeg mistet trænet'' (''So I missed the train'') (''Så kom jeg for sent til toget''); (5) *ofre* 'to sacrifice': ''Han ofrede mig 200 dollars'' (''He offered me 200 dollars'') (''Han tilbod mig 200 dollars''); (6) *stå* 'to stand': ''Hun stod der i fire dage'' (''She stayed there for four days'') (''Hun blev der i fire dage''); (7) *dejlig* 'lovely': ''Vi havde en dejlig tid'' (''We had a nice time'') (''Vi havde det rart''); (8) *hård* 'hard' (of objects) 'harsh' (of people, fate, and other things): ''Det er hårdt at sige'' (''That is hard to say'') (''Det er svært at sige''); (9) *smal* 'narrow': ''Giv mig et smalt glas'' (''Give me a small glass') :''Giv mig et lille glas''); (10) *spøg* 'joke': ''Det er ikke spøg'' (''That is no joke'') (''Det er ikke morsomt'').[7]

The rather mild degree of lexical and semantic interference seen here could be expected in the speech of immigrants themselves, individuals whose functional awareness of the Danish norm decreased according to individual combinations of factors. This is not the opportunity to review the linguistic and cultural factors that may generally have favored interference and a shift to English. These did not differ in kind from the factors observed in the case of other Scandinavian groups in the United States, although the greater extent and speed of a complete shift to English is a special characteristic of the Danish Americans. (See the information taken from the U.S. census report of 1970 below.) For most Danish Americans, strict bilingualism was an effort with few practical and psychological rewards. The educated members of the Danish-American intelligentsia, on the other hand—the ministers, educators, editors, and writers—gained self- and peer-esteem through a careful observation of language boundaries. Their steady contact through publications and correspondence with cultural life in Denmark was further reinforced by not infrequent trans-Atlantic travel. The popular image of the Danish-American immigrant singlemindedly at work on 320 acres of midwestern farmland does not fit those intellectuals who produced the bulk of the group's literature and expressed the greatest concern about the preservation of *danskhed*. Whatever else *danskhed* signified, it meant bilingualism in an American society where English monolingualism had the greatest practical value.

On the eve of the Civil War there were not yet ten thousand Danish-born residents of the United States, and a large portion of these were the result of the success experienced by Mormon missionaries in Denmark after 1850.[8] It was 1870 before the number of Danish-born exceeded thirty thousand. During the previous decade Swedish immigration was three times this number, and by 1870 the number of Norwegian-born residents had already passed one hundred thousand. The pattern of Danish settlement after 1865 was characterized by greater geographic dispersal than has been observed for the other main Scandinavian-American groups. In 1910, 57 percent of all Norwegian-born

Americans lived in the three bordering states of Wisconsin, Minnesota, and North Dakota. In the same census year 52 percent of the Swedish-born lived in Minnesota, Illinois and New York. The most Danish state in 1910, with slightly less than 10 percent of the Danish-born residents of the United States, was Iowa, and one must add Minnesota, the Dakotas, Nebraska, Kansas, Montana, Wyoming, and Colorado in order to encompass 37 percent of the first-generation Danish Americans. An additional 22 percent lived in the states of Michigan, Illinois, and Wisconsin. The distribution of Danes among the states of Illinois (primarily the Greater Chicago area), Wisconsin, Minnesota, Iowa, and Nebraska was rather even, and the last two states formed the southern boundary of heavy Danish settlement in the Midwest.[9]

Although most of Iowa and Minnesota does not belong to the Great Plains as the term is defined by geographers, both of these states are an integral part of the pattern and history of Danish settlement on the Great Plains proper. Consequently I use Great Plains here to mean Minnesota, Iowa, North and South Dakota, Nebraska, Kansas, Montana, Wyoming, and Colorado. One notes from the following figures that the proportion of Danish Americans in this region relative to the entire nation declines after 1900. (Reference in the following pages to ''Danish Americans,'' unless otherwise specified, is to the foreign-born only.) The decline in the more urban and industrial Great Lakes states of Michigan, Illinois and Wisconsin is less rapid.

	U.S. TOTAL	GREAT PLAINS	WESTERN GREAT LAKES
1870	30,107	22%	34%
1890	132,543	43	24
1910	181,649	37	22
1930	179,474	30	22
1950	107,982	25	20
1970	61,410	18	16

Lacking studies that suggest unusual migration patterns on the part of Scandinavian Americans within the United States in the twentieth century, one may assume that the more rapid decline on the agricultural Great Plains—so inhospitable to farmers in the dust bowl and depression of the 1930s—reflects the general American migration westward and away from the land. Moreover, new immigrants after 1920 have settled primarily in metropolitan areas on both coasts and in the Great Lakes states. By 1920, 10 percent of Danish Americans lived in California, and by 1960, 33% lived in western states.

The following table provides an overview of the absolute number of Danish Americans in these states and their proportion relative to other foreign-born residents. In this table there is no indication of the size of the category ''foreign stock,'' individuals with one or more foreign-born parents. Such statistics are omitted because the children and grandchildren of immigrants were the Americans who personally experienced the language shift. Their numbers as such would seem to tell little about the presence of Americans who were able to—indeed, who *had* to—use the foreign language rather than English in many, if not most, of life's situations. It was the presence of different groups of monolingual Americans which created the social requisite of bilingualism on the part of following generations. William F. Mackey summarizes the primary importance of the size and very presence of the monolingual, immigrant generation:

> An individual's use of two languages supposes the existence of two different language communities; it does not suppose the existence of a bilingual community. The bilingual community can only be regarded as a dependent collection of individuals who have reasons for being bilingual. A self-sufficient bilingual community has no reason to remain bilingual, since a closed community in which everyone is fluent in two languages could get along just as well with one language.[10]

DISTRIBUTION AND PROPORTION OF DANISH-BORN AMERICANS IN GREAT PLAINS STATES 1870–1970

	Population	Foreign-born as percent of population	Danish-born	Danish-born as percent of foreign-born
		Minnesota		
1870	439,706	36.5	1,910	1.2
1890	1,301,826	35.9	14,133	3.0
1910	2,075,708	26.2	16,137	3.0
1930	2,563,953	15.2	13,831	3.5
1950	2,982,483	7.0	7,374	3.5
1970	3,804,971	2.6	2,621	2.7
		Iowa		
1870	1,194,020	17.1	2,827	1.4
1890	1,911,986	16.9	15,519	4.8
1910	2,224,771	12.3	17,961	6.6
1930	2,470,939	16.8	14,698	8.7
1950	2,621,073	3.2	7,625	9.0
1970	2,824,376	1.4	2,658	6.6
		Dakota Territory		
1870	14,181	34.0	115	2.4
		North Dakota		
1890	182,719	44.6	2,860	3.5
1910	577,056	27.1	5,355	3.4
1930	680,845	15.5	2,936	2.8
1950	619,636	7.9	1,315	2.7
1970	617,761	3.0	410	2.2

	Population	Foreign-born as percent of population	Danish-born	Danish-born as percent of foreign-born
		South Dakota		
1890	328,808	27.7	4,369	4.8
1910	538,888	18.7	6,294	6.3
1930	692,849	9.5	5,298	8.0
1950	652,740	4.7	2,528	8.2
1970	665,507	1.6	916	8.4
		Nebraska		
1870	122,993	25.0	1,129	3.7
1890	1,058,910	19.1	14,345	7.1
1910	1,192,214	14.8	13,674	7.8
1930	1,377,963	8.7	10,210	8.6
1950	1,325,510	4.3	4,555	8.0
1970	1,482,412	1.9	1,651	5.7
		Kansas		
1870	364,399	13.6	502	1.0
1890	1,427,096	10.4	3,136	2.1
1910	1,690,949	8.0	2,760	2.0
1930	1,880,999	4.3	1,727	2.1
1950	1,905,299	2.0	649	1.7
1970	2,246,578	1.2	303	1.1
		Montana		
1870	20,595	38.7	95	1.2
1890	132,159	32.6	683	1.6
1910	376,053	24.4	1,943	2.1
1930	537,606	13.6	2,541	3.5
1950	591,024	7.3	1,398	3.2
1970	694,409	2.7	594	2.7
		Wyoming		
1870	9,118	38.5	54	1.5
1890	60,705	24.6	680	4.6
1910	145,965	18.6	962	3.5
1930	225,565	8.7	775	3.9
1950	290,529	4.6	444	3.3
1970	332,416	2.0	190	2.8
		Colorado		
1870	39,864	16.6	77	1.2
1890	412,198	19.3	1,650	3.8
1910	799,024	16.0	2,755	4.4
1930	1,035,791	8.2	2,373	2.8
1950	1,325,089	4.5	1,381	2.3
1970	2,207,259	2.7	1,487	2.5

Note: The raw data are taken from United States census reports for the years in question. Percentage calculations are my own. Before 1930 Icelandic-born Americans were included with the Danish-born. This significantly affects the data for North Dakota in 1910. The proportion of Icelandic- to Danish-born North Dakotans in 1930 suggests that the figure for 1910 may include 20 percent Icelandic-born.

It is interesting as a social statistic to know, for instance, that in addition to the 57,301 foreign-born Germans in Nebraska in 1910, there were 94,249 residents both of whose parents were German born, and 50,163 one of whose parents was native German. While the German stock in Nebraska in 1910 thus constituted 37.5 percent of the total population, the statistic is uninformative on the question of language usage by this portion of the population. As a statistical estimate of the possible or probable viability of a foreign language in an American community, the number and proportion of foreign born in local populations (counties and townships) are most telling. This is admittedly an inference after the fact and is based on observations by linguists of communities where foreign-language use and bilingualism persisted long after English prevailed elsewhere. It also would seem to assume the absence of social barriers and prejudices that actively promote bilingualism in that separate monolingual groups remain distinct socially and linguistically. Those social barriers were absent in the case of the Scandinavian immigrants, whose children had to be bilingual only so long as the monolingual foreign born were a significant presence in the community. The third-generation Scandinavian Americans seldom perceived a pressing need to be bilingual.

Diachronic statistics for the individual states provide a very general idea of Danish-American demography in the Great Plains. A close look at the patterns of residence in 1910 is much more informative. I choose the census year 1910 because at this time the number of first-generation Danish Americans in the United States was reaching its peak. Settlements in the prairie states were well established, although the size of the Danish population grew and its focal points shifted somewhat in both Montana and North Dakota after 1910. The census of 1910 defined urban population as residents of incorporated places having twenty-five hundred inhabitants or more. Only 24% of Danish Americans in the nine-state region fit this broad definition of urban. Rurality thus typified the group, and the rural population was particularly high in the Dakotas and Wyoming, where no boom towns, such as Denver and Butte, attracted immigrants to centers of industry.[11]

	Rural	Urban
Minnesota	64%	36%
Iowa	73	27
North Dakota	92	8
South Dakota	91	9
Nebraska	71	29
Kansas	78	22
Montana	78	22
Wyoming	85	15
Colorado	52	48

In fact, from the Great Lakes to the Rocky Mountains only six cities had more than 1,000 Danish-born inhabitants: Chicago (11,484), Racine (3,145),

Omaha (2,924), Minneapolis (2,030), Saint Paul (1,412), and Council Bluffs (1,155). To speak of other cities with relatively large numbers of Danes exaggerates the local weight of this group in relation to much larger groups: Oshkosh (373) and Green Bay (241) in Wisconsin; Duluth, Minnesota (405); Sioux City (517), Clinton (494), Des Moines (353) and Waterloo (237) in Iowa; and Denver, Colorado (892).

The impression one might gain from the information presented so far is that most Danish Americans in the Great Plains states were dispersed over a vast area of prairie. Yet quite a different picture emerges from a study, county by county, of the populations of the nine-state region. In the case of Iowa and Nebraska, some 40 percent of the two states' Danish population lived in a limited contiguous area—ten counties in Iowa, four in Nebraska—around the urban focal point of the sister cities on the Missouri River, Omaha and Council Bluffs. Another 40 percent of Iowa's Danish population lived in twenty-one contiguous counties extending northeasterly and northwesterly from Des Moines to the Minnesota border. Thus more than three-quarters of the Danes in Iowa lived in one-third of the state's geographical area, and these Danish areas extended into Nebraska and Minnesota to create enclaves of Danish-American population in the Midwest. It is also typical of Danish-American demography that these enclaves were shared with other Scandinavians; approximately 60 percent of the foreign-born Norwegians and Swedes in Iowa in 1910 lived in the same area as did 80 percent of the Danish born.

When those counties with the greatest concentrations of foreign-born Danes plus second-generation Danish Americans (both parents foreign born) are indicated on a map, the localized character of Danish American residence is quite striking. The following chart and table identify the forty-three most Danish counties. The Danish-American population of these relatively few counties constituted 49 percent of the total of first- and second-generation Danes in Great Plains states in 1910. One may view these counties as focal points surrounded by counties in which most of the remaining 51 percent of Danish Americans lived.

In order to suggest the density of the local (county) Danish-American population, the counties are ranked in descending order according to the Danish proportion in the local population. In this respect it is not altogether inappropriate or misleading to compare a small Iowa county with, for instance, the expanses of Valley County, Montana. Viewed as residents of townships, an important unit of social organization in rural America of the past, the Danish contingent in both counties may be comparably localized and cohesive in a manner which supported the viability of the Danish language in the American environment. In 1915 a Danish resident of Sheridan County, Montana, (which measures about forty by fifty miles) reported that the Danish colony near the town of Dagmar was "twelve miles wide and twenty miles long,

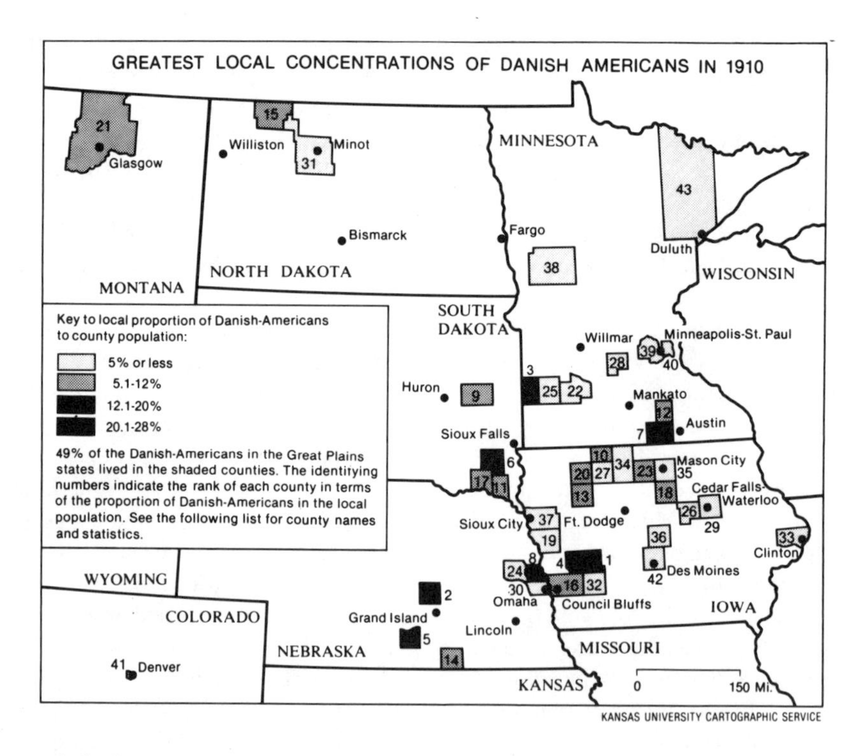

settled almost exclusively by Danes, some seven hundred in all.''[12] The dimensions of the Dagmar settlement correspond to those of most counties in Iowa.

For the purpose of describing the growth of these concentrations of Danish Americans, a distinction should be made between a settlement and a colony. The settlements came into being gradually and without a single organizational impetus, although a settlement might later increase in size as the result of an attractive institution within its borders, such as a Danish-American folk high school. The colonies were originally planned and financed by cooperating individuals who formed a land company or by cultural organizations whose overriding interest was the creation of cohesive Danish-American communities in the interests of *danskhed*. The church-related organization Dansk Folkesamfund (1887), The Danish Church, and The United Church all spearheaded such colonies.

The historically largest rural concentration of Danes in the United States, occupying a thirty-five by eighty-five mile area in Audubon, Cass, Shelby, and Pottawattamie counties in Iowa, came into being as a settlement. In the late 1860s a small number of Danes from Moline, Illinois settled in the Elk Horn area of Shelby County. Through the Danish-American grapevine that kept the

GREATEST CONCENTRATIONS, BY COUNTIES, OF DANISH AMERICANS IN 1910

Percent of local population: rank	Number of Danish Americans	Percent of local population	Size of local Danish-American population: rank
1. Audubon, Iowa	3487	27.5	4
2. Howard, Nebr.	2336	25.7	8
3. Lincoln, Minn.	1914	19.4	10
4. Shelby, Iowa	2996	18.1	6
5. Kearney, Nebr.	1539	16.9	14
6. Turner, S.Dak.	2067	14.9	9
7. Freeborn, Minn.	3277	14.7	5
8. Washington, Nebr.	1772	13.9	12
9. Kingsbury, S.Dak.	1186	9.4	19
10. Emmet, Iowa	915	9.3	26
11. Clay, S.Dak.	746	8.6	33
12. Steele, Minn.	1232	7.6	17
13. Buena Vista, Iowa	1198	7.5	18
14. Nuckolls, Nebr.	976	7.5	23
15. Burke, N.Dak.	634	7.0	40
16. Pottawattamie, Iowa	3785	6.8	3
17. Yankton, S.Dak.	876	6.6	27
18. Franklin, Iowa	917	6.2	25
19. Monona, Iowa	997	6.0	22
20. Clay, Iowa	764	6.0	32
21. Valley, Mont.	779	5.7	30
22. Redwood, Minn.	1035	5.6	21
23. Hancock, Iowa	654	5.1	36
24. Dodge, Nebr.	1109	5.0	20
25. Lyon, Minn.	765	4.9	31
26. Grundy, Iowa	645	4.8	37
27. Palo Alto, Iowa	643	4.6	39
28. McLoed, Minn.	825	4.4	29
29. Black Hawk, Iowa	1832	4.1	11
30. Douglas, Nebr.	6414	3.8	1
31. Ward, N.Dak.	943	3.7	24
32. Cass, Iowa	606	3.2	43
33. Clinton, Iowa	1318	2.9	16
34. Kossuth, Iowa	615	2.8	42
35. Cerro Gordo, Iowa	659	2.6	35
36. Story, Iowa	619	2.6	41
37. Woodbury, Iowa	1577	2.3	13
38. Otter Tail, Minn.	704	1.5	34
39. Hennepin, Minn.	4164	1.2	2
40. Ramsey, Minn.	2732	1.2	7
41. Denver, Colo.	1392	0.65	15
42. Polk, Iowa	644	0.6	38
43. St. Louis, Minn.	827	0.5	28

Total: 65,115 (49% of the nine-state total)

Note: "Danish American" here describes the foreign-born and the native-born children of two foreign-born parents. Approximately 50% of 133,167 Danish Americans in these states belonged to the second generation.

settlers in touch with friends and acquaintances in Denmark and the older Danish-American communities, the four-county area attracted newcomers from Europe, Wisconsin, Illinois, and eastern Iowa. The actual size of the Danish population cannot be gleaned from census data, for a considerable portion, perhaps 25 percent of the "German-born" residents of these counties (5,254 in 1910) were in fact Danish-speaking natives of Slesvig, the duchy lost by Denmark to Prussia in 1864. The creation in 1878 of the Danish-language Elk Horn Folk High School (to the discontent of many Danes originally called "Leif Eriksens Minde" by its Norwegian principal, Olav Kirkebert) added a cultural magnet to other attractive elements in the area: the fertility of the soil, proximity by rail to the market center of Omaha–Council Bluffs, and financial security provided by such cooperative ventures as the Danish Mutual Assurance Company for Elk Horn and Environs (1882).[13]

In 1871, 180 miles west of the Elk Horn settlement, lay the frontier in Nebraska. Land could be had in this region for four dollars an acre, and here in the valley of the Loup River in Howard County, representatives of the Milwaukee-based Danish Land and Homestead Company found conditions that invited the creation of a second colony on the fertile Great Plains. In 1875 the Danish town of Dannebrog vied with the American town of Saint Paul for the location of the county seat. Saint Paul won that election, but both towns gained greater commercial benefit from the track built by the Union Pacific Railroad from Grand Island into Howard County in 1880. Such mundane facts are not secondary when discussing Scandinavian-American colonies with respect to language use, for they remind one that the primary concern of the foreign-born Americans was to create economic security. The rigors of making a living must have relieved most Danish-Americans of time and energy to contemplate their Danish heritage and its value to the coming generation. One gathers from scattered comments by pioneer settlers of Howard County that the foundation in 1888 of Nysted Folk High School was less understood by the practical Danes than was the cooperative dairy formed in Nysted in 1884 or the Horse Breeders Association in 1891. The necessity for the Danish-owned Dannebrog State Bank was never in doubt, but there apparently was not enough local incentive to revive the Danish-language newspaper of Dannebrog, *Stjernen* (founded in 1888), when its printing plant burned in 1896. *Stjernen* was succeeded by the English-language *Dannebrog News,* edited by P. S. Petersen.[14]

In 1884 a committee on colonization was formed within the Danish Council to locate favorable sites for Danish settlements. The method used is exemplified by the arrangement made in 1884, when thirty-five thousand acres of land in Lincoln County, Minnesota were reserved by the church under an agreement with a land agent. For a period of three years the land was to be sold to Danes only.[15] In 1910 Danish Americans represented 20 percent of the county's population. Other colonies initiated by the Danish Church in Great

Plains states were those in the vicinity of Larimore, North Dakota; Dagmar, Montana; and Askov, Minnesota. Following the schism of 1894, the United Church also organized colonies: Kenmare, North Dakota; Daneville, North Dakota; and Dane Valley (Culbertson), Montana. As western states and Canada became increasingly attractive regions for settlement, the synods extended their colonizing efforts to California, Oregon, Washington, and Alberta. By making geographically cohesive Danish-American communities possible, the churchmen may have furthered in some measure the preservation of *danskhed* in America, but one suspects that the average Danish American saw the matter as one of economy. In Lincoln County, Minnesota, land sold in 1895 for $14–20 an acre; by 1916 the price had risen to $100–$125. The top asking price in the older Elk Horn settlement had inflated by 1916 to $250 an acre. Both the newly arrived immigrant and the mobile Danish-American farmer would know where to go when they learned that agricultural land in Roosevelt County, Montana—the Dane Valley colony—sold in 1916 for $15–$25 an acre.[16] Brief descriptions of Danish settlements sent to the editor of *Salomons almanak* graphically tell us of the priorities of the Danish American on the Great Plains.

> Flaxton, North Dakota—We had a good harvest again this year. In many places wheat is yielding twenty bushels to the acre, and the price is good. Land can still be bought for $25 an acre, and some perhaps a little cheaper. Danes will not regret buying land in this area, but one should not wait too long—A. J. Nygaard.
>
> Ida Grove, Iowa—No uncultivated land here. Cultivated land costs from $150–225 an acre. Hogs, cattle, pop corn, oats, wheat, barley. The Danes are usually tenant farmers; they pay about $10 an acre in rent. Only rarely do the children speak Danish. The first Danes here were Peder and Christian Lund from Lolland (in 1873). Undersigned came here in 1880—C. A. L. Jensen.
>
> Rothsay, Minnesota—The town is Norwegian; very few Danes; Norwegian, Norwegian, Norwegian; but they are second to none and will always lend a hand—A. Hendricksen.
>
> Mullen, Nebraska—There are only a few Danes here, ten to twelve families at most. The region is thinly populated because it was settled under the Kincaid Law, which requires a 640-acre claim per family. Mullen is about in the center of the so-called sand hill district of Nebraska and for its size (about 200 inhabitants) I dare say it is the best trading center in Nebraska. Extensive hog and cattle shipping. The grass here is amazingly nutritious and keeps longer than in the so-called better areas—William Nelson.[17]

One of the ironies of the effort by Danish-American synods to create and maintain colonies in North America is the fact that so few Danish Americans joined a Danish or any church. Church historians estimate that in 1910 approximately 20 percent of the Danish-born and 8 percent of the later generations of Danish Americans belonged to either of the two Danish churches (40,737 members in 1910).[18] This educated appraisal puts a sober perspective on the efforts by the synods to bolster the situation of Danish language and culture in America. One must suppose that the unchurched Danish Americans, the great majority, were not reached by spokesmen for *danskheden* unless they belonged to a Danish-American organization with cultural goals. In this regard one doubts that the activities, for example, of the rather exclusive and definitely urban Dansk-Amerikansk Selskab ever touched the lives of small-town and rural Danes in the Midwest.

Cultural and educational organizations could not create basic social conditions favoring bilingualism. The number of pupils attending folk high schools was, in the first place, a minuscule portion of the young Danish Americans. During the ten years of its existence, Brorson Folk High School at Kenmare, North Dakota had an average annual attendance of fewer than forty students. The record attendance was achieved by Danebod Folk High School in Tyler, Minnesota, which for a few years attracted more than one hundred students. The prominent minister, educator, and writer Kristian Østergaard, one of the early teachers at Elk Horn Folk High School, noted that the educational institution attracted settlers "because many wanted to be in the vicinity of the school."[19] This comment expresses the passive appreciation of most Danish Americans for culture in the community. It was respected, but the education offered by this and the other folk high schools was probably viewed as totally impractical in an American era when a grade school education—and sometimes less—was adequate for working-class occupations. Today, Dana College in Blair, Nebraska and Grand View College in Des Moines, Iowa are the extant colleges in Great Plains states which have their origins in the years when Danish-American educators, mostly churchmen, founded twelve schools.

The churches were the primary social organization most Danish Americans knew, yet the two synods were not alike in their concern for Danish-language retention. That the Danish Church made greater efforts to support the language is reflected by the percentage of church services conducted in Danish as late as 1940: Danish Church (approximately 19,000 members): 45 percent; United Church (approximately 57,500 members): 16 percent. Church services are primarily directed at adults, and listening to the pastor is a passive use of language at best. Information on the language of Sunday schools, on the other hand, tells what was happening in a situation requiring the active use of Danish by children. In 1923, 80 percent of children attending Sunday school in the Danish Church did so in the Danish-language classes; in 1927, 55 percent; in 1930, 44 percent. The downward trend continues until 1950, when fewer than 1 percent of Sunday school children were using Danish in that basic educational situation.[20] Many ministers in the Danish Church clung to their mother tongue and resisted the use of English long after it was clear that bilingualism was not functional among the postimmigrant generations of Danish Americans. But the practical necessity for using English in the church was, inevitably, the stronger force. Adult voices in the Danish church in 1922 describe the language gap between the older and younger generations.

> The language problem is most urgent in the cities and then again mostly in the Middle West. . . . The general development is that they begin with English in the Sunday schools. Then the instruction for confirmation is given in English, and last come the services. In general I will say that the language must serve life. If we cannot make ourselves understood by the children in Danish, then I believe we should use the English language instead of letting them go elsewhere.
>
> It is no longer possible to avoid it, especially in city congregations. Here we have, nearly everywhere, children who do not understand Danish well enough to follow the instruction in an entirely Danish Sunday school. What shall we do then? Shall we let them go elsewhere or try to meet them on their own ground?[21]

I have attempted here to suggest the distribution of the Danish-American population around the turn of the century and to present sociolinguistic factors that seem generally to have affected the viability of Danish-English bilingualism. From our perspective in the late 1970s it is an exercise in hindsight to discover in Danish-American history the social conditions which foretold the quite rapid linguistic assimilation of this relatively small group. Without strong clan feelings and culturally undifferentiated from the dominant Western European population of the United States, the Danish Americans encountered no closed doors as they adjusted to life in the English-speaking nation. The ease with which the postimmigrant generations slipped their ties with the Danish language was heightened by the constant shrinkage of the foreign-born generations who, in their day, had founded communities all over the Midwest.

Today the foreign-born Americans of Danish origin, equally distributed across the country, number some 60,000. Their median age in 1970 was sixty-six years. The median age of the 265,000 native Americans of Danish parentage was fifty-six years. Of the second-generation Danish Americans, 41 percent claimed Danish as their mother tongue. One can consequently estimate that 108,000 Americans born around 1921 used Danish as their first language. This statistical speculation tells nothing about language maintenance in later life, but the bare data do demonstrate the close relationship between generation and mother tongue in the case of the Danish Americans. Data in the 1970 census can be interpreted to estimate to what generation claimants to a Scandinavian mother tongue belong.[22]

Mother Tongue:	Danish	Norwegian	Swedish
Number of claimants:	194,462	612,862	626,102
Foreign born:	30%	15.4%	21%
Second generation:	55	51.2	61
Later Generations:	15	33.4	18

Generations later than the second are identified in the census as "native of native parentage." Only 29,000 Americans in this category claimed Danish as their mother tongue.

This evidence of the assimilation, socially and linguistically, of Scandinavian Americans is dramatized by comparison with the generational breakdown of the eight million Americans who claimed Spanish as their mother tongue in 1970. No fewer than 53 percent of these were natives of native parentage. Furthermore, the median age of second-generation Hispanic Americans of Mexican and Cuban origin was fifteen years, that of the foreign born thirty-eight years.

In fact, the situations of the speakers of Scandinavian languages and of Spanish have never been comparable. The extralinguistic, sociocultural factors which for generations have created resistance to linguistic assimilation on the part of Hispanic Americans were experienced only for a brief time by the Scandinavians. Some of the benign factors have to do with the local size of the foreign-born population, its renewal by constant immigration, and the stability of extended families within a traditional homeland in the United States.

Spanish also has acquired powerful status as a language of proud resistance because of the traditional treatment of Hispanic Americans in many cities and states as an inferior minority. The Scandinavian immigrants, in sharp contrast, were welcomed to the United States by all but the supporters of the various Know-Nothing movements, secret societies which viewed immigrants in general as religious and social threats to true American institutions. In the Great Plains states, however, where the proportion of European Americans approached or exceeded 50 percent for many decades following the Civil War, the Scandinavian Americans' accommodation to English-language culture developed in a social climate where the main resistance to a shift to English lay in the immigrant generations' wish to bequeath the languages of Scandinavia to their American children.

NOTES

1. Ray Allen Billington, *Westward Expansion: A History of the American Frontier,* 4th ed. (New York: Macmillan, 1974), pp. 279–96, 392–407.

2. P. S. Vig, ed., *Danske i Amerika,* 2 vols. (Minneapolis: C. Rasmussen Publishing Co., 1907–14), 1(B): 205–26.

3. The church organization that was later named the Danish Evangelical Lutheran Church in America (the Danish Church) was founded in 1872. Various differences among the clergy led in the course of the 1880s to the formal creation, in 1896, of the United Danish Evangelical Lutheran Church in America (the United Church). Putting the theological differences aside, one may say that the (Grundtvigian) Danish Church

saw greater importance in the preservation of Danish culture than did the (Inner Mission) United Church. In numbers of congregations, the United Church was twice as large as the Danish Church throughout the history of the two synods (now merged with the Lutheran Church in America and the American Lutheran Church, respectively). For a concise description of the attitudes toward Danish culture which contributed to the schism, see Thorvald Hansen, *School in the Woods: The Story of an Immigrant Seminary* (Des Moines, Iowa: Grand View College, 1977). Major studies of Danish-American church history are Paul C. Nyholm, *The Americanization of the Danish Lutheran Churches* (Copenhagen: Institute for Danish Church History, University of Copenhagen, 1963); Enok Mortensen, *The Danish Lutheran Church in America: The History and Heritage of the American Evangelical Lutheran Church* (Philadelphia: Lutheran Church in America, 1967).

4. It has been estimated that around 1900 no less than one-third of the Danish-born in the United States subscribed to Danish-American newspapers (Marion T. Marzolf, "The Pioneer Danish Press in Midwest America," *Scandinavian Studies* 48 [1976]: 437–38; Marion T. Marzolf, "The Danish-Language Press in America" [Ph.D. diss., University of Michigan, 1972]). The perfect ease with which a Dane could read Norwegian-American newspapers limits the usefulness of Danish circulations as an indication of language loyalty. One wonders how many Danish-born read local Norwegian papers, such as *Visergutten* in Story City, Iowa (circulation 9,600 in 1910) or *Posten og Ved Arnen* in Decorah, Iowa (circulation 36,821 in 1910) (*N. W. Ayer and Sons's American Newspaper Annual and Directory* [Philadelphia: Ayer and Son, 1910], pp. 1153, 1161–12).

5. Einar Haugen, "Norm and Deviation in Bilingual Communities," in *Bilingualism: Psychological, Social, and Educational Implications,* ed. Peter A. Hornby (New York: Academic Press, 1977), pp. 91–102.

6. Nils Hasselmo, *Amerikasvenska: en bok om språkutvecklingen i Svensk-Amerika* (Stockholm: Esselte Studium, 1974); Einar Haugen, *The Norwegian Language in America: A Study in Bilingual Behavior,* 2 vols. (Philadelphia: University of Pennsylvania Press, 1953).

7. These examples of American Danish are taken from Henrik Cavling, *Fra Amerika,* 2 vols. (Copenhagen: Gyldendal, 1897), 1:350–54; Nikotin [pseud.], "Det mærkelige Sprog, Dansk-Amerikansk," in *Salomons almanak for 1916* (Seattle: Danish Publishing House of the Pacific Coast), pp. 128–30; Karl Larsen, *De, der tog hjemmefra,* 4 vols. (Copenhagen: Gyldendal, 1910–14).

8. Kristian Hvidt, *Danske veje vestpå: en bog om udvandringen til Amerika* (Copenhagen: Politiken, 1976), pp. 100–14; English-language edition, *Danes Go West* (Copenhagen: Rebild National Park Society, 1976).

9. U.S. Bureau of the Census, *Thirteenth Census of the United States, 1910* vol. 1. *Population*, pp. 998–1006.

10. William F. Mackey, "The Description of Bilingualism," in *Readings in the Sociology of Language,* ed. Joshua A. Fishman (The Hague: Mouton, 1968), pp. 554–56.

11. Nationwide, 35 percent of the Danish-born lived in cities of more than twenty-five thousand. In the Great Lakes states, the rural and urban proportion of Danes

reflected the greater industrialization in those states (rural population: Illinois, 22 percent; Michigan, 61 percent; Wisconsin, 58 percent).

12. *Salomons almanak: de Forenede Staters danske almanak, haand- og aarbog for 1915,* ed. Michael Salomon (Seattle: Danish Publishing House of the Pacific Coast, 1915), p. 54.

13. "Danske Settlements," *Salomons almanak for 1917,* pp. 135–38; Enok Mortensen, "Den danske højskole i U.S.A.," *Kirke og folk,* 26, no. 13 (15 August 1977): pp. 1–3; 26, no. 14 (10 September 1977): pp. 3–5; 26, no. 15 (25 September 1977): pp. 2–4.

14. Ludvig Petersen, "Nysted og Dannebrog, Nebraska," *Salomons almanak for 1916,* pp. 159–63.

15. Enok Mortensen, *Stories from Our Church: A Popular History of the Danish Evangelical Lutheran Church of America* (Des Moines: Danish Evangelical Lutheran Church of America 1952), pp. 69–82.

16. "Danske Settlements," *Salomons almanak for 1916,* pp. 147–52.

17. "Korrespondancer," *Salomons almanak for 1915,* pp. 51–58 (Translation mine).

18. Nyholm, *Americanization,* pp. 284–89.

19. Vig, ed., *Danske i Amerika,* 1(B): 333.

20. Nyholm, *Americanization,* pp. 296–300. For comparable information concerning the status of Swedish in churches, see Sture Lindmark, *Swedish America, 1914–1932: Studies in Ethnicity with Emphasis on Illinois and Minnesota* (Uppsala: Läromedelsförlagen, 1971), pp. 236–304.

21. Nyholm, *Americanization,* p. 297.

22. U.S. Bureau of the Census, *Census of Population: 1970: Subject Reports: Final Report PC(2)-1A, National Origin and Language,* pp. 66–71, 492. This is a reference to Table 10, "Age of the Foreign Stock by Nativity, Country of Origin and Sex," and Table 19, "Mother Tongue of the Population by Nativity and Parentage" (data based on a 15 percent sample of the population).

The Impact of English on a Low German Dialect in Nebraska

JAN E. BENDER

Prospective immigrants to a country of foreign speech are probably not overly concerned about the future language problem. For some, there is no serious problem since they often settle among people of similar linguistic background. Others may already have some knowledge of the foreign tongue. In either case the immigrants may well expect to pick up the language after a period of several years in their new home. Once they arrive, however, they soon discover that native fluency is not so easy to acquire.

Thus it was, at least with most of the immigrants from East Frisia, the northwestern corner of Germany near the Netherlands border, who began arriving on the Great Plains in 1847. The influx of East Frisians peaked in the 1880s, as did that of the rest of the German immigrants.[1] Whether the East Frisians had earned their living as millers, bakers, fishermen, or artisans, they all became farmers after their arrival in the southeastern quarter of Nebraska.

The acquisition of English was not difficult for the youngest among the immigrants. For adults, however, East Frisian remained dominant throughout their lives. Even when they achieved fluency in English, they spoke it with a marked Low German accent.

The situation was quite different for members of the second generation. If their parents spoke Low German at home, they learned it as their first language. Many acquired English by playing with English-speaking children; others learned it upon entering school. The speech of such children usually developed without foreign accent in both languages. Like most bilinguals, however, they made differential use of their two languages. Low German was basically restricted to the farm and to home and family life. English was the written language, the language of education, science, technology, business, and government.

Consequently, second-generation teen-agers began to develop a negative attitude toward the use of the parental language, which seemed not to be of much use outside the home. Then, too, children whose skill in the use of English was inferior to that of native speakers of English or of older bilinguals could easily become the laughing stock of the one-room school. Teachers in such one-room schools were usually too busy to create an atmosphere of sympathy and tolerance for pupils with such language problems.

Later on in life the adherence to a non-English tongue marked the speakers as members of a minority group whose life goals might well remain restricted to a relatively small community. It was well known that a number of prominent German Americans—John Jacob Astor, August Busch, Henry Steinweg, Friedrich Weyerhaeuser—had early abandoned their mother tongue. Was there a causal relationship between the nonuse of German and success in this country? Considerations such as these caused many to wonder whether their ancestral language was an asset or a liability.

The superpatriotic hysteria generated by World War I was the source of great suffering for American speakers of German.[2] During and after the war many were branded as traitors by their neighbors of other tongues, whether their forefathers had come from the Kaiser's Germany or from another German-speaking country. Ironically, some who were most severely persecuted were the descendants of German-speaking immigrants from Russia, whither their forebears had fled to escape the very tryanny with which they were now being unjustly associated. The use of German became so unacceptable socially that it could not be employed outside the home without evoking disapproving glances, reprimands, and even harassment. Indeed, for a period of four years (1919–23) it was illegal to speak German over much of the Great Plains. Small wonder, then, that American-born generations should question the desirability of passing on their ancestral language to their children.

Thus it is not difficult to understand the sharp drop in the overall number of third-generation speakers of East Frisian Low German. To find a fluent speaker in the fourth generation is rare indeed. Today only a few hundred descendants of the several thousand immigrants of eighty to ninety years ago can still speak the dialect. Where it has survived, however, it is of particular interest to linguists.

The primary linguistic problem for bilinguals is keeping the two language systems apart. Most do not fully succeed in doing so. Nearly all bilinguals experience a certain degree of linguistic interference, which Uriel Weinreich has defined as "deviation from the norms of either language which occcur in the speech of bilinguals as a result of their familiarity with more than one language."[3]

In the following, various forms of interference characteristic of the speech of third-generation descendants of East Frisian immigrants will be described.

All examples were excerpted from a series of tape recordings of interviews (made in Gage County between 1969 and 1975) with several members of selected families. The selection of informants was made with a view toward ascertaining the consistency in the use of these examples within the speech community. The interviews were structured to include forty English sentences to be translated into East Frisian Low German, a vocabulary list, and free discussion of various topics including home and family, farming, business, government, and others.[4]

The most common form of interference in this Nebraska dialect is borrowing. An English word is used to fill a real or apparent vacuum in East Frisian Low German. The reasons for borrowing may be unconsious or deliberate. At the moment when a word or expression is needed, it is not available. Perhaps it is lacking in East Frisian Low German, or the native term may not have the same range of connotations as the English one, or else it may be unsatisfactory in some other way.

The process of borrowing is a linguistic habit modified by personal attitudes toward the purity of the language or the acceptance of borrowed words and phrases within the East Frisian Low German community or both. In general the older the borrowed term is, the more thoroughly it has been adapted to the phonological pattern of East Frisian Low German.

Borrowing began, of course, when the immigrants encountered items and situations that were new to them. In order to talk about such things they used the English labels within an East Frisian Low German context, pronouncing the foreign words as best they could, but usually substituting their native phones for the English ones. The second generation imitated their parents' version of the borrowed vocabulary, thinking the loanwords to be Low German since they were composed of Low German sounds and were used in a Low German context. The third generation was even less conscious of the fact that they were using components of two different languages simultaneously. Furthermore it is clear that each generation added its share of borrowed words to the East Frisian Low German vocabulary.

Today, when someone's attention is called to the use of a foreign term in his speech, his reaction is often a shrug of the shoulder and a comment like, "Well, that's what Pa always used to say," or, "Mama always said it like that." Those who are aware of the infiltration of English terms recognize as such only those which have not been phonologically assimilated and rarely consider as foreign those English expressions that have been germanized.

Probably the unassimilated importation is the most frequent type of innovation in East Frisian Low German. Such importations are commonly called *foreign words*, a term suitable here to distinguish them from loanwords that have undergone adaptation to the East Frisian Low German sound system. It is difficult to estimate their frequency in number or percentage. They are relatively infrequent in conversations about daily life in home, farm, and family, but their number can increase greatly when talk turns to the technical terminology of machine parts and repairs or to local business transactions. In fact, if the percentage of foreign words reaches a certain density and, as it were, overloads the Low German sentence structure, the speaker will momentarily shift to the English language entirely. Importations can be classified as foreign words only on the basis of phones that are *not* part of the East Frisian Low German sound system.

Thus the nouns [slap] 'slop' ("hog feed"), [bakət] 'bucket', and [hɛnl] 'handle' can be classified as assimilated borrowings even though they share all phones with the English sound system.[5] (The East Frisian Low German speakers' pronunciation of English does not differ perceptively from that of monolingual members of their community.) The consistent use of these three terms on every farm indicates that they are early borrowings.

For the most part, foreign words are nouns and interjections. The following examples are a small representative selection taken out of the context of free conversations. Since their pronunciation conforms to English usage on the Great Plains, they are given without phonetic transcription.

It is not always clear why foreign words were taken over by the informants or their parents or grandparents. Some items like *television, refrigerator, mixer,* and *pressure system* have a certain modernity, and clearly they, and therefore their labels, did not exist in the 1880s. *County, town, coop, farmer union,* and *government spending* are typical terms of American local government, as *real estate, competition, difference* (of cost and earnings), and *yield* (returns) are terms representative of American business, and *footing* (foundation), *loading chute, speed wrench,* and *preplanting tool* are technical terms connected with local farming. Other foreign terms, like *milo, possum,* and *cottonwood* (tree), were imported because their referents did not exist on German soil, and *pantry, driveway, sliding door,* and *cardboard* may, while extant in Germany, still warrant importation if one assumes a degree of novelty within the last eighty to ninety years. But it is difficult to explain why *coffee pot, coat, keg,* (pig) *pen,* and *fence* are used, since there are fitting labels in Low German for these items.

Loanwords differ from foreign words in that they have been adapted to the East Frisian Low German sound system. Speakers are usually unaware of the fact that they are of English origin. It is reasonable to assume that loanwords that differ most widely from English were borrowed early. Most loanwords by far are nouns, but even adjectives and adverbs also occur, and there is even a borrowed preposition. Typical examples are [pa:sdə] 'pasture', [pik] 'pig', [sœpə] or [sypə] 'supper', [pʊŋkŋ] 'pumpkin', [kʊ̃:fət] 'comforter (blanket)', [ʃgəra::f] 'sheriff'. Adjectives in predicate position are [tʊf] 'tough', [fɔni] 'funny', [rɛgələ] 'regular', and [ʃgu:ə] 'sure, surely'. The borrowed preposition is [dœ:gŋ] 'during'. Small wonder that the English origin of some of these loanwords remains obscure to most East Frisian Low German speakers.[6]

English words and phrases were used as models for East Frisian Low German compounds which would probably be incomprehensible to East Frisians in Germany today. These new loan formations include *loan translations, loan renditions,* and *idiomatic loans*.[7]

Loan translations are compound nouns, verbs, or adjectives based on an English model such as [bɛsmʃdɔk] 'broomstick', [aeəklɔpə] 'eggbeater', [ʃdœ:əmfɛnsdəs] 'stormwindows', and [a:bəlsdaklɛeə] 'workday clothes'.

The following verbs show an English compound pattern with the position of the prefix being last in order as is common in German usage: [ʊpnɛ:m:] 'to take up': [dat nɛ:md nɪ so bɔt ɪn ʃgɛ:ed ʊp] 'That doesn't take up so (much) room in the shed'.

In the present perfect tense, the prefix is combined with the past participle at the end of the sentence as in [ɪnbrɔ:kŋ] 'to break in': [di:əs ʃgɔo sʏnd mənɛt e:əs gɔod ɪnbrɔ:kŋ] 'These shoes have only just been broken in'. East Frisian Low German [vəzi:tn mɪt] copies the colloquial preposition *with* in "to visit with someone": [vi hɛb mɪt ʊ̃:s fəva:ntn vəzi:t] 'We visited with our relatives'. Modifying present participles resembling infinitive forms can precede nouns, such as [ɔfvi:zn] 'to show off' as in [hɛe ɪs n ɔfvi:zn gəzɛ:əl] 'He is a show-off fellow'.

Translated compound adjectives like [rɔot hɛet] 'red-hot' or [bu:tsi:t ga:ŋk] 'outside corridor' seem rarities.

Loan renditions are more liberal translations that correspond to the foreign model only in part, like [ʃwoəsɔkŋ] for "sweatsocks," literally "heavy socks," and the widely used verb [ʊpmɔ:kŋ] 'to put up (wood)', that is "split and stack wood," as in [kã:s du nɪ vat brɛnhɔlt ʊpmɔ:kŋ] 'Can't you put up some firewood?'

The term *idiomatic loan* in its widest sense is the imitation of a foreign expression and may or may not contain English morphemes. The following combinations, although consisting of only Low German words, are unheard of in Germany: [dɛn vɛ] 'that way', [klo:ə tə bru:kŋ] 'ready to use', [a:l bi hœ syəs] 'all by themselves'.

[dat ɪs vat hɛe krɛ:gŋ hɛt] 'That's what he received' would be rendered in the German homeland as *[dat hɛt hɛe krɛ:gŋ]. [dat ɪs ɛen dɪŋ vat ɪk nɪ dɔo] 'That's one thing I don't do' would be heard as *[dat dɔo ɪk nɪ]. But the continental Low German version of [du kã:s gi:n lɛ:bm mɛ:ə mɔ:kŋ ʊpm lɛekŋ fa::m] 'You can't make a living on a small farm any more' would have to be reproduced in an entirely different way.

Other idiomatic loans, like [dɔol hɪl] 'downhill' and [raet nu] 'right now' contain borrowed English morphemes which have been adjusted to the East Frisian Low German sound system. In [vat so:ət fœ:gəls mεens du] the model "What sort of birds do you mean?" is evident; the speaker's relatives abroad would say *[vat fœ fœ:gəls mεens du]. The phrasing of [vi ha:dn kraots to ʃbɔos mɔ:kŋ] 'We had crowds to have fun' is entirely unique to East Frisian Low German in this country.

Both languages supply parts for *hybrid compounds* whose model usually is an English noun.[8] As before, the borrowed part has been adapted to the East Frisian Low German sound system. Hybrid formations, with either the first or second part of the compound being English, are relatively frequent. In [fo:əkrɔp] 'feedcrop', [ʃda:lflo:ə] 'barnfloor', [tu:nrεek] 'gardenrake', and [rɔompɪtʃə] 'creampitcher' the second part is of English origin; in the triple compounds [seεsdu:mɔ::gə] 'six-inch-auger' and [ʃdikəlvi:əfεns] 'barbed-wire-fence' the last element is English. Note that the word [vi:ə] 'wire' is an East Frisian Low German cognate.

In the following compounds, the second part is Low German: [sœpətit] 'suppertime', [kɪtʃnʃga:p] 'kitchen cabinet', [fi:də swi:n] 'feeder hog', [plεesdɪkʃgɔot] 'plaster wall'.

Hybrid derivative is the term for words consisting of an English lexeme and a foreign affix.[9] East Frisian Low German readily assimilates English verbs by adding infinitive, participle, or conjugational endings. The English verb stem is often altered to fit the East Frisian Low German phonological system as in [bɔodən] 'to bother', [ʃdεn::] 'to stand (endure)', but not always, as in [kju:ʀn] 'to cure (meat)', and [ʀi'ʃεepm] 'to reshape'.

Most participles, including those with strong past (that is, gradation) formation, receive the regular weak ending [-t] or allophonic [-d]: [dεe syn dɔa mɪt bɔltn anbɔlt] 'They are bolted on there with bolts'. [nɔ:də hεt hεe ʊpha:ŋt] 'Afterwards he hung up (the telephone receiver)'. A past participle recorded with strong formation is this: [hεd hεe di a:l ʊprʊŋ: tədɔ:] 'Has he already called you up today?'

Many English verb stems are used with East Frisian Low German separable prefixes. [ʊp-] and [ut-] are the most frequent: [ʊprɪŋ::] 'to ring up (telephone)', [utʃmu:dn] 'to smooth out', [vεɣmεltn] 'to melt away', [œ:vətɪpm] 'to tip over'.

Some borrowed nouns receive for their plural formation the East Frisian German ending [-n] ([-ŋ] after [g, k], [-m] after [b, p]), as in [hi:əln] 'hills', [lεekŋ] 'lakes', [krɔpm] 'crops'. Even [pɔon::] 'ponds' shows the German ending in the compensatory lengthening of the nasal, while [frʏn:s] 'friends' evidently sports a double bilingual plural ending.

If the East Frisian Low German sentence structure is altered so that it matches the English word order, we have a case of *loan syntax*. This phenomenon is especially noticeable when the characteristic German final position of past participles, infinitives, and separable prefixes is disturbed. In the following, adverbs and prepositional phrases are final elements according to the pattern: [sɛe hɛt brɔot bakŋ dɔon gʏsdə] 'She baked bread yesterday'; [hɛe pɪk meɛlk hi:ərʊm ʊp ɔok] 'He picks up milk around here, too'; [dat hɔlt mʊs du ʊpmɔ:kŋ bi ʊp krɪk] 'You have to put up wood up the creek'.

Inverted order of subject and verb (if the first element in the main clause is one other than the subject) is another syntactical rule in German. The following examples show no inversion after an adverb and after an initial dependent clause: [dɛn hɛe fəkɔopt dɛe] 'Then he sells them'; [vɛn dʊ nɔ taon hɛn vʊs du nɛ:ms rɔot ɔos fən hi:ə] 'If you want to go to town, you take the road east from here'.

English syntax left its mark on East Frisian Low German also in infinitive phrases. English sentence structure has both *to* and the infinitive form at the beginning of the infinitive phrase, while German puts both equivalents in sentence-final position. In Nebraska East Frisian Low German, these parts are unexpectedly separated as [tɔo] *to* is used at the beginning of the inifinitive clause while the infinitive is retained in final position: [dat nɪmp mɛ:ə mã:ly tɔo dat dɔon] 'It takes more men to do that' or [sə hɛet tɔo də keidls va:sn] 'She hates to wash the kettles (pots)'.

When an East Frisian Low German word receives a new meaning under the influence of a similar English word, we speak of *semantic borrowing*. Whether the old meaning is actually replaced is difficult to ascertain. We can assume a passive or merely cognitive stage for an archaic meaning of a term before it falls into disuse and oblivion. Paul Schach has pointed out that as prerequisites for semantic borrowing the physical forms of the two items need to be similar (*Sachähnlichkeit*), the two word structures have to be the same (*Baugleichheit*), and the individual parts of both terms should concur semantically (*semantische Übereinstimmung*).[10]

Especially nouns and verbs, but also some adjectives, are subject to this semantic transfer. [hɛnl] 'handle' has replaced distinct vocabulary for handles of brooms, pots, knives, cups, and other things. [baks] 'box' takes the place of designations of boxes of different sizes and materials. The verb [nɛ:m:] 'to take' wins out over many verbs with specific meaning in a process of vocabulary simplification. In the following sentence, for instance, [nɛ:m:] stands for 'require', a meaning usually not covered by it elsewhere: [dat nɪmp so la:ŋ dat se fo:ət vo:ən dɔot] 'It takes so long for them (the animals) to be fed'. The verb [rɛn::] 'to run' normally refers to the physical activity, while it is applied now to running an enterprise: [ʊ̃:s jʊŋ rɛnt ʊ̃s fa::m] 'Our son runs our farm'.

Among the nouns acquiring new meanings are [tuʊŋ] for 'wagon tongue', formerly designating the anatomical member only, [ka::n] meaning 'tin can', formerly 'pitcher' or 'container with a handle for pouring', [kɔp] meaning 'head of wheat', formerly only the 'head on the shoulders', and so forth.

The adjective [ʃma:l] now means ''small'' instead of ''narrow'': [si hu:s ɪs tɔo ʃma:l fœə mɛ:ə dɛn fi::f ly: tɔoɪn lɛ:bm] 'His house is too small for more than five people to live in'.

Our examples have demonstrated some of the developments in bilingual individuals of East Frisian Low German and English. While the East Frisian Low German dialect has changed under the impact of English in Nebraska, the speech relatives in Germany changed in approximation to High German, which East Frisian Low German children in Germany often learn as a foreign language upon entering public school. Many of the processes of borrowing mentioned above apply here as well, albeit with different outcome.[11]

The frequency of English borrowings spread throughout an East Frisian Low German conversation should not be misleading, however. To speak of a language mixture or language fusion would be overstating the phenomenon. The basic structure and the phonology of East Frisian Low German remain intact; the percentage of English morphemes occurring within the East Frisian Low German context is usually not more than 5–7 percent, but may rise to 10 percent or more depending on the topic discussed, as explained earlier. Nevertheless, the borrowings and other influences from English evident in every tenth to twentieth word on the average are quite conspicuous to the interested listener, who may be amazed at the receptiveness and flexibility of East Frisian Low German in absorbing foreign material and integrating it to fit its grammatical and phonological structures. Perhaps the relatively close ''language distance'' (Einar Haugen's term for the presence or absence of a historicolinguistic relationship) between Low German and English is a decisive factor here.[12] It may be because of this proximity also that this colonial derivative of East Frisian Low German with all its loans, hybrid formations, and semantic borrowings does not appear arbitrary or willful in the flow of its words, but sounds smooth and organic to a listener given to impressionistic judgment, while it is intriguing to the linguist interested in the dynamics of language change.

Notes

1. George Schnücker, *Die Ostfriesen in Amerika* (Cleveland, Ohio: Central Publishing House, 1917), p. 3. The census of 1890 shows a high of seventy-two thousand German immigrants in Nebraska, or 6.8 percent of the total population of the state. On this see Frederick C. Luebke, *Immigrants and Politics: The Germans of Nebraska 1880–1900* (Lincoln: University of Nebraska Press, 1969), pp. 190–91. My own conservative estimate puts the East Frisian Low German portion of this total at 3–4 percent, or between two thousand and three thousand immigrants. By comparison, for 1915 Schnücker (p. 311) assumed a total of eighty thousand East Frisians and their descendants in the states of Illinois, Iowa, Nebraska, South Dakota, and Minnesota.

2. On this see Frederick C. Luebke, *Bonds of Loyalty: German Americans and World War I* (De Kalb: Northern Illinois University Press, 1974), pp. 225–65.

3. Uriel Weinreich, *Languages in Contact: Findings and Problems,* Publications of the Linguistic Circle of New York, no. 1 (New York, 1953), p. 1.

4. For a detailed description of interviewing methods and procedures see Jan E. Bender, ''Die getrennte Entwicklung gleichen niederdeutschen Sprachgutes in Deutschland und Nebraska,'' (Ph.D. diss., University of Nebraska, 1970).

5. The phonetic transcriptions make use of the International Phonetic Alphabet as listed in Hans-Heinrich Wängler, *Grundriß einer Phonetik des Deutschen,* 2d ed. (Marburg: N. G. Elwert Verlag, 1967); and Robert H. Hall, Jr., *Introductory Linguistics* (Philadelphia: Chilton, 1964).

6. The phonetic symbol [r] represents the alveolar trill, whereas [ɾ] represents the American retroflex *r*. The stem (usually the first) syllable carries primary stress; [ə] is never accented. If the first syllable is not the (accented) stem syllable, a preceding (′) will mark primary stress.

7. The terminology follows Werner Betz, *Deutsch und Lateinisch: Die Lehnbildungen der althochdeutschen Benediktinerregel* (Bonn: H. Bouvier, 1965) and Weinreich, *Languages in Contact*. To the extent that these three formations do not involve the importation of English morphemes, they can be subsumed under the concept *loanshift* as used by Einar Haugen, ''The Analysis of Linguistic Borrowing,'' *Language* 26(1950): 215; and *Bilingualism in the Americas: A Bibliography and Research Guide, Publication of the American Dialect Society,* no. 26(1956), p. 52. See also Paul Schach, ''Types of Loan Translations in Pennsylvania German,'' *Modern Language Quarterly* 13(1952): 268–76; and ''Die Lehnprägungen der pennsylvania-deutschen Mundart,'' *Zeitschrift für Mundartforschung* 22(1955): 215–22.

8. Paul Schach, ''Hybrid Compounds in Pennsylvania German,'' *American Speech* 23(1948): 121–34.

9. Paul Schach, ''The Formation of Hybrid Derivations in Pennsylvania German,'' *Symposium* 3(1949): 114–29.

10. Paul Schach, ''Semantic Borrowing in Pennsylvania German,'' *American Speech* 26(1951): 257–67.

11. For a detailed discussion and comparison see Bender, "Die getrennte Entwicklung gleichen niederdeutschen Sprachgutes."

12. Haugen, *Bilingualism in the Americas,* p. 49.

Hungarian and American Borrowings in a Twice Transplanted Fulda Dialect

ANDREAS GOMMERMANN

Following the Turkish occupation of southeastern Europe, Hungarian landowners sought to repopulate their devastated estates with German farmers and artisans. Through their favorable settlement contracts—religious freedom, exemption from statute labor, settlement by groups from the same region of Germany, and so forth—they succeeded in resettling the area between the Danube, the Drave, and Lake Balaton in a relatively short period of time. Until 1946 this region was known as the *Schwäbische Türkei* ("Swabian Turkey") although most of the Germans there were not Swabians. Since 1922 these people were called *Donauschwaben* ("Danube Swabians") to distinguish them from the Swabians of the mother country.

Among the German emigrants were a number of families from the bishopric of Fulda in Hesse, who were settled at a place called Mucsi in the administrative district of Tolnau. By 1946 this village had grown to about 460 households with roughly twenty-three hundred individuals. The inhabitants of Mucsi lived their own lives, isolated from their surroundings.[1] In spring, summer, and fall they worked on their fields and in their vineyards; winter was the time for recreation and preparation. Only the major religious holidays—Christmas, Easter, church-dedication anniversary—brought variety into their daily lives. Since the village community enjoyed a strong degree of independence through their agricultural production and since their geographical situation (no railroad or through highway) isolated them from the neighboring villages, they could maintain their dialect almost completely intact until the time of their expulsion in 1946.

This dialect is characterized by forms that are also characteristic of the dialects spoken in the former bishopric of Fulda.[2] These include the diminutive suffix [-jə], plural [-ərjə], as in [ha:esjə] *Häuschen* 'little house'—plural [ha:ezərjə]. In these dialects the Middle High German vowels *î* and *û* appear consistently as diphthongs. Characteristic features of the dialects south of Fulda are the open *ä* in words like [fąlḍ] *Feld 'field'* and [ġəląnḍ] *gelernt 'learned'* as well as the *u* before *r* plus consonant in such words as [khʊən] *Korn 'grain'*, [ḍʊəḍ] *dort* 'there', and [ḍu:ərf] *Dorf* 'village'. Furthermore the interrogatives have initial [b] as in [ḅą:r] *wer* 'who', [ḅo:s] *was* 'what', and [ḅąm] *wem* 'to whom'.

On a recent visit to Germany I explored the region south of the city of Fulda, conversed with people there, and visited several cemeteries. On gravestones I found family names that were current in Mucsi and are now found in the Middle West, such as Bott, Gensler, Keidl, Ruppert, and Erb. Since there seem to have been no earlier group emigrations from Fulda to the United States, family names common to Fulda and the Middle West must have been brought here by way of Mucsi, Hungary.

Although Hungarian became the language of the schools in Mucsi in the twentieth century, its impact on the transplanted Fulda dialect was slight, compared with that of English. The following Hungarian loanwords, some of which were replaced by English loans later on, are typical.

Since births were registered in Hungarian, the people of Mucsi frequently retained the Hungarian forms of given names such as [jɔuʃġɔ] *Jóska* for *József;* [jʊri] *Gyuri* for *György* 'Georg'; [fęręnds] or [fęri] *Ferenc* or *Feri* 'Franz'; and and [jɒ:nʊʃ] *Janos* 'Johann'.

After the dissolution of the Austro-Hungarian monarchy in 1918 Germans in Hungary had to serve in the army. A number of words were borrowed by the dialects from army language. Typical loanwords of this kind are [hɔunvẹ:ḍ] *honvéd* 'army'; [ḅɒgɒ] *baka* 'infantryman'; [ḍɪze:r] *tüzér* 'artillery man'; [fɔjɒme:r] *folyamör* 'river fleet'; [hʊso:ɐr] *huszár* 'cavalry man'.[3] Not only the designations of branches of the service, but also designations of rank and commands were borrowed from Hungarian, as, for example, [e:rmęʃḍṛ] *ör-mester* 'sergeant' and the command [ʃɔrɒġɔzo:] *Sorakozó!* 'Fall in!' The soldiers' cooking utensil was known as [ʃɔjġɔ] *sajka,* the canteen as [ġʊlɒḍʃ] *kulacs,* and the lace boots as [ḅɒgɒnḍʃ] *bakancs.*

Before induction into the Hungarian army German speakers had to participate in a premilitary course, which they called in the Mucsi dialect [lęvęnḍə] *levente.* The training ground was called a [lęvęnḍəḅlɒḍs], a hybrid compound composed of Hungarian *leventetér* and the dialect form of German *Platz* 'place'.

Borrowings from Hungarian, of course, were not limited to military language, but included loans of various kinds dealing with agriculture, food, clothing, and the like. The field name [sąląʃ] *szállás* 'shelter' was used in many villages of Swabian Turkey. The boundary name [ho:uzəjɒ:nʊʃ] "trouser

John'' is a hybrid formation with a humorous semantic change, being an adaptation of Hungarian *Hosszú János* 'Long John' with substitution of the dialect word for *trousers* for the Hungarian adjective. Various hybrid compounds are formed with [d̥sɪrɔġ] *cirok* 'foxtail millet'. The shaft of the millet is known as [d̥sɪrɔġʃd̥ąŋl̩], the second element of which is the dialect form of German *Stengel*. The housewife swept the floors with a broom (German *Besen*) made of such shafts which she called a [d̥sɪrɔgb̊ą:zə]. The Hungarian food names *paprikás, gulyás,* and *pörkölt* occur in many names of dishes such as [hɪŋl̩sb̥ɒb̥rɪġą:ʃ] *Hühnerpaprikasch* 'chicken paprika soup', [feʃ-b̥ɒb̥rɪġa:ʃ] *Fischpaprika* 'fish paprika soup', [reŋsġʊlą:ʃ] *Rindersuppe* 'beef soup', and [khɒlb̥sb̥ɛrġɛld̥] *Kalbfleischgulasch* 'veal goulash'.

Few translation loans have been attested for the Mucsi dialect. The beadle (*Gemeindediener*) was called [ġlã:ə̃rɪçd̥r̩], a translation of Hungarian *kisbiró,* literally *Kleinrichter* 'little judge'. [ʃdã:ə̃ʃdrɔs], literally *Steinstraße,* seems to be a translation of *köves út,* which literally means ''stony street'' but is used to designate a graveled road or street, as is the Mucsi translation also.

A marked semantic shift is shown in the loanward [vɪd̥ɒm], which has the phonetic form of Hungarian *vidám* 'happy, glad, merry'. In the dialect, however, it is used to designate an unusually lively boy. Since this word is pronounced [vɪd̥ɒŋ] by some dialect speakers, its meaning may have been influenced by *bitang,* which means ''rascal.'' A similar semantic shift has occurred in [b̥ed̥ją:r], the dialect form of *betyár* 'robber, highwayman', which is used as a designation for a rude or disobedient boy.

Hungarian seems to have had no impact on verb conjugation or sentence structure. The following adverbs and interjections have been attested: [ɔgɒrb̥ɪ] from *akár milyen* 'even though'; [d̥ɛhɔd̥j nɛd̥] from *dehogy* 'by no means' plus the native negative adverb; [hɒd̥] *hát* 'thus, so'; and [ʊd̥jə] *ugye* 'nicht wahr'.

Around the turn of the century the population of Mucsi was almost two thousand, and the farms had become so small that they could no longer support a family. In order to make a living many dialect speakers had to seek supplementary employment. They worked as day laborers or harvest laborers on nearby estates or joined threshing crews. Some of them emigrated to the United States shortly before or immediately after World War I. Their goal was Milwaukee, Wisconsin, a city many Germans had heard about as early as the middle of the nineteenth century and that bore the name ''German Athens.''[4]

The first emigrants from Mucsi, numbering about two hundred persons, intended to remain in America for only a few years. They soon came to feel at home in the United States, however, and most of them decided to remain permanently in Milwaukee. The main contingent of Mucsi dialect speakers came to America between 1949 and 1955 by way of West Germany, to which they had been banished in 1946 by the Hungarian government. Most of these immigrants also settled in Milwaukee, although smaller groups settled elsewhere, mainly in Aurora, Illinois.

Today there are about two hundred persons in Milwaukee who still speak their twice displaced Fulda dialect. The main factors contributing to the survival of their mother tongue seem to be family traditions, a common culture and religion, and a strong feeling of group unity. From the very beginning the immigrants met in each other's homes every Sunday to play cards, whereby they enjoyed their homemade wine. This custom has been preserved to the present day.

In 1929 the Mucsi Family Club was founded. In 1966 this club and three other Danube Swabian clubs were invited to form the organization Vereinigte Donauschwaben (United Danube Swabians). In their clubhouse, Schwabenhof, which they purchased in 1968, they still celebrate festivals in the style of their old home in Hungary.

The close contact with English in the United States intensified the process of linguistic borrowing. The impact of English can be seen primarily in the lexicon of the language. The incorporation of English words has not affected the structure of the dialect. The borrowed lexical items are adapted phonologically and morphologically. Loan verbs are conjugated like native ones, and borrowed nouns usually are declined like dialect ones. In spite of these borrowings, the dialect has essentially retained the vocabulary of the community of Mucsi.

As already mentioned, some of the borrowings from Hungarian have been replaced by English loanwords. Thus Josef, Georg, Franz, and Johann are now called [ḍʃo:], [ʃɔrʃ], [frɛŋk], and [ḍʃa̧:n]. Young male dialect speakers now serve in the [a̧:rmɪ] or the [nẹ:vɪ]. Some of them achieve the rank of [sa̧rʃənḍ]. Instead of [bɒġɒnḍʃ] they now wear [ḅu:ḍs], and some of them receive their premilitary training in the [arɔḍɪsɪ] *ROTC* (Reserve Officer's Training Corps). The housewife no longer sweeps with a broom made of millet shafts, but with a [ma̧ḅ], and she now cooks [ḍʃɪgṇḅɒḅrɪġa:ʃ] *chicken paprika soup*. Today one does not go to the *Gemeindehaus,* but to the [sɪḍɪhɒl] *city hall.* Instead of the former Hungarian adverbs and interjections we now hear [vel] *well,* [ɔġẹ:] *okay,* [jUno:] *you know,* [ḅlenḍɪ] *plenty,* and [ʃu:r] *sure*.

In addition to these replacements of Hungarian borrowings, there was a rather extensive importation of English loanwords. The chief reason for this is the fact that dialect speakers in America felt a need for words that were lacking in their Fulda dialect in Mucsi—words with which to accommodate themselves linguistically to a radically different environment. It is doubtful that most of these loanwords came directly from English; rather, we must assume that they were taken over from other German dialects. The Fulda dialect, after all, has been spoken in America—primarily in Milwaukee, but also in Aurora, Illinois—for a relatively short time. The earliest immigrants spoke no English and worked and socialized among other Danube Swabians or Germans who had immigrated earlier. Whenever possible, adult dialect speakers sought work at places where other Germans were employed. Thus it is clear that most of the borrowings were adapted to the Fulda dialect from other German dialects.

There follows a discussion of a number of characteristic lexical borrowings from English in keeping with the terminology proposed by Werner Betz, Einar Haugen, and Paul Schach.[5]

Loanwords represent the most common type of borrowing. An interesting example is the loanword *corn* in the American sense of "maize" (German *Mais*). This borrowing has been attested also in Pennsylvania German and in German dialects spoken in Texas. In these dialects the borrowed word represents a semantic loan.[6] This, I discovered, holds true also for other dialects spoken in Milwaukee. In the case of this word the colonial Fulda dialect is unique. As already mentioned, Standard German [ɔ] corresponds to [ʊə] in this dialect. [khʊən] *Korn* 'grain' has been preserved. The English loanword *corn*, however, is pronounced [khɔrn]. A compound of this borrowing is [ḅaḅkhɔrn] *popcorn* (German *Puffmais*). Since the speakers of this dialect no longer engage in agriculture, they lack further compounds such as those listed by Schach for Pennsylvania German.[7]

Various borrowed designations for food and drink, house and garden, commodities, and other things owe their existence to the fact that corresponding words were lacking in the dialect or its Hungarian variety. Since cranberries were unknown in Mucsi, the word [ġrenḅɛrɪ] was borrowed in America. American fruit pies bear such names as [ęḅḷḅa:e] 'apple pie', [ḍʃęrɪḅa:e] 'cherry pie', and so forth. Since the dialect came under English influence relatively late, native appellations alternate with borrowed ones. Doughnuts bought at the market are called [ḍo:unąḍs], whereas the homemade variety are known as [ġrąbl] (German *Krapfen*). Gravy is alternately designated by the loanword [ġrẹ:vɪ] and by the dialect term [so:us] (German *Soße*). As a dessert applesauce is called [ąḅḷsḅra:e] (German *Apfelbrei*); as a side dish it is known by its American name [ęḅḷsɒ:s].

Since American houses differ essentially from the German peasant houses in the Swabian Turkey both in construction and arrangements, the Fulda dialect speakers use a number of loanwords that are found also in other American-German dialects, such as [ḅẹ:sməṇḍ] 'basement' (*Keller*), [ḅel] *'bell' (Hausklingel)*, [ḅɔrdʃ] 'porch' (*Vorbau, Veranda*), and [ḍa:enɪŋru:m] 'dining room (*Speisezimmer*).

Translation loanwords or loan translations are relatively infrequent. They include [ḅɒŋkḅu:əx] 'bank book' (*Sparbuch*), [ʃḍʊrəmḍi:ər] 'storm door' (*Außentür, Doppeltür, Wintertür*), [hã:əġəmɔiçḍə nʊl] 'homemade noodles' (*selbsthergestellte Nudeln*), and [hã:əgəmɔiçḍə vã:ẽ] 'homemade wine' (*selbsthergestellter Wein*). Various verbs illustrate semantic borrowing, including the following three interesting examples. If a young man wishes to go out with a girl, he asks if he may *take her out* [a:osnɒ:m]. The dialect word in Europe had nothing to do with an invitation to go out; it was used only to designate dressing poultry or animals. [ɔḅlẹ:ç] 'to lay off' has acquired the additional meaning of ''to dismiss temporarily from work'' (*vorübergehend entlassen*), just as *ablegen* has quite generally in American-German dialects. [ɔḅnɒ:m] 'to take (time) off' (*sich vom Dienst oder von der Arbeit befreien lassen*) originally meant ''to lose weight'' or ''to photograph.'' All three verbs used in the manner above would be incomprehensible in Europe.

Translations of phrases or loan phrases have also been attested; this phenomenon can be illustrated by the following examples. [s nɪmḍ ḍsa:eḍ] 'It takes time' (''Es dauert''); [hą mɒxḍ sae lɒ:və] 'He makes his living' (''Er kommt in wirtschaftlicher Hinsicht verhältnismäßig gut aus''); [vɪsḍ khɒ:lḍ / vɔərəm] 'Are you cold / warm?' ''Ist dir kalt / (zu) warm?''). The last example illustrates semantic changes that can lead to misunderstandings in colloquial German.

In regard to loan creations, one must agree with the observations made by Schach about Pennsylvania German: they represent the least common form of borrowing.[8] To the extent that nouns derived from English verbs by means of the prefix [ġə-] can be regarded as loan creations, the following qualify: [ġəkhɪġ] '(repeated) kicking' (*wiederholtes Stoßen mit dem Fuß*); [gəphʊʃ] 'pushing' (*Schieben, Drängen, Gedränge*); [ġədʃi:ḍ] 'cheating' (*Betrug, Betrügen, Betrügerei*); and [ġədʃɒmḅ] 'jumping' (*Springen*).

Far more numerous than the loan creations are hybrid word formations, most of which are either nouns or verbs. Of the many hybrid compounds only a few, formed from German *Mann* and English *box*, will be listed here: [ɪnʃu:rənsmɒn] 'insurance man' (*Versicherungsvertreter*); [ḅɪsnɪsmɒn] 'business man' (*Kaufmann*);[mẹ:lmɒn] 'mailman' (*Briefträger, Briefzusteller*); and [ḅɔli:smɒn] 'policeman' (*Polizist*). Examples of hybrid compounds of *box* are [hɔlḍsḅɒġs] 'wooden box' (*Holzkiste*); [ḍsɔuġṛrḅɒġs] 'sugar box' (*Zuckerdose*); and [mą:lḅɒġs] 'flour box' (*Mehldose*). Hybrid derivatives are represented by the following verbs with separable prefixes: [õ:ũseḍḷ] 'to settle' (*niederlassen*); [a:osphɪġ] 'to pick out' (*auslesen*); [fəmɪġs] 'to mix up' (*vermischen*); [rẹmfu:l] 'to fool around' (*Unsinn machen*). The hybrid derivative [ɔḅfɪġs] 'to fix up' (*anordnen, arrangieren, unterbringen, [ein Haus] renovieren*) is undergoing semantic change and means about the same thing as slang *to fix (someone)* (*jemanden fertig machen, jemandem aufs Dach steigen*). It should be noted that most of the attested hybrid verbs in this dialect are of the type with separable prefixes.

Among the most interesting examples of semantic borrowing are [ɒġṛ] 'acre' (*Acker*), [ġlaeç] 'to like' (*gleichen*), [ʃḅenḍ] 'to spend' (*spenden*), and [ʃɒf] 'to work' (*schaffen*). In the home dialect (as in standard German) [ɒġṛ] designated a cultivated field; in America it became synonymous with its English cognate. *Gleichen,* which in Europe means "to be like," has come to mean "to like." *Spenden* is now used predominantly in the sense of "to spend," whereas it originally meant "dispense, donate, contribute, bestow." In the original Mucsi dialect *schaffen* did not have the sense of the weak verb "to be active, to achieve," which in South German means "to work." Rather it meant "to prevail upon someone (to do something)," a meaning that Kupper has attested for south Germany.[9] In view of the fact that the Fulda-Mucsi dialect, as mentioned above, has been spoken in America for a relatively short period of time, these semantic borrowings must stem from contact with other German dialects, since these meanings have been attested not only for Pennsylvania German but also for American-German dialects in general.[10] In the case of *schaffen,* at least, this must hold true.

Sometimes such semantic loans can be puzzling to visitors from abroad. Recently a speaker of the Mucsi dialect, now living in West Germany, made a visit to Milwaukee. His hostess asked him to hang his overcoat in the [ġlązəḍ]. Astonished and somewhat embarrassed, he put his coat in the bathroom. When someone expressed surprise at finding his overcoat in the bathroom, the guest from Germany said he had been asked to put it in the [ġlązəḍ], which in the original dialect, as in standard German (*Klosett*), means "toilet."

In regard to the borrowings in the American Fulda-Mucsi dialect, let me quote in closing a comment made by Moser about standard German: "A radical struggle against words of foreign origin would be a sign of narrowness; it would mean a danger for the richness of linguistic possibilities of expression. Often words of foreign provenance cannot be replaced, as they permit finer semantic nuances. . . . As Goethe said, 'Language should not reject that which is foreign, but consume it.' "[11]

[Translated from the German by Paul Schach]

NOTES

1. Johann Weidlein, *Die schwäbische Türkei,* vol. 1 (Munich: Landsmannschaft der Deutschen aus Ungarn, 1967), p. 157; Fritz Noack, *Die Mundart der Landschaft um Fulda, Deutsche Dialektgeographie* no. 27 (Marburg: N. G. Elwert, 1938), pp. 1–5, emphasizes the conservative nature of the Hessian dialect speakers in the Fulda region as well as their linguistic isolation and independence.

2. See Andreas Gommermann, "Oberhessische Siedlungsmundart in Milwaukee, Wisconsin, USA: Tochtermundart einer in Mucsi (Ungarn) gesprochenen fuldischen Siedlungsmundart" (Ph.D. diss., University of Nebraska 1965).

3. On the etymology and history of standard German *Husar,* see Walther Mitzka, ed., *Etymologisches Wörterbuch der deutschen Sprache,* 17th ed. (Berlin: Walter de Gruyter & Co. 1957), p. 321.

4. Kate Asaphine Everest, "How Wisconsin Came by Its Large German Element," *Collections of the State Historical Society of Wisconsin* 12 (1892): 323.

5. Werner Betz, *Deutsch und Lateinisch: Die Lehnbildungen der althochdeutschen Benediktinerregel* (Bonn: H. Bouvier, 1965), pp. 27–35; Einar Haugen, *Bilingualism in the Americas: A Bibliography and Research Guide,* Publication of the American Dialect Society, no. 26, p. 157; Paul Schach, "Hybrid Compounds in Pennsylvania German," *American Speech* 23 (1948): 121–34; "The Formation of Hybrid Derivatives in Pennsylvania German," *Symposium* 3 (1949): 114–29; "Semantic Borrowing in Pennsylvania German," *American Speech* 26 (1951): 257–67; "Types of Loan Translations in Pennsylvania German," *Modern Language Quarterly* 13 (1952): 268–76; "Die Lehnprägungen der pennsylvania-deutschen Mundart," *Zeitschrift für Mundartforschung* 22 (1955): 215–22.

6. Schach, "Semantic Borrowing," p. 263; Joseph Wilson, "The German Language in Texas," *Schatzkammer* 2 (1976): 47.

7. Schach, "Types of Loan Translations," p. 271.

8. Schach, "Die Lehnprägungen," p. 218.

9. *Wörterbuch der deutschen Umgangssprache,* vol. 2 (Hamburg: Claassen Verlag, 1966), p. 245. See also *Der große Duden,* vol. 7 (Mannheim: Bibliographisches Institut, 1963), p. 593.

10. Schach, "Semantic Borrowing," p. 258.

11. Hugo Moser, *Deutsche Sprachgeschichte* (Tübingen: Niemeyer, 1969), p. 174.

German Dialects in Anabaptist Colonies on the Great Plains

KURT REIN

Although German is still spoken widely throughout the United States, the number of its German speakers has declined appreciably in recent years. Whereas the greatest concentrations of German speakers were formerly in Pennsylvania, Maryland, Missouri, and Wisconsin, the preponderance of such speakers seems to have shifted to the Great Plains, and especially to the former frontier states of North and South Dakota, Nebraska, and Kansas. Here large numbers of German-speaking immigrants settled during the last quarter of the previous century. Thanks to special circumstances, appreciable numbers of their descendants have retained their native tongue to this very day.[1]

Historical Background

The German speech islands of the Great Plains are of interest to the linguist not only because of their size but also because of the varied histories of their origins. In contrast to most Americans of German descent, these people have maintained a remarkably strong loyalty to their ancestral language. Their loyalty to German can be attributed largely to the fact that their forebears were so-called *Auslandsdeutsche,* that is, German-speaking people from eastern and southeastern Europe (Galicia, Volhynia, areas along the Volga and the Black Sea, the Banat, Bukovina, Transylvania), who lived for generations in more or less closed speech enclaves, where they became accustomed to a form of bilingualism in which the foreign tongue was the national or at least the dominant language.[2]

A second factor in the preservation of German on the Great Plains was the circumstance (not unusual in the United States) that a large proportion of the numerous immigrants of the late nineteenth century belonged to strongly cohesive and exclusive religious groups. This was especially true of the Germans from Russia, who received numerous reinforcements in the early 1920s following the Russian Revolution. The Mennonites are the best known and numerically the largest group who migrated to America for religious reasons. In origin they were Dutch Anabaptists, who through persecution beginning in the sixteenth century were scattered across northern Germany. In West Prussia they found a spirit of tolerance as well as employment in the construction of dikes on the delta of the Vistula. Here they remained for almost three hundred years until the introduction of compulsory military service in Prussia brought about their emigration to Russia.[3]

In addition to these Low German Mennonites, found today from Canada to Paraguay, there is on the Great Plains a small separate group of at most five thousand so-called Swiss, or Volhynian, Mennonites, who live in two settlements in southeastern South Dakota and northeastern Kansas.[4] In both origin and language this group differs strongly from the Low German Mennonites. As the name suggests, the Swiss Mennonites are closely related in spirit and origin to the Swiss Anabaptists in Pennsylvania known as the Amish. The history of this sect, which can be reconstructed from the stirring family histories of its present-day members, leads back to the birthplace of the Anabaptist movement—to Zürich. Here, in 1525 under the leadership of Konrad Grebel and Jörg Blaurock, the Anabaptist movement split off from the Zwingli reformation through renewed emphasis on adult baptism.[5]

Like the forebears of the Amish, those of the Swiss Mennonites, persecuted and driven from the Swiss Alps, had retreated into Alsace and subsequently into the Palatinate. Whereas the Amish in the seventeenth and eighteenth centuries emigrated directly to the New World, however, the forebears of the Swiss joined the colonization movement under Maria Theresa to southeastern Europe in the last quarter of the eighteenth century. They settled first in Galicia and later in Volhynia. Here in Russia they came into close association with the Low German Mennonites, who were closely akin to them in their Anabaptist faith; but although their settlements were close to each other, they maintained the manner of speech they had acquired during their sojourn in the Palatinate.

The retention of their Palatine speech prevented a rapid assimilation to the Low German–speaking Mennonites and enabled this group to become a very interesting and unique language island. In 1876 the Swiss Mennonites emigrated from Russia to the United States—again for religious reasons. The settlement of the immigrants in two communities—one near Freeman, South Dakota and one near Moundridge and Pretty Prairie, Kansas—fortified the preservation and development of this dialect, since the use of German in church until the First World War and their traditional religious and linguistic dissimilarity from other German settlers in the vicinity (Swabian Black Sea Germans, Hessian-speaking Volga Germans, Bavarian-Austrian Hutterites) was not conducive either to their amalgamation within the German-speaking community or to their absorption into the English-speaking one.

Today, of course, this assimilation process is well under way. When the author in 1965 first came in contact with this dialect, the youngest bilingual informant who was fluent in both "Swiss" and English was already beyond school age. This means that the dialect will probably disappear in the foreseeable future. Therefore it is urgent to record and study it before it has become a matter of linguistic history.

The situation among the Hutterite Brethren, on the other hand, is quite different.[6] The Hutterites arrived on the Great Plains in 1876 with about the same number of individuals as the Volhynian Mennonites. Today the Hutterites, in colonies (*Bruderhöfe*) throughout North and South Dakota and neighboring provinces of Canada, number about twenty thousand. Not only do their colonies comprise one of the most vigorous German speech islands in North America, they are also distinguished by a much stricter adherence to and observation of the Anabaptist doctrine, which enabled them to become one of the oldest extant communal religious and social communities on the continent.

In origin the Hutterites go back to the South Tirolian hatmaker Jakob Huter, who at an early age had come in contact with the left wing of the Zwingli reformation. Fleeing from the persecution that soon began, he led his numerous followers from the Tirol, Austria, and Bavaria to safety in Moravia, which was more tolerant. Although Huter was burned at the stake in Innsbruck in 1536, his brief activity and his charismic personality had created the spiritual and organizational bases that enabled his scattered adherents to organize a free church bearing his name. Following the Thirty Years War the Hutterites were banished from Bohemia by the victorious Catholic emperor. The thirty thousand members, known as the Moravian Brethren, developed a lively, notable cultural life that was distinguished by an extensive literature of devotion and vindication and by choice craftsmanship (for example, cutlery and pottery—later to become famous as *Habanerware*).[7]

The next stages of their stirring history led the Hutterite Brethren in their craving for religious freedom into western Slovakia where, in three villages east of Pressburg, a considerably more modest way of life developed for the Anabaptists, here known as *Habaner*. Threatened by the forced conversion to Catholicism of Maria Theresa, the group, greatly reduced by the Counter Reformation, divided. The majority became Catholic and, in the course of the next century and a half, Slovak. The remainder succeeded in fleeing to Transylvania and there were able to preserve their religious faith and the German language.

In Winz in Transylvania the remaining Habaner came in contact with a group of people from Carinthia, who as cryptoprotestants had also been forcibly resettled. These Carinthians, who were also the spiritual heirs of Jakob Huter, joined with the Habaner to form what became the modern *Huttertum*, which is flourishing today in America.[8]

To be sure, there was still another migration, this time from Transylvania to Russia where, in Volhynia, for barely a century a new vigorous community life developed in the vicinity of the Swiss and other Mennonites. The strict centralist development in the Russian politics of the 1870s compelled the Hutterites as well as the Mennonites to emigrate once more. Following the general trend of the times, this emigration now brought them to the New World.

These two religious groups—the Hutterites, of course, more so than the Swiss—can be regarded as the hard-core nucleus of the German language on the Great Plains. Indeed, the Hutterites, who within their *Bruderhöfe* speak only German, permit the prognosis that the use of German will persist on the American continent for quite a few years to come.

State of Research

For (comparative) linguists—and especially for those professionally interested in the German language—these groups of speakers or language enclaves represent a most interesting and timely area of study.[9] For they permit us to observe at first hand linguistic change and assimilation in a systematic context—a process which, at least for the relationship between German and English, can scarcely be observed and studied so explicitly anywhere else today.

Even more interesting than these processes and results of English-German linguistic interference are the phenomena of strategies of linguistic preservation and survival within a foreign linguistic environment. This holds true especially for the Hutterites, who have succeeded in preserving their ancestral language in its astonishing multiplicity practically unadulterated for over two hundred years, both within the individual colonies and throughout the entire Hutterite speech community of almost twenty thousand speakers.

Linguistic interest is not confined to the synchronic level with its interesting sociolinguistic problems. Equally interesting are the diachronic-historical phenomena that one encounters in the investigation of speech islands, such as the development of new dialects through the mixing and leveling of the dialects of the individuals and groups in the new settlement. A modern universalistic-methodic interpretation of these phenomena is still lacking in German speech-island dialectology.[10]

Of the numerous aspects of research connected with linguistic minority groups of religious origin, only two will be investigated here. The first of these is interference linguistics, associated especially with the name of Uriel Weinreich.[11] In my opinion interference linguistics has not yet found appropriate consideration and methodical evaluation in spite of the investigations already carried out—some of them, in the United States before the introduction of the term by Weinreich. Such investigations have been made of Pennsylvania German by Carroll E. Reed, Lester W. Seifert, and Paul Schach, and of Texas German by Fred Eikel, Jr. and Glenn G. Gilbert. It will be worth while to undertake similar studies of our two dialects with modern methods. Although these groups have been investigated in detail from the standpoint of history, sociology, and medicine, their languages remain to a large extent unstudied or at best have been inadequately represented (as in the relevant entries of the *Mennonite Encyclopedia,* for example, which otherwise are quite good).[12]

Linguistic Analysis

The linguistic development and the result of that development, the present-day idioms, reflect the briefly sketched features of the very stirring religious and secular history of these people with their repeated migrations and religious transformations.

A linguistic analysis or reconstruction must begin with an exact synchronic description of the main features of the present-day manner of speaking in the two speech communities. Only then can the task of elucidating the diachronic development be undertaken with the goal of reconstructing earlier stages of the dialect.

In accordance with the dual purpose of this study—a precise description of the linguistic, dialectal, and sociolinguistic structures of these two languages as spoken today and a careful reconstruction of their linguistic prestages and formative processes—a compromise must be found in regard to both the explicitness of the description and the parameters employed. Of the classical levels of description—phonemic, morphemic, syntactic, and lexical—the first and last prove to be the most fruitful for our purposes of comparison. The phonemic system (and to a lesser degree the morphemic one) permits a concise but sufficient characterization of the linguistic or dialectal variants and provides a good indication of beginning changes. The lexicon clearly reveals historical changes in the form of interference.

In accordance with these restrictions a summary synchronic description of both dialects will be given. The method used is essentially that of Noam Chomsky and Morris Halle in the descriptive apparatus of their study, *The Sound Pattern of English*. The slight modifications necessary for its application to German were depicted in detail by the author in his monograph *Religiöse Minderheiten als Sprachgesellschaftsmodelle*.[13] Detailed demonstrations of the phonemes of both dialects established on the basis of numerous examples of oppositions are provided here. Thus only the results of that investigation need be presented here.

The Dialect of the Swiss Mennonites

As already stated, the language spoken by the Volhynian Mennonites is a West Middle German (Palatine) dialect, which can be characterized briefly through the following phonemic inventory.

"Swiss" has the following vowel phonemes that occur in syllables of primary stress: /i:≈i ≈e:≈e≈ɛ:≈o:≈o≈u:≈u/. Most of these vowels can also occur in pretonic position—for example, /dsu'rig/ *zurück* 'back'; /vi'fi:l/ *wieviel* 'how much'; /he'le:n/ *Helene;* /ge'le:s/ *gelesen* 'read'; /tra'ra/ *Aufhebens, Lärm* 'noise, hullabaloo'. It also has the diphthongs /ai, au, ui/ and two vowel phonemes that occur only in unaccented position: /ə/ and /ɨ/. This Mennonite dialect, which has undergone the High German sound shift except for the bilabial voiceless stop, exhibits twenty consonant phonemes. The dialect briefly characterized here is obviously not "Swiss" or high Alemannic, as the speakers themselves assume it to be, since it has undergone the New High German diphthongization of the Middle High German vowels and since initial *p* has not been shifted to *pf*.

The vowel system of this American-Palatine dialect can be represented as follows:

		Front				Back	
High	i(:)			ɨ			u(:)
Mid		e(:)		ə		o(:)	
			<ai>		<au>		
		ɛ:					
Low				a(:)			

The consonant system can be represented as follows:

	Labials	Alveolars	Velars
Nasals	m	n	-ŋ(-)
Occlusives			
Fortes	p-	–	k-
Lenes	b	d	g
Lenes aspiratae	-B-	-D-	-G-
Fricatives			
Voiceless	f	s ʃ	x
Voiced	v-		
Liquids	r l		
Glides		j	h

These Mennonites today speak the dialect that their forebears acquired during their sojourn in the Palatinate in the seventeenth and eighteenth centuries. Here the "Swiss" speakers experienced during a period of about 150 years a language displacement, that is, an assimilation to the dominant language. As the author has demonstrated in detail by means of "diasystematic comparisons" (according to the method of Uriel Weinreich or G. R. Cochrane), this temporary home of the Mennonites can be determined very precisely by linguistic means.[14] Their dialect exhibits the greatest degree of agreement with the characteristic features of the present-day Northeast Palatinate (*Nordostpfalz*). This linguistic determination can be verified by historical documentation: the forebears of our "Swiss" speakers are known to have set out on their second migration—the one to Eastern Europe—from several villages in the vicinity of Ludwigshafen.

This American *Pfälzisch*, however, differs somewhat from the present-day dialects of the Northeast Palatinate both in vocabulary and phonology. A diasystematic comparison of each of the six investigated subsystems can provide a concise summary of both correspondences and deviations. In accordance with the procedure used by William G. Moulton,[15] the indices refer to correspondences of the Middle High German vowels and the pre-High German (*voralthochdeutsch*) or West Germanic consonants: for example, the Middle High German short vowels /i_1 ü_2 e_3 ë_4 ö_5 ä_6 a_7 o_8 u_9/; the Middle High German long vowels /î_1 iu_2 ê_4 œ_5 æ_6 â_7 ô_8 û_9/; the Middle High German diphthongs /$(\text{iu})_{10}$, ie_{11}, üe_{12}, uo_{13}, ei_{14}, öu_{15}, ou_{16}/; and the West Germanic consonants:

Labial	*Dental*	*Velar*
p_1	t_4	k_8
b-	d-	g-
-b-_2	-d-_5	-g-_9
f_3	þ_6	h x_{10}
	s,z_7	
m_{11}	n_{12}	
	l_{13}	
	r_{14}	
w_{15}		j_{16}

Such a diasystematic comparison of Northeast Palatine (NP) with Swiss Mennonite (SM) can elucidate these differences concisely and accurately:

VOWELS

Short Vowels

$$\text{NP, SM: i}_{1,2}\ \frac{\text{NP e}_{1,2,3,4,5,6}-\approx\varepsilon_{4,2,5,6}}{\text{SM e}_{[\varepsilon]\ 3-6,\ 1,2}} \approx \text{a}_7 \approx \text{o}_{8,9} \approx \text{u}_{\frac{9,8}{9}}$$

Long Vowels

$$\text{NP, SM: i:}_{1,2,10,11,12} \approx \text{e:}_{1,2,3,5,6} \approx \varepsilon\text{:}_{4,3,5,6} \approx \text{a:}\ \frac{\text{NP}\ _{7,14,15,16}}{\text{SM}\ _{7,\ (16)}} \approx \text{o:}_{8,7} \approx \text{u:}_9$$

Diphthongs

$$\text{NP, SM: } \frac{\text{NP ai}_{1,2,10,14,15} \sim \text{a:i} \approx \text{au}_{9,16} \sim \text{a:u}}{\text{SM ai}_{1,2,1,14,15} \quad \approx \text{au}_{9,16}}$$

CONSONANTS

Labials

$$\text{NP, SM: } p_{(-)1(-)} \approx b_{(-)2(-)} \approx {-}\text{B}{-}_{-2-,-3-} \approx f_{3(-),1} \approx v_{(-)15} \approx m_{11}$$

Dentals

$$\text{NP, SM: } \frac{\text{NP } d_5}{\text{SM } d_{5 \approx \text{D}_{6-}}} \approx s_{7,4} \approx \int_{7+8} \approx n_{12} \approx l_{13} \approx r\, \frac{\text{NP}_{14,-5,-6}}{\text{SM}_{14}}$$

Velars

$$\text{NP, SM: } k_{-8-\approx} \frac{\text{NP } g_{(-)8(-),9-}\, x_{-9-,(-)8(-)}}{\text{SM } g_{(-)8(-),9-\approx}\, \text{G}_{-9-\approx}\, x_{(-)8(-)}} \approx \eta_{12+8,9} \approx j\, \frac{\text{NP}_{16,-9-}}{\text{SM}_{16}} \approx h_{10}$$

An explicit interpretation of this schematic representation can be paraphrased as follows:

In the short vowel system there is extensive agreement between the Palatine mother dialect and the American daughter dialect. Only in the *e* range are there substantial deviations: whereas the Palatine dialect distinguishes between a tense *e* phoneme and a more open ε phoneme, there is in the American dialect only one short *e* phoneme—to be sure, with a variant [æ] from Middle High German *e* as an allophone before *r*.

This deviation, which is essential for the total sound impression of the dialect, may well be an innovation similar to those innovations in other speech islands of Palatine and other southwest German genesis, which in each case led to a methodically quite interesting simplification or to the elimination of only slightly represented phonemic oppositions.[16]

In the case of the long vowels the Palatine characteristics have been better preserved. This holds true also for the typically Palatine lengthening before *r*, as in /ge:ʀn/ *gern* 'gladly' and for the West Middle German shortening, lowering, and rounding of Middle High German *â* to [ɔ], as in Middle High German *lâzzen* > /lɔse/ *lassen* 'to permit, to cause'.

In the vowel system—and indeed, in the correspondences of Middle High German *ei*—there occurs the only important, immediately noticeable sound difference between the two American settlement areas of the Swiss. In Kansas /e:/ is pronounced as in the Palatinate; in the larger speech island of South Dakota one hears /ai/ as in standard German. This is probably due to the influence of Alsatian, which also has /ai/ < Middle High German *ei,* since a considerable number of the forebears of these people had their interim home in Alsace before continuing their migration to Volhynia.

In the consonant system "Swiss" has given up the rhotacism common to older Palatine dialects (that is, the substitution of [r] for the dental stops *d* and *t*) and has returned to its preliminary stage, a strongly spirantized dental stop.

Correspondingly, in the velar range the strongly endangered lenis stop was either changed to a fricative or lost completely in the Palatinate, as in Middle High German *nagel* /naxəl/ or /na:l/ *Nagel* 'nail', Middle High German *vliegen* /fli:jə/ or /fli:ə/ *fliegen* 'to fly'. Here the daughter language has a slightly spirantized voiced velar stop: /naɢəl/, /fli:ɢə/.

The phonological characteristics sketched here can be interpreted as follows: (1) the so-called Swiss Mennonite dialect has nothing to do with Swiss Alemannic, but is essentially a Palatine dialect; (2) its West Middle German (Palatine) characteristic features prove it to be a composite or compromise dialect (*Ausgleichsmundart*), similar to those dialects spoken in many southwest German speech islands in southeastern Europe that date back to the seventeenth and eighteenth centuries. In spite of the typical amalgamation process, however, this dialect possesses a substantial number of unique features.

An outstanding characteristic of religiously motivated mobile speech islands of this kind is the relative stability of the language after leaving the homeland (or, in this case, the second homeland). The amalgamation process took place far from the homeland and independent of its linguistic influence, yet because of the Mennonites' intensive study of the Bible this process was similar to that of the European speech islands of German provenance and led to a completely autonomous manner of speaking.

The Hutterites

The linguistic development of the Hutterites parallels that of the Swiss in the repeated change of home and language and in the five-hundred-year adherence to anabaptism. Yet there are also interesting, basically different features. These features are manifested by the present-day Hutterite as spoken in a colony (*Hutterhof*). Not only English and German can be heard here, but several different varieties or levels of speech side by side. These variants are by no means accidental or capricious; they occur side by side in a systematic and functional manner.

The extent of this variation can be illustrated by means of a so-called shibboleth sentence, in which the differences occur in combination. Thus the sentence *Ihr lieben Brüder, hört meiner Geschichte von einer Rose gut zu* ("Dear Brethren, listen carefully to my story about a rose") can be heard in the following variants or speech levels: Standard German (SG), Preachers' Hutterite (PH), Standard Hutterite (SH), and Basic Hutterite (BH):

SG: /i:r li:bn bri:dr hɛ:rt mainr gəʃixt fon ainr ro:s gu:t tsu:/
PH: /i:r liɐbm briɐdr hɛ:rt main kʃixtl fun a:nr ru:sn guət tsuə/
SH: /ös liɐm priɐdr hɛ:rts main kʃixtleɐn funr ru:sn guət tsuɐ/
BH: /ɛös liɐm priɐdr hɛɐrts (loɐsts) main kʃixtleɐn funr roɐsn güət tsüɐ/

These phonemic variations must not be interpreted as a sort of ad hoc unassimilated language mixture, but structurally in the sense of a language system; that is, they always appear in the same position in a given environment. This permits their classification as variation types of so-called subuses or codes that can be formally defined and functionally described. Basic Hutterite, which represents the lowest dialectical speech level, is used actively, especially by women and children, in all situations of family life.

Standard Hutterite, the most comprehensive speech form (corresponding approximately to the status of a regional dialect), differs markedly in phonology from Basic Hutterite. Standard Hutterite is understood by all, but used actively more by men in discussing general matters.

Preachers' Hutterite is a relatively specialized "high" language, or cult form, not identical with High German, which is also spoken by some of the older Hutterites. Completely autonomous in phonology and vocabulary, this language is used primarily by preachers and elders in religious functions, but also for the discussion of community affairs.

The following description is based on Standard Hutterite since it is the most extensive and comprehensive speech form and also occupies an intermediate position between the extremes of Basic and Preachers' Hutterite.

The phoneme inventory of Standard Hutterite is as follows: /i≈e≈ɛ: ≈a≈o≈u≈ə≈æ/. The diphthongs are /ai≈au≈ui≈iɐ≈eɐ≈uɐ/. The eighteen consonants can be depicted thus:

	Labials	Dentals	Velars
Nasals	m	n	-ŋ(-)
Occlusives			
Fortes	p	t	k
Lenes	-b(-)	-d(-)	(-)g-
Fricatives			
Voiceless	f	sʃ	x
Voiced	v		
Liquids		r l	
Glides		h-	j-

The unique relationship of the individual functional speech variants which is typical of Hutterite can be illustrated with the help of the following Venn diagram. According to this diagram Standard Hutterite (*Umgangssprache*) equals the intersection of the basic quantities Basic Hutterite (*Mundart*) and Preachers' Hutterite (*Hochsprache*) or of the elements common to both of them.

Through the inclusion of the two additional idioms that help comprise the Hutterite linguistic reality, the German written language (*Schriftsprache*) and English, additional areas can be defined:

1. The English influence equates the intersection of English (USE) and Basic Hutterite (including a portion of Standard Hutterite). This is most readily seen on the basis of the English loan words: English Loanwords (LW) = BH ∩ USE.
2. Analogously, the substantial number of features common to Preachers' Hutterite and the German written language (*Hochsprache;* GWL), as seen especially in correspondence among the colonies, can be depicted as the intersection between the quantities. This specifically Hutterite written language (HWL) could be formalized: HWL = PH ∩ GWL.

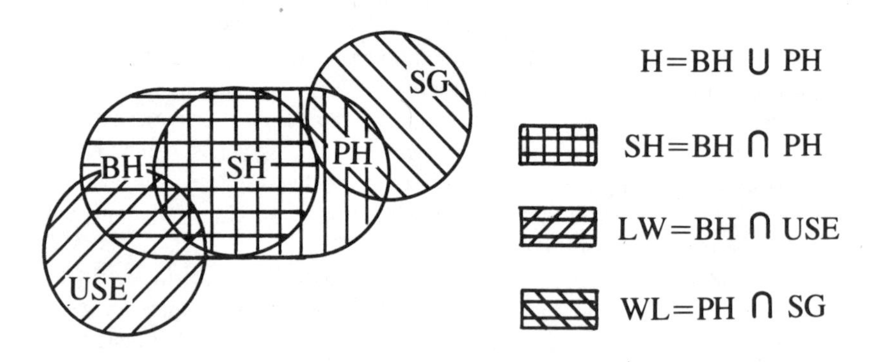

Historical Analysis of Hutterite. As is to be expected from the extraordinarily dramatic history of the Hutterites, their historical development has been precipitated out in their linguistic history and can still be recognized in their present-day language. In order to treat these hypotheses we can avail ourselves of a diasystematic comparison of the characteristic features of present-day Hutterite and its subcodes with those of the historically documented original homeland as well as of the intermediate homelands, that is, the dialects of Tyrol, northern Moravia, and Transylvania.

Comparison of Hutterite with Tyrolian. A comparison of Hutterite with Tyrolian is suggestd by the fact that the Hutterites themselves call their idiom "Tyrolian," and this designation was also used uncritically in the older literature.

A diasystematic comparison like the one used above is extremely difficult because of the great phonological diversity of the Tyrol, which with regard to its linguistic geography is strongly splintered. An attempt at such a comparison on the basis of detailed tabular listing of individual phonetic features reveals a relatively great linguistic distance between Hutterite and Tyrolian and only a slight agreement that scarcely goes beyond general South Bavarian mutualities.

In the diasystematic manner of presentation, similarities and differences can be clearly brought out, whereby the relationship becomes evident. Thereby the diasystem is to be understood "diastratally," that is, as a characterization of various simultaneously present partial systems of the total system Hutterite.

Vowels

		(")		(")	(")	(")
BH:		/iə/ /eεo/		/eou/	/oa ~ u(:)/	
SH:	/i(:)/ ≈	/e(:)/ /ε(o)/ ≈	a(:) ≈	/o(:)/ ≈	/u(:)/	
PH:		/ε(:)/				
SG:		e(:)		/a(:)/	/a(:) ~ u(:)/	

Diphthongs

BH:		/εo/	/aei/	/ui/	/au/	
SH:	/ia/ ≈	/ε(ɐ)/ ≈	/ai/ ≈	___ ≈		≈ /uo/
PH:	___	/ε(:)			/au/	___
SG:	/i(:)/	/e(:)/ ≈ /oi/		/ai/		/u:/

Comparison of Hutterite with Habanic. As explained above, Habanic is a daughter dialect of the Tyrolian exiles who settled in Moravia, a dialect that has died out as a consequence of World War II and that could be reconstructed from sparse speech remnants of the Habaner descendants in western Slovakia. A detailed comparison that I have made shows unequivocal correspondences and differences among High German (HG), Habanic (H), and Middle Bavarian (MB), which are revealed in the lexicon and especially in the vowel system:

HG:		HG $e_{3,4,5,6} \approx a_7$	H7		
H:	$i_{1,2} \approx$	H $e_{3,4,5} \approx a_6 \approx$ H, HG o	HG8	≈ u	H 8,9
MB:		MB e_5 ~ $\varepsilon_{3,4}$ ~ a_6 ~	MB ~ $ɔ_7$ ~ o_8		HG, MB 9

As a diasystematic comparison makes clear, the differences are in the region of the mid vowels. The raising of Middle High German *o* to /*u* / (customary otherwise only in East Middle German), which is shared by Hutterite and Habanic, is foreign to the vowel system of Bavarian. This phenomenon was diffused into Habanic during the Moravian-Silesian sojourn and was taken over, together with the new faith, by the Carinthians. The striking fact that only the mid back vowel was raised and not the mid front vowel (*e* > *i*), as is the case with the Middle German donor, is probably to be explained on the basis of articulatory phonetics and structure, respectively.

Comparison of Habanic with Carinthian. A comparison of Habanic with Carinthian is suggested by the fact that the last Habaner community in Winz in

Transylvania, greatly reduced in numbers, was strengthened numerically and religiously by newly converted transmigrants from Carinthia in 1755.[17]

Whereas there is far-reaching agreement in the consonants, the vowel system reveals the strong influence on modern-day Hutterite by Carinthian on the one hand (for example, the long vowel [a:] < MHG *ei*) and by Habanish on the other (for example, the raising of *o* > *u*) in the following diasystem, which includes Tirolian (T), Carinthian (C), Hutterite (Ht), and Habanish (H):

```
T:
               T,C e(:) ~ ε(:)                T(-)     T o(:) (-)≈u(:)
C: i(:) ≈            3,4    5         ≈ a(:)___ 6 ≈    ______7,8_______9____
               _____________________
Ht:            Ht e(:)   ~ [ε̈ = ε ]       C         C o(:) (-)~o ~u(:)
                    3,4,5      3,4    3,4                      7     8    9
               ______________________      Ht(-)     ____________________
H:             H e(:) (-)                       6,14
                       3,4,5               H         Ht, H [ɔ=o] (-)≈u(:) (-)
                                                                  7        8,9
```

The origin and subsequent development of Hutterite, which was demonstrated above on the basis of several selected but conclusive phonological phenomena and corroborated in detail by lexical evidence, can be summarized as follows: like other new speech communities which arise through the coming together of individuals and groups who speak heterogeneous dialects, Hutterite also underwent numerous linguistic processes of adaptation and leveling on the various stages of the peregrination of its speakers. In contrast to most of the processes known to and recorded by students of German dialect enclaves, the interference in this case did not occur on one level, that is, through a blending of the individual dialects, but rather in the form of a diastratification (*Durchschichtung*), whereby essential features of the donor dialects are retained and exist side by side on various levels and in various functions. More specifically, when the Carinthians joined the remnants of the Hutterites in Transylvania, the former were in the majority, and their dialect became the foundation for the family language of the newly formed community. The religious superstructure of the future speech community, however, was determined in its linguistic form by the Habaner as the last protectors of the pure Hutterite faith. These linguistic forms then logically became the higher or more highly regarded speech variety according to Ferguson's diglossia concept.[18] Between these two poles, which were supported by specific functions and therefore could readily be kept apart, there developed the real, or standard, Hutterite as the interference and finally the compromise dialect, as is usually the case with such immigrant tongues. Through its functional openness it is the most widespread speech form today, from which the other two varieties can be delimited in regard to phonology and lexicon.

Summary of the Linguistic Analysis. An interpretive summary of these striking linguistic findings can be made only through the application of social, or at least sociolinguistic, considerations. If one (with certain reservations) regards a Hutterite colony (*Bruderhof*) as a small group and as a small speech community, one can attribute its linguistic circumstances to the following basic sociological structures. In contrast to the social or occupational classification of a social group, which is generally regarded as the cause of linguistic differentiation, it is in the case of the Hutterites, who have practiced Christian communism for centuries, primarily the functional and instrumental aspects of language that bring about its differentiation: the sex-specific one, which has occasioned the continuance of Carinthian dialectal traits as a women's language, so to speak, in the form of Basic Hutterite; and the religious function of Habanic, the relics of which survive in Preachers' Hutterite as a lingua sacra.

Summary

The purpose of this discussion was to stress the exemplary value of German language vestiges on the Great Plains as an interesting means of studying all kinds of linguistic interference, from both a synchronic and a diachronic viewpoint. As objects of diachronic linguistic investigation these two groups of German speakers are especially valuable as mobile linguistic speech islands in the midst of a sea of constantly changing dominant languages. Linguistic reconstruction, and thus language history in general, is possible only over such relatively safely reconstructible stages as those of the Hutterites. Such reconstructions permit fairly reliable analogical conclusions about the development of similarly archaic groups and circumstances about which we possess no direct information.

The two problems treated here, however, are only two of a whole series of possible aspects from which the language remnants on the Great Plains can be investigated.

In conclusion one such aspect can be referred to briefly, and that is the matter of psychological problems—for individuals and for the group as a whole—related to their bilingual situation. Among the Hutterites this problem is intensified by the fact that in the colonies there is a German school (*daitsche Schuel*) in addition to the exclusively English grade school. The German school, which is conducted by the minister or one of the elders, is not very effective and represents no competition for the English school—partly because of the unfavorable time (late afternoon) and partly because of the methods: reading practice based on Hutterite devotional tracts.

A careful consideration of the most recent developments shows that the average Hutterer's use of the various languages or speech variants changes considerably during his or her lifetime and that this change is different for men and for women. The schematic overview shows the relative use of English (including English loanwords in Hutterite) and of the German dialect variants (Basic Hutterite, Standard Hutterite, Preachers' Hutterite, Standard German) among the male and female population.

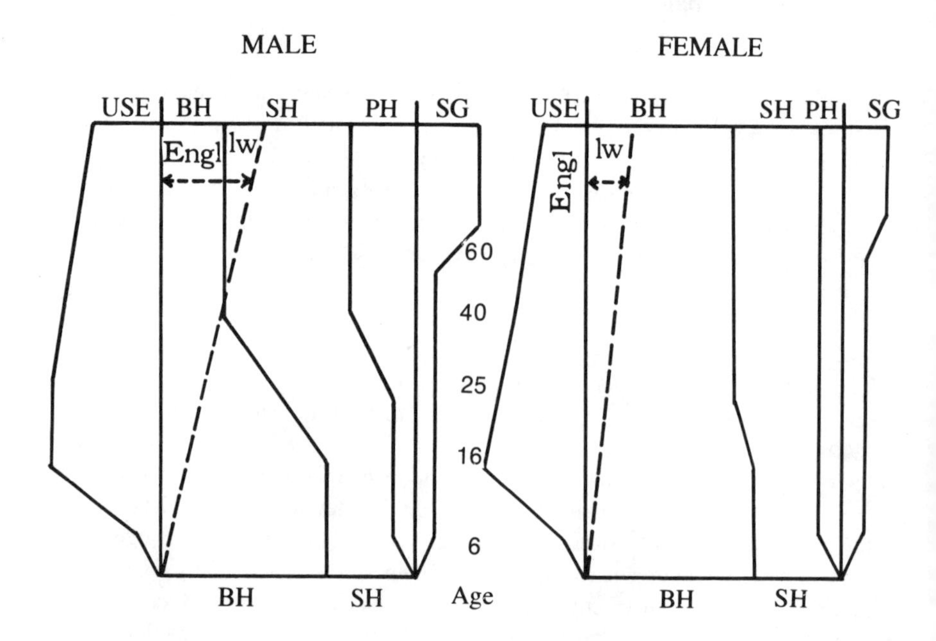

This diagram reveals that the German language enjoys a relatively favorable—yes, a unique position—among the Hutterites, comparable at best with that among the Old Order Amish. Nevertheless it cannot be denied that the preponderance of German, at least among young people, is beginning to shift somewhat in favor of English.

This tendency could be observed in 1965 in several colonies with the aid of a series of association tests using German and English homophones, such as *find* (≈*Feind* 'enemy'), *hunt* (≈*Hand* 'hand') and homographs, such as *hear* and *nest*. These tests showed that young Hutterites usually responded in German when they were spoken to—for example, *nest* usually elicited *Ei* ("egg"), *Vogel* ("bird"), and so forth. When they read the same words, however, their associations were English; *nest,* for example, called forth *a bird.*[19]

The results of these tests reveal a very delicate equilibrium in which German in its variant forms remains unassailed as the spoken language even among young people, while English is advancing to replace the retreating standard German in its partial function as the language of education and writing.

In spite of this, the German language is in no immediate danger among the Hutterites, even if one cannot agree with Kloss's denial of any bilingualism among these people.[20] And so it is not difficult to venture the prognosis that in the distant or not so distant future, after the German language has been absorbed in the American melting pot, the last German-speaking Americans will be the Old Order Amish of Pennsylvania or, what is more likely, the Hutterites in their colonies on the Great Plains.

[Translated from the German by Paul Schach]

NOTES

1. This paper is based in large part on field work done in 1963–65 and on my book *Religiöse Minderheiten als Sprachgemeinschaftsmodelle: Deutsche Sprachinseln täuferischen Ursprungs in den Vereinigten Staaten von Amerika, Zeitschrift für Dialektologie und Linguistik,* n.s., supplement no. 15 (Wiesbaden: Franz Steiner Verlag, 1977). For information on German speakers in North America see Glenn G. Gilbert, ed. and introd., *The German Language in America: A Symposium,* (Austin: University of Texas Press, 1971); Wolfgang Viereck, "German Dialects Spoken in the United States and Canada and Problems of German-English Contact Especially in North America: A Bibliography," *Orbis* 16 (1967): 549–68; 17 (1968): 532–35; Otto Springer, "Die Erforschung des Pennsylvania-Deutschen," *Arbeiten zur germanischen Philologie und zur Literatur des Mittelalters* (Munich: Wilhelm Fink Verlag, 1975), pp. 35–74; Heinz Kloss, "German-American Language Maintenance Efforts," in *Language Loyalty in the United States: The Maintenance and Perpetuation of Non-English Mother Tongues by American Ethnic and Religious Groups,* ed. Joshua A. Fishman, Vladimir C. Nahirny, John E. Hoffman, and Robert G. Hayden, Janua Linguarum, series maior no. 21 (The Hague: Mouton, 1966), pp. 206–52; and Einar Haugen, *Bilingualism in the Americas: A Bibliography and Research Guide, Publication of the American Dialect Society,* no. 26 (1956).

For further information and literature, see Rein, *Religiöse Minderheiten,* pp. 7–15.

2. On immigration from these regions see Richard Sallet, "Rußlanddeutsche Siedlungen in den Vereinigten Staaten," in *Jahrbuch der Deutsch-Amerikanischen Historischen Gesellschaft,* ed. Max Baum, vol. 3 (Chicago: University of Chicago Press, 1931), pp. 5–126.

3. On the Mennonites in the United States see C. W. Redekop, *The Old Colony Mennonites: Dilemma of Ethnic Minority Life* (Baltimore, Md.: John Hopkins Press, 1969).

4. On the background of these people see Martin H. Schrag, "European History of the Swiss-Volhynian Mennonite Ancestors Now Living in Communities in Kansas and South Dakota," (Master's thesis, Freeman College, South Dakota, 1956).

5. See the pertinent entries in the *Mennonite Encyclopedia: A Comprehensive Reference Work on the Anabaptist-Mennonite Movement* (Hillsboro, Kans.: Mennonite Brethren Publishing House, 1955 ff.).

6. For information on this religious group see John A. Hostetler and Gertrude Enders Huntingdon, *The Hutterites in North America* (New York: Holt, Rinehart & Winston, 1967); John Unruh, "The Hutterites During World War I," *Mennonite Life* 24 (1969): 130–37; Norman Thomas, "The Hutterian Brethren," *South Dakota Historical Collections* 25 (1951): 265–99; Victor Peters, *All Things Common: The Hutterian Way of Life* (Minneapolis: University of Minnesota Press, 1965; and Rein, *Religiöse Minderheiten,* pp. 321–29.

7. See Christiane Rein-Hedrich and Kurt Rein, "Name and Herkunft der 'Habaner' und ihrer Keramik," *Südostdeutsches Arkiv* 16–17 (1972–73): 36–65.

8. Kurt Rein, "Die Hutterer in Siebenbürgen," *Südostdeutsche Vierteljahrsblätter* 14 (1965): 96–103.

9. For the more theoretical aspects of speech-island dialectology see Rein, *Religiöse Minderheiten,* pp. 6–52.

10. On this, see Rein, *Religiöse Minderheiten;* and Anton Schwob, *Wege und Formen des Sprachausgleichs in neuzeitlichen ost- und südostdeutschen Sprachinseln,* Buchreihe der Südostdeutschen Historischen Komission, no. 25 (München: R. Oldenbourg, 1971).

11. Uriel Weinreich, *Languages in Contact: Findings and Problems,* Publications of the Linguistic Circle of New York, no. 1 (New York, 1953).

12. For a detailed discussion see Rein, *Religiöse Minderheiten,* pp. 53–69, 114–79.

13. Noam Chomsky and Morris Halle, *The Sound Pattern of English* (New York: Harper and Row, 1968); Rein, *Religiöse Minderheiten,* pp. 45–48, 115–41, 143–78.

14. Uriel Weinreich, "Is a Structural Dialectology Possible?" *Word* 14 (1957): 1–15.

15. William G. Moulton, "Zur Geschichte des deutschen Vokalsystems," *Beiträge* 83 (1961): 1–35; and "The Consonant System of Old High German," in *Mélanges Fourquet,* ed. Paul Valentine and Georges Zink (Paris: Klincksiek), pp. 247–59.

16. For an alternative explanation of this phenomenon see Paul Schach, "Zum Lautwandel im Rheinpfälzischen: die Senkung von kurzem Vokal zu *a* vor *r*-Verbindung," *Zeitschrift für Mundartforschung* 26 (1958): 200–228.

17. See Rein, "Die Hutterer in Siebenbürgen," pp. 96–103.

18. Charles A. Ferguson, "Diglossia," *Word* 15 (1956): 325–40.

19. For a detailed description and interpretation of these tests see Rein, *Religiöse Minderheiten,* pp. 282–88.

20. See Kloss, "German-American Language Maintenance Efforts."

Czech in Nebraska

Bruce Kochis

Since so little work has been done on the language of Czech Americans, and particularly Czech Americans of Nebraska, this study can, of necessity, be only an introduction to the subject.[1] Of particular concern to this writer is to prepare the ground by sketching the general outlines of the problems involved and posing some of the more interesting questions to be answered by future research. It will be clear from what follows, for example, that a thorough study of American Czech can contribute to the more general theoretical discussion of the evolution of dialects, the history of the literary language, interference phenomena, and sociolinguistics. Here, however, it will suffice to set the sociocultural stage for Czech in Nebraska and to indicate some of the more general factors operating in the speech of Nebraska Czechs.

The first permanent Czech settler to Nebraska arrived in 1856, and from then until about 1910 the immigration of Czechs grew steadily to a total of about fifty-one thousand—about one-tenth of the state's population.[2] After 1910 the flow was severely restricted by World War I, the founding of the Czechoslovak Republic, and new, stricter immigration laws. It is this immigrant population, 1860–1910, which has served as the basis of American-Czech speech in Nebraska.

This segment of the population has served not only as a linguistic base virtually unaltered by later immigration, but also as the social base that has promoted the preservation of Czech culture, mainly through the language, in the face of pressures for americanization.[3] The linguistic consciousness of this group, therefore, acquires added importance in a description of Nebraska Czech.

The peoples that emigrated from Bohemia to America were, for the most part, from the central and southern regions. This fact is significant in that these regions are defined linguistically by relatively minor dialectal differences. Furthermore, in the structure of Czech there exists between the dialects and the literary language an interdialect known as *obecná čeština,* or common Czech.[4] In Bohemia itself common Czech functions in two directions: in relation to the dialects it functions as the unifying code; and in relation to the literary language it functions as the nonliterary pole in the opposition literary-nonliterary. In addition, there exists in Czech a fourth subcode, *hovorová čeština,* or colloquial Czech, which serves as the spoken variant of the literary language and is composed of elements from both the literary language and common Czech.

Thus a literate farmer from eastern Bohemia could potentially be in command of four dialects, or subcodes, of Czech: local dialect, common Czech, colloquial Czech, and the literary language. This repertoire of subcodes cannot but provide the immigrant Czechs with a valuable linguistic flexibility as their language comes into conflict with English. And so, even prior to migration, the language of the emigrants contained as a subcode a dialect that could be used to unite the various regional dialects; and therefore the problems of interdialectical communication that often encourage interference from, and eventual replacement by, the new language were greatly reduced.[5] Furthermore, it appears that the Czechs, in part owing to this status and function of common Czech, have tended to group themselves in American communities not on the basis of regional dialect (a process that produces fragmentation of an immigrant population) but on the basis of a more unifying criterion, such as profession or religion. This is true in the case of Nebraska Czechs, who are predominantly farmers or agricultural workers—regional dialect plays no role in the population of the rural villages. In Texas, on the other hand, it seems that religion was the primary factor of communality.

The Czechs who came to Nebraska were literate—a fact suggested not only by the mandatory education existing in the Austro-Hungarian Empire or immigration statistics that list Czechs as having the lowest percentage of illiteracy but also by the extensive Czech language publication carried on in the United States.[6] The language of these publications was almost universally standard literary Czech, a dialect of Czech that, apart from stylistic discrepancies in vocabulary, presented few problems to a literate Czech farmer. As is proper to most literary dialects, the literary language is rather conservative, and this fact, in conjunction with the role of common Czech, has provided a remarkably stable code among Nebraska Czechs. Furthermore, based on the number and content of primers and language aids published in the period 1860–1910, it appears that the literary language continued to act as the arbiter in language preservation among the immigrants.[7] In other words, the Czechs always had at their disposal an institutionalized and universal code as model, while their spoken language was continually subjected to pressures for americanization.

First and foremost, Czech was the language of the home, and, in the case of Nebraska, this home tended to be isolated from the influence of English that would have been felt in a more urban setting. Because of the concentration of Czechs in smaller communities and the popularity of social, religious, and business organizations catering only to Czechs, it tended also to be the language of the community.[8]

Furthermore, even the Nebraska-Czech farmer's intellectual needs were met by the above-mentioned widespread publication in Czech of journals, newspapers, and books. In the late nineteenth and early twentieth centuries about eighty-five Czech newspapers and periodicals were published in Nebraska. Most were village weeklies, and most were rather short-lived; but some, for example, *Pokrok západu* [Progress of the West] and *Hospodář* [The Husbandman], claimed wide readership and long life. The latter reached a total circulation of thirty thousand and is now published in Texas.

The one enormously influential arena where Czech was completely supplanted by English was, of course, the classroom. But even here the influence of English was reduced by competition with the Czech-language school and by the fact that the student body of the small rural school often was composed only of Czechs, or predominantly so, who spoke Czech among themselves outside the classroom.[9]

Thus, though Czech came under the same pressures from English as other immigrant languages, its particular situation in the rural environment and the unity and stability of its code have tended to retard the process of succumbing to that influence, without, of course, winning the battle. Nevertheless, Czech, especially in relation to other Slavic languages, has proven to be very resilient in an alien environment.

The material used in this study was taken from the tape recordings made by Joseph G. Svoboda, University of Nebraska–Lincoln archivist, as part of the Czech Heritage Project. The informants are, in general, from the older strata of the Czech population in Nebraska and include members of the first, second, and third generations. The level of proficiency in Czech ranges from complete fluency to virtually little knowledge of Czech.

The informants were interviewed informally in their homes and encouraged to narrate on various topics, including experiences in Bohemia, childhood, education, religion, politics, food, social events, farm life, and so forth.

In general Nebraska Czech manifests the same range of interference phenomena as other immigrant languages.[10] As the preceding discussion suggests, however, the particular structure of interference is unique owing to the different structure of Czech itself and to the particular sociocultural setting in which American Czech has thrived. To determine exactly to which of these two factors a given phenomenon owes its existence is very complex. For example, does the tendency to replace Czech numerals with English ones (especially in second generation, but also in first) derive from the importance of numerals in everyday speech, or from the particular phonetic makeup of Czech numerals, which stands in marked contrast to English? Czech numerals in the teens, for example, contain the particularly non-English consonant cluster in final position [-tst]. Before advancing even the most tentative answers to these questions, we will need a description of the Czech used by Nebraskans.

As mentioned above, Czech offers a solution to dialectal divergences in the form of the interdialect common Czech and the transitional subcode colloquial Czech. They replace individual dialects and then enter into a colloquial-standard relation vis-à-vis literary Czech. In other words, the opposition (dialect versus common Czech) is replaced by another (common Czech versus literary language). In three speakers from eastern Bohemia, for example, expected northeastern dialect features, voiced consonant in word-final position and initial *i*, do not occur and are replaced by features of common Czech—voiceless consonant in word-final position and initial [ji], for example, [zabaf] 'amusements' and [jídlo] 'food' in place of [zabav] and [ídlo]. Even in a second-generation speaker whose parents came from Moravia, conspicuous Moravian features, such as [šč] and [ó] for Czech [šť] and [ou], are absent.

On the other hand, it seems that of the eight features used to define common Czech only four are used, while four are replaced by literary language elements.[11] This signifies a narrowing of the function of common Czech and consequent expansion of the function of the literary language—in other words the shift to colloquial Czech as the base dialect of Nebraska Czech. This shift may be explained in sociocultural terms by the situation that in a population relatively homogenous by social class (that is, the dominance of farmers and agricultural workers), isolated from the native linguistic environment, the system of subcodes and their functions is subjected to a reorganization on teleological principles. Because of the felt need both for stability in an alien linguistic environment and for overcoming broader dialectical differences than would be necessary in Bohemia, the language moves in the direction of greatest uniformity and invariability, that is, toward the literary language.

This move to colloquial Czech as the base dialect of Nebraska Czech is also evident in the morphology, where common Czech and the literary language (with a dominance of the former) replace dialect forms. On the one hand, common Czech replaces the literary language, for example, common Czech *můžu* 'I can' versus literary language *mohů, pracuju* 'I work' versus *pracuji;* instrumental plural *čechama* 'by the Czechs' versus *čechy;* infinitive common Czech *říct* 'to speak' versus literary language *říci;* and on the other hand, common Czech–literary language *bratovi* 'to the brother' versus dialect *bratroj;* instrumental singular feminine common Czech–literary language *ulicí* 'street' versus dialect *ulicej.*

While based on common Czech and colloquial Czech, Nebraska Czech cannot be completely identified with either because the impact of English has caused significant shifts in the structure and functions of the subcodes that constitute the Bohemian Czech base. Furthermore, English has contributed its own features and elements to form a new language that is in reality a spectrum of elements and codes within a Czech and an English pole.

An appreciation of the complexity of this new structure—part Czech, part English—can best be attained if we begin examination of English interference in larger units of discourse, and especially units of English discourse. In addition, by looking at the larger units we may more closely see the relationship between the sociocultural factors and the linguistic results.

At the English end of the spectrum we have a group of unassimilated English segments and sentences that are simply transposed into the Czech utterance without any transformation. This first applies to second-generation speakers, who will begin a sentence or segment of discourse in English and continue in English for up to several minutes. These segments in English were usually accompanied by one or more of the following three factors: (1) opportunity, that is, the bilingualism of the interviewer, (2) dominance of the metalingual function, that is, where possible misunderstandings could arise, English was resorted to as the language of explanation, and (3) situation, that is, a specifically American experience, custom, or event. While these factors played a significant role in the language of the speakers recorded in 1975, one can easily imagine that situation in rural Nebraska, especially prior to the advent of mass communication technology, would play a relatively minor role. Even the third factor, American experience, would be weakened in the rural communities, where social and personal experiences would be isolated from the specifically American and related to the farm or village.

Next on the spectrum we have English phrases, again without transformation, being incorporated into a context of Czech. These usually relate to specifically American phenomena or places: *Gage County, country school, District 54, money order, nursing home, Historical Society, Ellis Island, Ford Sedan, son of a bitch, Mary's husband.* It is interesting to note that in these random examples a trochaic stress pattern dominates, for example, *móney órder, Máry's húsband.* This is very likely caused by the dominance of trochaic and dactylic patterns in Czech, where stress is fixed on the first syllable of polysyllabic words. This points to an interesting set of questions surrounding the relationship between phonological features (stress in English) and nonphonological features (stress in Czech), and the role of that relation in interference phenomena.

Further down on the English-Czech spectrum we have individual words, undergoing no transformations, but incorporated directly into an otherwise completely Czech context. In the first-generation speakers these lexical items relate almost exclusively to things and events specifically American: *ranch,*

Medicare, Foundation, greenhorn, television, prairie, and, of course, geographical designations like *Wilbur* and *Dodge*. Another group is those words that, though they have equivalents in Czech, are associated in the mind of the speaker with his or her American experience: *alfalfa, house, pony, butcher shop, uncle, pork, corn, Western.*

With variable frequency, speakers also incorporated English interjections, exclamations, and introductory words and phrases, like *well; see; oh, yes; no; you know; sure; my God; let's see.* This group of words was marked by automatization, that is, they did not trip the English switch in the linguistic consciousness of the speaker.

Among almost all speakers there were examples from an anomalous class of English words that seem to be motivated by the speaker's forgetting the Czech original. Many of these words were introduced or followed by metalingual phrases in Czech or English, such as *Jak se říká?* or *How do you say?*, or by immediate translation: "housekeeper—hospodyně," or "business—obchod."

The above examples are taken for the most part from the speech of first-generation Czechs. Though quantitative analysis was not attempted, it is clear that in the language of such speakers these categories constitute a very low percentage of the total discourse. For second-generation speakers all the above categories increase in frequency, at least doubling the percentage for first-generation.

The preceding constitutes the English end of the spectrum of codes that is Nebraska Czech. Next we have that interesting segment of the spectrum which is composed of transitional cases where English makes itself felt and then (1) is rejected, (2) is accepted and coexists with Czech, or (3) supplants Czech.

In the first case we have those instances already mentioned where the English word is used in lieu of a forgotten Czech word but the former is rejected when the latter comes to mind. This occurred in the utterances of both generations, but was more frequent in the second (where the Czech word was more often forgotten or not known): for example, "Můj—jak se říká česky *cousin*?" "Bratranec." "Ano, můj bratranec. . . ." "My—how do you say *cousin* in Czech?" "Bratranec." "Yes, my cousin. . . .")

Where English and Czech coexist, we have the feature that sets Nebraska Czech in opposition to both English and Czech. The coexistence can occur on the phonological level as partial overlapping of the phonological systems and be found in several homologous Czech-English diamorphs: [klarinet] and [klærinet] *clarinet,* [farma] and [farm] *farm,* [bušl] and [bušəl] *bushel.*

On the morphological level we have the declension of English words using Czech morphemes: [pankejky] "pancakes," [sajdvaky] "sidewalks," [po trejnu] "by train," [kornu] "of corn," [na rentu] "on rent," [na ranči] "on the ranch,'' [hausu] ''of the house.'' And similarly we have the conjugation of English verbal stems with Czech morphemes: [vizitovat] ''to visit,'' [stompovat] ''to stomp,'' [čejnžovat] ''to change,'' [organajzoval] ''he organized.''

On the level of phrase we have the inclusion in one linguistic context of seemingly unmotivated phrases from the other language as in *She mluvila německy to me* (''She spoke German to me'') and *do South Omahy* (''to South Omaha''). At times one can hear the shift to the other language occur as in the phrase *dvacet dolarů cash,* where the loan word *dolarů* trips the English switch in the discourse and English takes over. Other examples of the coexistence on the phrasal level are such constructions as: *nice lide* (''nice people''), *česky language* (''Czech language''), *Koupili jsme house* (''We bought a house''), *public škola* (''public school'').

A particular category of coexistence is the use, especially in second generation, but also in the first, of numerals in English within a Czech context: *až do forty-five* (''up until forty-five''), *Byla jsem eleven* (''I was eleven''), *To bylo v 1909* (''That was in 1909''). Indeed, most speakers had difficulty rendering Czech numerals, and one could postulate that the cause lies in the importance, even the necessity, of mastering the English numerical system for business and everyday affairs. And, because of the phonological discrepancy in the Czech and English systems, the Czech system is supplanted as the English one is mastered. Degree of assimilation, then, may be directly related to communicative need times phonological discrepancy. This may also account for the otherwise unmotivated use of English designations for days of the week and months.

In conclusion we may tentatively suggest that the particular structure of Nebraska Czech is a spectrum of Czech and English, where the Czech base is constituted by a reorganization of the subcodes of Bohemian Czech, and the English component is a stock of predominantly lexical and phrasal components, the use of which seems motivated by the exigencies of life in an English environment. Nebraska Czech, however, appears to differ from other European immigrant languages in the degree of its resistance to americanization, and that resistance seems to be motivated by the following factors: (1) existence of the subcodes common Czech and colloquial Czech, which reduce to a minimum the weakening effects on the parent language of dialectal differences among the immigrant population; (2) stability and conservative character of literary Czech, which acts as a unifying base and supports the common Czech interdialect; (3) the rural setting, especially the small village, which avoids the linguistic pressures of the urban environment; (4) the popularity of social, religious, and business organizations which served only Czechs and did so in Czech.

NOTES

1. Most studies touching on the subject of Czech in America are embedded in general cultural surveys, where the subject is treated nonlinguistically. Some studies that do employ certain linguistic criteria are the following: J. B. Dudek, "The Czech Language in America," *American Mercury* 5 (1925): 116–20; Reinhold Olesch, "The West Slavic Languages in Texas with Special Regard to Sorbian in Serbin, Lee County," in *Texas Studies in Bilingualism: Spanish, French, German, Czech, Polish, Sorbian, and Norwegian in the Southwest, with a Concluding Chapter on Code-Switching and Modes of Speaking in American Swedish,* ed. Glenn G. Gilbert, Studia Linguistica Germanica, no. 3 (Berlin: Walter de Gruyter & Co., 1970) pp. 151–62; Jan L. Perkowski, "A Survey of the West Slavic Immigrant Languages in Texas," in *Texas Studies in Bilingualism,* pp. 163–69. See also the helpful article by Goldie Piroch Meyerstein, "Bilingualism among American Slovaks: An Analysis of Loans," *Publications of the American Dialect Society,* no. 46 (1966): pp. 1–19.

2. My discussion of the sociocultural situation of Czechs in Nebraska is based on Thomas Čapek, *The Czechs in America* (Boston: Houghton Mifflin Co., 1920); Vladimir Kučera, ed., *Czechs and Nebraska* (Ord, Nebraska: Quiz Graphic Arts, Inc., 1967); and Joseph G. Svoboda, "Czechs: The Love of Liberty," in *Broken Hoops and Plains People,* ed. Paul A. Olson (Lincoln: Nebraska Curriculum Development Center, 1976), pp. 153–92.

3. Svoboda, *Czechs: The Love of Liberty,* p. 166.

4. On emigration, see Čapek, *Czechs in America,* p. 28. On dialectal differences, see Bohuslav Havránek, "Nářeči česká," *Československá vlastivěda 3* (1934): 84–218. On common Czech, see Henry Kučera, *The Phonology of Czech* (The Hague: Mouton, 1961), pp. 11–20.

5. For an example of the opposite, see Einar Haugen, "Language and Immigration," *Norwegian-American Studies and Records* 10 (1938), pp. 1–43; reprinted in Einar Haugen, *The Ecology of Language: Essays by Einar Haugen,* sel. and introd. Anwar S. Dil (Stanford Calif.: Stanford University Press, 1972), pp. 1–36.

6. Svoboda, "Czechs: The Love of Liberty," pp. 158–61.

7. Ibid., pp. 161–62.

8. Ibid., p. 159, and especially the catalogue of organizations and resources at the end of his article.

9. Ibid., pp. 165–66; Kučera, *The Phonology of Czech,* pp. 52–63.

10. Uriel Weinreich, *Languages in Contact: Findings and Problems,* Publications of the Linguistic Circle of New York, no. 1 (The Hague: Mouton, 1970).

11. Kučera, *The Phonology of Czech,* pp. 87–92; and K. Kravčišnová and B. Bednářová, "Z výzkumu bežně mluvené češtiny," *Slavica Pragensia* 10 (1968): 305–20.

Aspects of Lakota Bilingualism

Elizabeth S. Grobsmith

The impact of modern American culture and technology on Native American society has been a major object of anthropological investigation for nearly half a century. One concern in documenting acculturation has been the influence of English on the languages of America's indigenous tribes. The results of the impact of English on native language use have been far from uniform. Some native tongues, such as Yahi, a Yana language once spoken in California, have suffered extinction. Others have been able to persist with varying degrees of vitality and integrity. An example of a language which has remained remarkably intact is Lakota [la'kxo:ta], a Siouan tongue spoken by Brule and Oglala Sioux of the Pine Ridge and Rosebud Reservations in South Dakota. Although linguistic acculturation has occurred, Lakota continues to be used almost exclusively by some Indians and at least occasionally by others.

It will be the purpose of this paper to study the differential persistence of Lakota and the circumstances that characterize its maintenance on the Rosebud Reservation and to discuss a phenomenon that derives from and contributes to continued bilingualism. The nature and extent of the simultaneous use of English and Lakota on the reservation will be assessed by comparing two reservation communities in which linguistic acculturation differs widely. The paper will explore contact between the two languages with emphasis on the manner in which the native speaker utilizes each for different purposes. The differential use of Lakota and English results in frequent bilingual shifts that have come to characterize reservation speech. This facet of linguistic acculturation—code-switching—will be considered in some detail below. The alternation between Lakota and English within the sentence will be seen to be a new acculturative linguistic form that insures maximal precision and effectiveness in communication.

These sociolinguistic concerns focus specifically on the concept of functional bilingualism developed by Joshua A. Fishman, that is, the simultaneous use of two languages in a single speech community, each appropriate for use in specific social contexts.[1] The functional separation of Lakota and English indicates that English has not replaced the native language despite the important role it plays in reservation communication; furthermore, since there is a separation of languages according to the domains in which each is deemed appropriate, it appears that Lakota almost certainly will not become an extinct language even though many assimilative changes have occurred in the speech of younger Indians.

The Rosebud Reservation in south central South Dakota is the home of approximately seventy-two hundred Western, or Teton, Sioux and three times as many non-Indians. Most of the Indians are descendants of the Brule bands, with fewer residents representing the Oglala bands. The twenty-one communities on the reservation are grouped geographically into five regions. Linguistically these communities range from virtually all-English-speaking villages where only the elderly know and speak the native language to indigenous communities where English is seldom spoken except to outsiders. The two communities represented in this study were originally selected for intensive investigation specifically because they appeared to be on opposite ends of a continuum of linguistic assimilation. A brief sketch of each community will illustrate their contrasting natures.

Spring Creek is an indigenous community of fewer than three hundred persons, located seventeen miles from the Rosebud agency town and thirty-three miles from the predominantly non-Indian town of Mission, South Dakota. Spring Creek residents are dependent upon this town for merchandise, heating fuel, electricity, and general commercial and recreational services. Spring Creek is considered by most reservation residents to be a traditional community, both because it is an indigenous settlement and because much activity relevant to native religious tradition occurs there. Most families dwell in bilateral extended households where grandparents and grandchildren live in proximity. Because of its geographical isolation, Spring Creek receives few visitors from the outside except for health workers and employees of the elementary school. Since residents go to town only once a week for services, there is little interaction with more assimilated communities.

Nearly all of Spring Creek's residents were born and reared in their community, growing up in homes where parents were all strictly monolingual Lakota speakers. With the exception of one non-Lakota Indian, all claim to be native speakers. Despite the fact that all but the oldest Spring Creek residents had several years of formal education, both adults and children communicate primarily in Lakota. The extended family structure is at least partly responsible for the high degree of native-language maintenance, since elderly monolingual grandparents often care for children while their parents are away at work, and as a result the children are reared in a nearly all-Lakota-speaking environment. Another factor which appears to correlate with the high degree of linguistic preservation is a high unemployment rate—55 percent. The joblessness among Spring Creek residents is partly circumstantial, partly deliberate, for these people are oriented more toward the routines of traditional life and are less likely to seek employment from a non-Indian employer. Few individuals seek income reliability or job security as do the Indians in more assimilated communities and the surrounding white population. Those who are employed tend to prefer jobs which enable them to speak their native language and to remain in or near their home community, such as road construction, janitorial work, and bus driving. This low employment rate contributes to or reinforces the high degree of native-language maintenance, for it limits exposure to non-Indian working situations.

The Antelope community contrasts sharply with Spring Creek in that it was never an indigenous community. Rather, it was originally a federal housing project, which drew people from rural areas. Antelope was built in the mid-1960s and has a more urban appearance, with gridlike paved streets, lawns, and speed bumps. Lacking the dispersed rural nature of the Spring Creek settlement, Antelope is located directly on a main state throughway, which bisects the state from its eastern to its western boundaries. Located only one mile from the town of Mission, Antelope depends on its proximity for services, schools, and recreational facilities. The public school complex attracts local non-Indians as well as those Indian people for whom education is a high priority, for it is considered both by the state and by local residents to have the highest academic standards in the reservation area. Since it is equipped with boarding facilities, many students from outside the Mission-Antelope area attend this school; however, it serves primarily the Indians residing in the vicinity. It is difficult to determine whether Antelope's more assimilated character can be attributed to its proximity and exposure to town and school—and thus to employment and middle-class values—or whether the population moved to this area because they already shared those values and chose to bring up their children in this somewhat more cosmopolitan environment.

At Antelope only half of the population (represented in the sample community) claimed to be native speakers of Lakota—a marked difference from the native-language fluency of Spring Creek residents. Formal interviews conducted in both communities reveal that only 12.5 percent of the Antelope community claimed to rely primarily on Lakota as the language of the home, whereas 47.5 percent of the Spring Creek population claimed to rely on Lakota exclusively. Similar differences between the two communities hold true also for the children: while only 22.5 percent of respondents from Antelope stated that their children were native speakers, nearly 80 percent of Spring Creek's residents asserted that their children were fluent in the native language. Antelope is more linguistically assimilated than Spring Creek, since fewer adults have maintained their native language and even fewer have provided a Lakota-speaking environment in which to rear their children.

The unemployment rates for the two populations also differ radically—55 percent for Spring Creek as opposed to only 15 percent for the Antelope population. Employment is more acceptable in Antelope and represents less of a deviation from expected behavior. Working is less incompatible with local values and may, in fact, be an accurate index of the degree of assimilation. It is difficult to determine whether higher employment rates can be attributed to increased opportunity and proximity to the town of Mission, or to the more assimilated nature of most of the inhabitants of Antelope.

Antelope and Spring Creek differ not only in their use of Lakota but also in their attitudes toward maintenance of the native tongue. At Spring Creek few are conscious of a need to maintain Lakota; native-language use is so prevalent that concern for its loss is almost unimaginable. Consequently, little pressure exists for the development of native-language or bilingual instructional programs. The lower educational level of Spring Creek residents may also contribute to the general lack of conscious concern about educational policy, for in this village, school is still considered a government-imposed institution and not an integral part of Spring Creek tradition. The prevalent attitude at Antelope is the reverse: strong pressure exists to create native-language instruction programs and, indeed, an Indian studies program already exists. For most Antelope residents language instruction is a priority—a rather ironic situation in view of the fact that few parents have actually reared their children bilingually.

The reasons which account for this discrepancy in the two communities are very complex. Antelope residents are aware of their break with tradition, and they believe this loss will have damaging effects on the character development of their children. First, they believe language loss will markedly reduce or totally prevent communication between young and old, thereby severing a critical link to indigenous tradition. Second, they feel that this remoteness from native practices will deprive their children of an essential element in their personality development—ethnic pride. Consciousness of one's ethnicity and an appreciation for one's history, culture, and language, they say, give a child security, confidence, and the necessary personal resources for self-determination in adult life. They view language preservation as the basis of cultural stability, but have delegated the responsibility for such instruction to the school. For Spring Creek residents, linguistic and cultural preservation are taken for granted and thus are naturally considered part of the child's family upbringing within the home.

Antelope and Spring Creek differ not only in their cultural makeup; they are also very distinct regarding situational language choice. A comparative study of language preference for similar social contexts in the two sample communities illustrates this remarkable linguistic heterogeneity so typical of reservation communities. For purposes of comparison nine domains were selected which were considered typical of the range of activities in which most reservation residents, regardless of community affiliation, participated. Fishman explains how these domains are recognized:

> There are classes of occasions recognized by each speech network or community such that several seemingly different situations are classed as being of the same kind . . . just *where the boundaries come* that do differentiate between the classes of situations . . . must be empirically determined by the investigator.[2]

The domains included at the store, during business dealings, at work, with friends, at the hospital, during social occasions (for example, pow-wows, giveaways, and other community events), at *yuwipi* ceremonies, during Native American Church services, and at the Christian church. A total of eighty informants were interviewed, forty from each community. The results proved to be extremely interesting: despite radical differences in the character of the communities, residents of both Antelope and Spring Creek said they preferred to speak English for three of the specified domains: at the store, during business dealings, and at the hospital. For purposes of this discussion these three domains will constitute a class of situations involving public interaction, Class A. Only two domains were regarded in both communities as being strictly the province of the Lakota language: at *yuwipi* [ju'wipi] "they wrap *or* bind" ceremonies and during Native American Church services.[3] These two domains will be grouped as Class B, those requiring exclusively the native language, even for the more assimilated community residents. The third group of domains, Class C, includes at work, with friends, during social occasions, and at Christian church services. Class C situations are extremely revealing, for here we can observe a true split between the two communities in language use. While Antelope residents are generally more comfortable speaking English for these occasions, Lakota individuals from Spring Creek stated that the native language was more appropriate for them. A brief look at the differences between the three classes of situations will clarify why, in some situations, respondents from both communities consistently chose English for certain occasions and Lakota for others, while for the last class of domains, Class C, the two communities diverged. Class A situations involve the necessity of communicating with authorities, merchants, and individuals in the health field. For most Indian people, English is the practical selection, for one can never be certain whether Lakota employees speak the language or not. In order to avoid possible embarrassment, therefore, Indians in these two communities prefer English for commercial or official transactions. Class B situations, those requiring exclusively the use of Lakota, are restricted for the sake of both efficacy and principle. Indigenous rituals, the *yuwipi* and *lowąpi* [lo'wã:pi] "they sing" healing and curing ceremonies, are expressions of highly formalized ritual prescription which must be conducted with utmost correctness and propriety in order to be effective.[4] Great care is taken to preserve the traditional character of these ceremonies—nonbelievers are barred as are menstruating women—and all efforts are directed toward insuring that the spirits summoned during these night-long rituals will be cooperative in their responses to supplication. Use of English for such religious activities is prohibited. Incorrect ritual is potentially hazardous. It may not only render attempted cures ineffective and spoil herbal medicines, but may even bring danger or harm to the shaman or ceremonial sponsor.

Native American Church services dictate the same general linguistic requirements even though this church is essentially an interreservation, pan-Indian phenomenon, one not at all restricted to the Lakota. The Native American Church is a particularly syncretic religion, employing basic beliefs of Christianity and simultaneously depending on Native American religious universals like the personification of natural forces such as Earth and Sky, use of the four cardinal directions, the drum, Indian music, and various items of Indian ritual paraphernalia. Native American Church rituals, in which peyote is taken as a sacrament, are always conducted in the language spoken on the reservation where the service is conducted, whether Lakota, Omaha, Winnebago, or any other. In contrast to the *yuwipi* ceremony, some English may be spoken by nonnative speakers in attendance, although this is considered undesirable and is avoided if at all possible.

Whereas bilingual speakers habitually use English for business transactions and Lakota for religious or ceremonial purposes, they choose the language in which they feel more comfortable for Class C situations. Since most of the Spring Creek residents work in their home community, they naturally prefer to speak Lakota while at work. Antelope residents, on the other hand, generally work in the town of Mission or in the tribal enterprises located in their community and therefore feel more comfortable speaking English. These contrasting preferences prevail also on social occasions and when with friends and here too reflect significant differences among the residents of both villages. Language use in the Christian church poses a very interesting question. Why should it be that in one community a congregation collectively prefers that English be spoken at church, while the other claims Lakota to be more appropriate for church services? The answer lies in the degree to which the Lakota have assimilated Christianity into their native way of life. Christianity, particularly Catholicism, has gained a strong place in Lakota life since the beginning of the reservation period. The influence began with the Jesuit missionaries who came to Rosebud in the 1870s and 1880s. Many Indians participate in both native and Christian ritual, finding neither contradiction nor incompatibility between them. Some participate in native ritual during the week and attend church faithfully on Sunday. Baptism, religious instruction, marriage, and burial are services performed by the Christian church. For an indigenous community like Spring Creek, the use of the native language for church activities reflects a natural merging of the two traditions. Lakota is used for sermons, prayers, and especially hymns. Antelope, on the other hand, regards the use of English as proper for Christian worship, since most of the inhabitants of the community do not have native language fluency and since most of the churches in the vicinity are located in the predominantly non-Indian town of Mission.

The variation in linguistic selection as described above strongly supports Fishman's concept of functional bilingualism. This simultaneous persistence of two distinct languages is explained by Fishman as follows:

> A speech community maintains its sociolinguistic pattern as long as the functional differentiation of the varieties in its linguistic repertoire is systematically and widely maintained. As long as each variety is associated with a separate class of situations there is good reason and established means for retaining them all, each in its place, notwithstanding the modicum of metaphorical switching that may occur. However, two or more varieties with the same societal function become difficult to maintain and, in the end, one must either displace the other or a new functional differentiation must be arrived at between them.[5]

For Rosebud, Lakota and English *are* separated functionally as illustrated by the domain division discussed above. It is precisely this separation which insures the persistence of the native tongue, for particular situations occur with regularity which must be dealt with in the language deemed more suitable. The inexchangeability of the two languages, even for a few domains, assures the separate persistence of the languages whose functions are, at least in part, mutually exclusive.

Let us turn now to another aspect of linguistic acculturation which is often a concomitant of the bilingual situation: *code-switching,* the alternation between one speech variety and another within the context of a single sentence. Bilingual switching among speakers of Lakota and English basically consists of utterances in Lakota into which a speaker interjects English words. While this may happen in the reverse manner, that is, an individual may interject Lakota terms into the context of an English sentence, most shifts occur in the context of Lakota conversation. Most native speakers' discourse is sprinkled with English vocabulary, for it is nearly impossible for the Lakota, under pressure to participate economically in an increasingly non-Indian world, to avoid reference to items of American technology or philosophy.

A careful examination of bilingual shifts reveals that such alternations do not occur randomly but appear to be highly patterned. The following brief excerpt from ethnographic texts is typical of the everyday speech in which bilingual shifts occur and illustrates some of the conditions precipitating such shifts:[6]

VISITOR: Now there's one thing too,[lɛ] regular size.
this

SALESLADY: [hã:]
Yes.

V: [na'kũ nijɛk ˀe ˀaʃ he'nũ oja'kihi ktɛ . . . lɛ . . . lɛ]
It's an adult size; you could wear it too . . . this . . . this. . . .

S: One and three-fourths yards [lɛ].

V: [o na ˀɛ ˀɛ 'lɛtkija] wide.
And this way it's really

S: ['lila] wide, [tʃa] I'll have to cut this.
Very and so

(*Later*)

V: It figured out to forty dollars. [ho'tʃa ɑ̃'ska . . . ˀi'juha ja'kaeʒu 'hãta ˀaʃ]
And so if you are going to pay half of it
it'll all be ready by fifteenth.

This excerpt is from a conversation in which the two women speak predominantly Lakota. They are discussing shawl making and the purchase of fabrics. Also they are discussing money, costs, and deadlines. Every time they need to make reference to a quantity, date, or cost, their flow of conversation switches from Lakota into English. Words such as "yard," "regular size," and "wide" are inserted in English within the context of a Lakota phrase. The explanation for this is quite apparent: while Lakota may be suitable for the general line of conversation, it is more effective and efficient to switch into English in order to convey the precise meaning intended at certain points in the conversation. Both women prefer to speak Lakota to each other, as do most native speakers. But when it is necessary to express concepts which have more precise English referents—things such as yard goods, money, and measurement for fit for commercially sold products—convenient English phrases are automatically inserted. Once this has been accomplished, the conversation returns to its predominantly Lakota flow.

The following is a summary of observations concerning bilingual shifts:

1. Bilingual shifts occur mostly in the speech of fluent native speakers and involve the interjection of English words and expressions into what is otherwise a Lakota sentence. While some shifting occurs in the reverse manner, that is, someone inserts Lakota words into the context of an English sentence, far more shifts occur among people conducting conversations which are, for the most part, in Lakota.
2. English is used to refer to items of European manufacture or concepts specifically characteristic of non-Indian ideology or material culture. Al-

though Lakota has undergone considerable acculturation and there are now words for things such as *sewing machine* [ma'zwitʃeɣe] (literally, "iron that sews"), *dresser* [juslu'wo:ganaka] (literally, "pull and store") and others of this nature, most Lakota prefer to use the English term, either because it is quicker, easier, shorter, or because it has a more precise referent. In other words, English also loses something in the translation.

3. English is used to refer to specific persons, for example Mr. and Mrs. White Hawk, the Menards. Ceremonial or Indian names are rarely used except during religious events.
4. English is used to refer to quantities or amounts, such as people's ages, dates, and the year. Numerical quantities are more easily expressed in English since Lakota numbers (above the number ten) consist of lengthy composite strings. For instance, a Lakota speaker considers it simpler to say "It will all be ready by fifteenth" than to substitute the Lakota lexical items for *fifteenth* [wik'tʃemna a'ke zap'tã] (literally, "ten again five"); the difference in convenience is one word in English as opposed to three in Lakota. Here English is more efficient.
5. Concepts of time lend themselves more readily to expression in English. This includes reference to minutes, hours, days, weeks, months, years, dates, future schedules, relative and absolute time—all concepts which are clearly Western in origin. While one can easily say *I will be there later* in Lakota, this is not usually considered specific enough in the time-oriented society in which the Lakota now live, for *late* could mean in ten minutes, in an hour, or in a week. Telling time has problems all its own: in Lakota, there is no word to designate *hour*—only [o'wapxe] (literally, "waiting period"). To say *three o'clock* in Lakota one would have to say ['mazaskaska 'jamni] (literally, "iron-that-moves three"). One cannot refer to minutes or seconds in Lakota; one refers, instead, to a *short time* or [o'wapxe 'pte:tʃela]. It is not difficult to see, then, why Lakota speakers interject precise English expressions into Lakota sentences. It enables the speaker to communicate in a manner he or she considers maximally effective without sacrificing the general use of Lakota and yet permits the accuracy or specificity expressed by certain English concepts. In other words, bilingual shifts accomplish what translation cannot.

Rather than indicating an increasing trend to use English and a simultaneous decreasing use of the native language, code-switching illustrates the complementarity of Lakota and English in a bicultural environment. More importantly, patterning in bilingual shifts provides corroborating evidence, along with domain-specific linguistic choices, of a persistent parallel use of two languages which remain of equal importance in a single speech community.

Certainly there is some overlap in language use; but the essential ingredient in flourishing bilingualism is the dual participation in a bicultural environment. Lakota tribal members do participate economically and politically in the Western society; but ideologically and socially, that is, culturally, their way of life is uniquely Lakota. It is not that of a quasi-assimilated group of Native Americans whose strongest links with their tradition are nostalgia. While Lakota society is undergoing acculturative changes in many spheres, such as housing, industrial development, and an increased dependence on commercially marketed products, it is conscious and deliberate conservatism which is responsible for the preference to live in a society with distinctly Indian values. Specifically, it is the adherence to Lakota cultural principles which, in turn, demands knowledge and retention of and instruction in the native language.

While many Indian languages have fallen into obsolescence because of replacement by English, this particular case of stable bilingualism provides us with considerable insight into the process and form of language maintenance and linguistic acculturation. Despite overwhelming pressures to participate in an increasingly non-Indian world, viable cultures such as Lakota society have actively resisted the process of total assimilation. It is through native-language maintenance that this situation has become at all possible.

Notes

Portions of this paper appeared in a paper delivered at the 74th Annual Meeting of the American Anthropological Association, December 1975, San Francisco, and the 35th Annual Plains Conference, November 1977, Lincoln, Nebraska.

1. Joshua A. Fishman, *Language in Sociocultural Change: Essays by Joshua A. Fishman,* sel. and introd. Anwar S. Dil (Stanford, Calif.: Stanford University Press, 1972); for a discussion of this linguistic phenomenon see Nils Hasselmo, "Code-Switching and Modes of Speaking," in *Texas Studies in Bilingualism: Spanish, French, German, Czech, Polish, Sorbian, and Norwegian in the Southwest, with a Concluding Chapter on Code-Switching and Modes of Speaking in American Swedish,* ed. Glenn G. Gilbert, Studia Linguistica Germanica no. 3 (Berlin: Walter de Gruyter & Co., 1970), pp. 179–208.

2. Fishman, *Language in Sociocultural Change,* p. 6.

3. *Yuwipi* refers to the wrapping and binding of the medicine man in a quilt, done in the healing ritual known by that name. See Luis Kemnitzer, "Structures, Content, and Cultural Meaning of *Yuwipi:* A Modern Lakota Healing Ritual," *American Ethnologist* 3 (May 1976): 261–80.

4. *Lowąpi* refers to a type of healing ceremony during which individuals sing in order to evoke supernatural help. *Lowąpi* ceremonies resemble *yuwipi* except that the former does not entail wrapping or binding the shaman.

5. Fishman, *Language in Sociocultural Change,* p. 7.

6. See Elizabeth S. Grobsmith, "Lakota Bilingualism: A Comparative Study of Language Use in Two Communities in the Rosebud Sioux Reservation" (Ph.D. diss., University of Arizona, 1976).

Language Change and Cultural Dynamics: A Study of Lakota Verbs of Movement

ELAINE JAHNER

Lakota is the dialect spoken by the Tetons, the western branch of the Sioux nation. Language classifications list Lakota as a dialect of Dakota, but the term *Dakota* also designates a specific dialect, with Nakota as the third major dialect of the language.[1] Spoken by several thousand persons, Lakota is the language of preference for many of middle age and older. It is still learned as a first language by children in some communities.[2] The most vital of the Siouan languages, Lakota presents intriguing possibilities for the study of language change as a result of contact with other languages. Some linguistic changes such as the increased use of contractions and the substitution of English lexical items are obvious to the researcher, who can also gather information about changes much more difficult to describe when Lakota people point out that "the old words are dying" and that "some young people use words differently." Speakers and scholars alike are aware that linguistic change is occurring on many levels, some easy to document and some almost impossible to describe accurately. In this paper I shall examine a methodology for studying one kind of relationship between language and culture change and illustrate the method by studying one lexical field—the Lakota verbs of movement.

Lakota verbs of movement exhibit some identifiable differences from the English pattern, and an examination of the Lakota world view shows that ideas related to movement served as pivotal concepts in articulating the prereservation relationship between social structure and world view. The verbs of movement, which are words with a high frequency of use, exhibit only minor dialectal change. Such facts suggest the problem area for this paper. Is there any way to identify correlations between changes in linguistic features of the Lakota verbs of movement and changes in the cultural relationship between social structure and world view?

Studying language change is always perilous when scholars have to rely on previous field work that can seldom be verified. Researchers who attempt diachronic studies of Lakota are extremely fortunate, though, in that they inherit the work of Ella C. Deloria, a native Dakota speaker who spent a lifetime doing careful linguistic and ethnographic field work.[3] She was born on the Yankton Sioux reservation in 1888. While attending high school in South Dakota, she won a scholarship to Oberlin College and went from there to Columbia University, where she worked with Franz Boas and those students of his who were interested in Sioux language and culture. In 1914 she received her B.A. from Columbia and returned to reservation schools to teach. Later she accepted a position at Haskell Institute in Lawrence, Kansas. Then in 1927 Boas wrote to her asking her to gather more Dakota data. Soon she was working full time recording and translating statements made by native speakers of all three Sioux dialects. She also translated manuscripts that J. Owen Dorsey had collected from Sioux informants, and her careful notes to all the manuscripts present invaluable data about Sioux culture and language. Much of her work is still unpublished. There are hundreds of pages of typescript in the American Philosophical Library of Manuscripts, and other materials can be found in the Ella C. Deloria Manuscript Collection at the Institute of Indian Studies, Vermillion, South Dakota. One collection of Dakota texts, originally published in 1932, has recently been reprinted by AMS Press.

It is thus possible to gather data about the verbs of movement and their turn-of-the-century contexts. We not only have translations of the words themselves, but we also have word-for-word transcriptions of texts recorded just as the informants presented them. These texts illustrate how concepts related to movement functioned to structure discourse. And this is a basic methodological point. We need examples of extended discourse because they are an essential source of data about semantic structures as they operated in various kinds of speech acts. The object of the present study is not to compare isolated features of Lakota to isolated features of English but rather to select certain Lakota linguistic properties and then to show a relation between these properties and their psychosocial environment. The entire process should suggest the kinds of data needed to show changes in the relationship between linguistic properties and environment that result from culture contact.

Although the data most pertinent to this study are those relating to the verbs of movement, a cursory statement on patterns of language change involving lexical substitution can serve to introduce the discussion. Clearly the frequency and the type of English lexical item substituted for Lakota varies from region to region, but the tendency toward substitution is present everywhere. An example can show the characteristics of the phenomenon. The following sentences were recorded during a conversation between an old woman and her middle-aged son. The woman spoke only Lakota, and her son used Lakota as his language of preference.

[Etãhã ehanni wowaglak ĩ kte. Wana le I am eighty-
Concerning long ago, I will speak. Now

three years old hena matʃatʃa. . . . Day school wã six miles
that I am. *a*
hatʃa. . . . Watʃitaka waũwajapi.
that's where it was. Patiently (enduring much) we went to
Hehã drop outs tuweni slolje ʃni. Witʃcoka hijaja ca
school. *never were known.* *When noon came*
ũ-si waũtapi. Beans na biscuit wãjila ũjutapi. Watʃĩtãka
pitifully we ate. *and* *one* *we ate.* *Patiently*
waũwajapi.
we went to school.]

As we examine the English terms, we see that "day school," "six miles," "beans," and "biscuit" are words for features of non-Indian culture, and it is entirely natural to use the English words rather than newly coined Lakota words. The phrase "I am eighty-three years old" presents a different problem though. One plausible explanation for its use derives from the fact that it is a phrase with a high frequency of usage, especially in situations involving both Indian and non-Indian. As a result, the informant is so familiar with it that she automatically uses the English in preference to Lakota. Predictably, English nouns are substituted more frequently than verbs, and it is interesting to note that the informant nominalizes the entire English phrase, "I am eighty-three years old" by the use of the Lakota verb *"hena matʃatʃa."* Continuing field work and research are needed to study emerging patterns of the way in which English words are substituted for Lakota ones before we can consider the nature of the relationship between these surface structure changes and the more abstract structural changes that are the focus of this paper, namely those changes that have to do with the way the verbs of movement condition discourse and therefore the cognitive framework of the traditional Lakota people.

Since the Lakota world view was, and to a certain extent still is, the context that provides the background for any semantic or cognitive analysis of the verbs of movement, I will preface analysis of the verbs of movement with an examination of the basic tenets of the Lakota world view in order to establish the cultural significance of point-to-point movement. The starting point for studying the world view has to be the idea that movement itself is the primal image for life. This idea is not unique to the Lakota, and the clearest articulation of the general outlines of the concept is found among the Omaha Indians, also Siouan in origin. In their classic study of the Omaha tribe, Alice Fletcher and Francis La Flesche give a clear statement of the principle.

> An invisible and continuous life was believed to permeate all things seen and unseen. This life manifests itself in two ways. First by causing to move—all motion, all actions of mind or body are because of this invisible life; second, by causing permanency of structure and form, as in the rock, the physical lakes, the animals and man. This invisible life was also conceived of as being similar to the will power of which man is conscious within himself—a power by which things are brought to pass.

The belief that permanency of structure is brought about by the same power that manifests itself as movement leads naturally to the belief that human movements need to be structured so that social life has some kind of permanent form consistent with the changes that must occur as the group and individuals adapt to changing circumstances. Form is completed movement, or movement at rest. Alice Fletcher has recorded an especially illuminating verbatim account of the relationship between movement and rest.

> Everything as it moves, now and then, makes stops. The bird, as it flies, stops in one place to make its nest, and in another to rest in its flight. A man when he goes forth stops when he wills. So the god has stopped. The sun which is so bright and beautiful is one place where he has stopped. The moon, the stars, the winds he has been with. The trees, animals, are all where he has stopped, and the Indian thinks of these places and sends his prayers there to reach the place where the god has stopped and win help and blessing.[5]

Ella Deloria's field notes include a specifically Lakota verification of the belief in movement as a manifestation of primal power.

> There is only one thing something like that which I have heard; it runs thus: It is the belief in the God of Movement. That thing they say is stone. Stone, but in pebble form, like hailstones, and it comes scattering on the tipi wall; this, when they sing to it and summon it. And that Stone was all-powerful, like nothing else; so whenever the race had to pursue anything very difficult, then faith was placed on it in prayer. . . . So the Dakotas lived, saying in such and similar ways by way of explanation, "Why say, the Something-in-Movement is Stones," so they will tell.[6]

The same interview records the belief that a person could receive messages from stones if that person "moved with them." To move with them means to arrange one's actions according to culturally defined standards of moral behavior, so that personal actions of moving and stopping reflect an archetypal pattern. Within the traditional Lakota world view, there is a complementary relationship between movement and rest. The completion of a prescribed pattern of movement results in a concrete realization of power that in turn gives rise to the need for further movement. Stone is movement held in abeyance, but its potential can be activated by someone whose own movements are in accord with prescribed patterns. The prescribed patterns of movement are determined by the way Lakota social structure determines individual actions.

Since the Lakota were a nomadic people, their social organization had to accommodate movement within territorial limits. Social structure and its way of directing movement were the stable form that gave order and system to the environment. The entire system reflects a complex play between environmental qualities, the belief system, and the symbolic system. This matching process among different levels of phenomena resulted in cultural categories that imposed order on diverse phenomena and created a valuation system. To describe the ordering quality of the cultural process, I use the term *spatial categories* and the term *spatial values* to denote its properties of valuation.[7]

We can determine the features of Sioux spatial categories by examining the fixed symbols that reflected the Sioux world view and helped people understand the way that various patterns of social organization related to each other. The basic fixed symbol of Sioux life was and still is the circle. Other core symbols such as the pipe and the buffalo are related to the circle image in that they subsume the same referential domain, and each set of forms is the key to the others. In trying to explain Sioux beliefs, one contemporary Sioux man began in the following way:

> The sun from the east and the moon from the west are all symbolic of a circle. Likewise our Lakota people are also symbolic of a strong circle. Whenever you see our people camp, it is always in a circle. When they sit and have a parley or a council of many fires, the pattern of their sitting is always in a circle. From this circle of our Lakota people comes the extended family. Whether they are cousins, brothers, sisters, or distant cousins, they are still bound by love, honor, respect and strong ties which symbolize a circle.[8]

Joseph Flying By's account of the circle image's semantic ambit indicates the large number of ideas included in it. The image is applicable to every one of the Sioux spatial categories. Within the Sioux world view the major spatial categories are the cosmos, the world, the camp circle, and the tipi. One of James R. Walker's informants commented on the cosmic implications of the circle image.

> Since the Great Spirit has caused everything to be round, mankind should look upon the circle as sacred because it is the symbol of all things in nature except stone. It is also the symbol of the circle that marks the edge of the world and therefore of the four winds that travel there.[9]

For the Lakota each of the four directions respresents specific sets of meanings. The north has to do with purification; the west, the home of thunder beings, is the direction of either constructive or destructive change; the east suggests wisdom, and the south, fertility. Ceremonial movement is generally clockwise beginning with the west, because the Lakota believed that within the cosmos movement of powers was clockwise. The one exception was the movement of the thunder beings, whose behavior was antinatural.[10] The directional meanings and the corresponding systems of ceremonial movement were the day-to-day reminders of the way the cosmos and the world as spatial realms with defined patterns impinged upon daily life.

The camp circle was another spatial category with prescribed systems of movement. The Sioux maintained ideal images of camp circle organization, and whenever the group was camped for ceremonial participation, the actual pattern reflected the ideal. Each tipi had its place within the circle determined by the role the family played within the group. Therefore, the position of the tipi in the circle automatically identified the role of its inhabitants relative to that of other group members.[11] As a family gained in prestige, a tipi could be moved, and whenever a family could not contribute to the group's welfare, its tipi had to be moved outside the circle.

The tipi was the fourth major spatial category. Within the tipi all space and all positions were meaningful and represented a plan of order that directed the family's movements within it. The area opposite the door behind the fire held the place of honor. (The center of any circle was always the position of honor, reserved for the sacred or for the activities of leaders.) The area to the right was allocated to family members, and the left central portion was for guests. Nearest to the left of the tipi's doorway was the area where the old people begging for food could rest. The direction of actual movement in the tipi was also culturally guided. The pattern of order that directed all movement within the tipi helped the family to visualize it as the cosmos in miniature, where movement had to follow culturally prescribed patterns.[12]

Because the Sioux visualized every level of social organization as a circle that unified members of the group and marked out the circumference of a prescribed pattern of movement, they could use features of space to conceptualize the place of the individual in the group. Every person could think of his or her personal identity as intimately related to the particular place occupied in the circles of social organization. But no individual's place was ever static. Many factors caused movement among the various circles of being. The one inescapable movement that every person had to submit to was the constant progression of time. The Sioux used spatial imagery to articulate their concept of time, which was seen as realized movement through space, so that the individual, starting from a particular point, had to follow culturally prescribed movements through the circles of social organization in order to inscribe the circle which was the circle of individual life.

> Is not the south the source of life, and does not the flowering stick truly come from there? And does not man advance from there toward the setting sun of his life? And does he not arrive, if he lives at the source of light and understanding which is in the east? Then, does he not return to the south where he began, to his second childhood, there to give back his life to all life and his flesh to the earth whence it came?[13]

Any study of the relationship between world view and discourse must concentrate on the various circles of a person's identity because the dynamic interrelationships among the circles provide the thematic content of the various kinds of discourse, and the principles of order and causality that determined action within the various spheres of being provide the motivation for basic cultural activities, including significant speech acts.

Now that we have sketched the operation of Sioux spatial categories, we can summarize these ideas in axiomatic statements that list the most fundamental cultural variables that can be associated with the semantic distinctive features of the Lakota verbs of movement.

1. Each person's identity is viewed as a specific point within a series of circles. His or her position defines a role relative to all other members of the tribe, and it defines the potential for movement from one social group to another.
2. Each circle constituting a person's social identity is defined by its degree of social organization. For example, the circle of the immediate family is more organized through kinship obligations than that of the camp circle, which is more controlled than that of the entire tribe. The tribe, in turn, is more organized than that largest camp—the entire earth.
3. Each degree of intensification of social organization is simultaneously an intensification of appropriated power. All power is procured and maintained through social organization, which is achieved through directed and culturally prescribed patterns of movement. The farther power is drawn into the circles of organization, the less random it becomes and the more accessible to the individual and the group.
4. Social organization is identical to the establishment of kinship bonds.
5. Those individuals most bound by the precepts of society are the leaders whose achievements have led them to the very center of the inmost circle. (The Council Lodge was in the center area of the camp circle, and all ceremonial activity took place in the same area, which was imaged as the "center of the world.") The position of leaders symbolizes their authority.
6. Only those can become leaders who have followed the culturally prescribed means of appropriating power available in circles outside the immediate one in order to bring it closer to the center of the hoop of the nation. (Leaders had to have been successful hunters or warriors or visionaries, and sometimes one man combined all three major ways of going outside the immediate circle of being to bring in what the group needed.)
7. All movement is potentially regressive as well as progressive. The misuse of power or the failure to comply with cultural prescriptions can result in the individual's being driven outside the camp circle. The less the degree of social organization surrounding the use of power, the more dangerous it is.

These principles of the Sioux system of belief are fundamental to an understanding of the factual regularities in Sioux life. They once conditioned the cognitive structure of all aesthetic constructs. The summarizing statements of the system of belief have the status of observational laws, and they provide the background knowledge for the model used to interpret both the prereservation and the current semantic data related to the verbs of movement. How does one relate these tenets of the system of belief to specific linguistic features? In her study of the cognitive features of the Papago language, Madeline Mathiot employs a terminology that clearly marks each level of abstraction needed to show how specific lexical items share features of meaning with nonlinguistic manifestations of culture.[14] By distinguishing between the semantic and the cognitive features of linguistic data, she can show how the cognitive features characterize the pragmatic component of the language model and, therefore, how these features are directly related to cultural dynamics. According to Mathiot, the semantic distinctive features of a given aspect of language are the invariant characteristics of that aspect as these are shown by lexical items related to the particular aspect. The cognitive distinctive features label the cognitive significance of a given aspect of language and its relationship to cultural themes.[15]

Mathiot's first step is to form sets with the naming units of pertinent data and to infer the semantic characteristics of particular categories from the contrastive patterns within the set. Then one can proceed to study the cognitive content of a given linguistic aspect. Once the primary semantic features have been identified, they are related to an underlying concept. Mathiot's basic terminology enables us to abstract two sets of distinctive features for lexical items and to study the interrelationship between the two sets. This is an especially important distinction to make in relation to the Lakota verbs of movement because current field data suggest that the semantic distinctive features of these verbs have remained relatively constant in spite of inevitable changes in the cognitive distinctive features. Because of the change in features in the cognitive domain, however, the way in which the verbs of movement structure discourse is changing dramatically. The verbs of movement are losing their metaphoric potential as they lose their connection with the dynamics of social organization. Such assertions as I have just made require careful justification through illustration, and the first kind of required data is a summary of the semantic distinctive features of the verbs of movement. The semantic features are inferred from the contrastive patterns in the data. Three semantic distinctive features are evident from the data. They can be labeled as *direction, stage of completion,* and *location*. Franz Boas, using Ella Deloria's data, has described the three aspects of the concept of movement.

> In movement Dakota distinguishes between thither and hither, completion of movement hither and thither, movement to a place formerly occupied (i.e., return); completion of movement thither and hither to a place previously occupied (i.e., arrival, returning). The combinations of the verbs of arrival and motion express the concept of starting, e.g., he went to arrive there, i.e., he started going thither, etc.[16]

The following tables present other characterizations of the Lakota verbs of movement:

Ella Deloria: 1933[17]

[u]	*to be coming*
[ku]	*to be coming back here*
[i]	*to arrive going*
[ki]	*to arrive going back there*
[gli]	*to arrive coming back there*
[glitʃu]	*to start coming back here*
[gla]	*to be going back there*
[ja]	*to be going*
[hi]	*to arrive coming*

Eugene Buechel: 1936[18]

[u]	(*to come*) *to be on the way to a place not one's own*. The fact is mentioned at that place.
[ku]	(*to come home*) *to be on the way to one's home*. The fact is mentioned at that home, or, in the first person, towards that home.
[i]	*to have gone to, to have been at a place not one's own*. The fact is mentioned away from that place.
[ki]	*to have arrived at one's home*. The fact is mentioned away from that home.
[gli]	(*to arrive at one's home*.) The fact is mentioned at that home.
[glitʃu]	(*to start to come home*.) This verb refers to past time and can be used only when the fact is mentioned *at the home* of the person in question.
[gla]	(*to go home*) *to be on the way to one's home*. The fact is mentioned away from that home.
[ja]	(*to go*) *to be on the way to a place not one's own*. The fact of going is mentioned away from that place.
[hi]	(*to arrive at a place not one's own*.) The fact is mentioned at that place.

Current Informants: 1977[19]

[u]	to come, no knowledge of who or where
[ku]	to come back with the knowledge that the subject left from the place or lives there
[i]	to have gone there, goal indefinite
[ki]	to return to a place once left
[gli]	to leave and return to one's place
[glitʃu]	to leave and to go home
[gla]	to go from somewhere to where one's residence is
[ja]	to go from anywhere to anywhere
[hi]	to arrive from a definite point of departure to a definite goal

A careful study of current informants' actual use of the verbs confirms what the translations suggest, namely, that contemporary Lakota speakers continue to mark semantic features of the verbs of movement in much the same way as earlier speakers did. Current informants are less precise than the Buechel translations, but they correspond very well with Ella Deloria's. In specific contexts current informants tend to note the position of speaker in relation to the goal as Buechel specifies. On the level of semantic distinctive features there has been little or no accommodation to the less precise English system. As I will demonstrate, however, the semantic features no longer match specific cognitive distinctive features as regularly as they once did. Change is occurring on the cognitive level without having significantly affected the level of semantic distinctive features. At least semantic change has not yet occurred to any great extent. But before analyzing cognitive feature changes, we must examine more linguistic data in order to show other manifestations of the same semantic distinctive features that the verbs of movement have. The nature of point-to-point movement is a cultural theme that is regularly manifested by the semantic features of direction, stage of completion, and location of movement.

The Lakota words referring to travel are distinguished from each other by the semantic feature of direction. The word *itʃimani* once had as one of its features of meaning "to return to the starting point." Deloria writes, "*Itʃi* occurs in several words and it always means something like looping back over itself. From that I think *itʃimani* which means to go on a journey, must mean *to walk–to return,* that is, to go somewhere on a visit." She also says, "Wayfarers, nomads are not said to *itʃimani*." The language has still a third word for travel—*omani* which can also mean "to roam about," but is often used to refer to an extended journey even though the intent is to return home.[20] Current informants maintain some sense of the original distinctions, but their use seems to imply a distinction between walking and traveling by other means. One informant said that *itʃimani* means "traveling far away" while *omani* means "just walking around."

One word that is seldom used now is the verb *manĩl*. This verb is particularly interesting because its direction feature implies that the starting point is the center of the camp circle. Deloria translates the verb to mean "living away from the center," and she mentions the old Lakota idiom *manĩl ijeja* which literally means "to send away from the center" but which had the force of "to send out of the picture as it were."[21]

Both the direction and the location features are illustrated by the verbs meaning "to bring" with the sense of a person in a particular sphere of being constituting a part of the meaning of the location feature. *Au* means "to bring here," while *kau* means "to bring here to someone." A comparable pair is *aja* meaning "to take there" and *kaaja* meaning "to take there to someone."[22]

Linguistic categories other than verbs illustrate further the importance of spatial distinctions. The demonstratives are more precise than the English ones in the way that they point out specific relationships. Boas briefly summarized the older meanings of the demonstratives. He prefaces his summary by remarking that exact definition of demonstratives is particularly difficult because it is always necessary to reconstruct the position in which the speaker images himself or herself to be.

> In Dakota we have the fundamental forms *le, he, ka, to* which express 'near me', 'away from me', 'away from me visible', 'somewhere'. The concepts 'near thee' and 'near him' are not distinguished. The particular place in reference to two persons is expressed by the suffix *-k'i* (after *e, -tʃ'i*). Thus *letʃ'i* means 'here and away from you or him', *hetʃ'i* means 'here and away from me', *kak'i* 'yonder visible, away from me'. With the ending *ja* these forms express a region rather than a spot.[23]

Another word of particular interest for showing cultural distinctions is *makoskãl* which as a noun can mean "wilderness" or "a place where no one dwells" but as an adverb means "for naught" or "in vain."[24] The different meanings of this word derive from the former cultural belief that although movement to and from the wilderness can be meaningful, life in the wilderness, outside the patterns of social organization, is meaningless.

Even from such a brief survey as this, one indisputable point emerges clearly. The language provides for precise description of point-to-point movement. The importance of point-to-point movement is the underlying concept that links the linguistic aspects that describe the movement to the cognitive aspects that correspond to specific linguistic features. The Lakota spatial categories and the interaction among the various spheres of being are the social and cultural factors that determine the significance of various kinds of movement. How can one proceed from analysis of semantic distinctive features to cognitive distinctive features? In describing her methodology, Mathiot writes, "For every linguistic variable, the question should be asked whether or not it is associated with one or several cultural variables." Mathiot defines cultural variables as the "cultural conditions that (a) affect the form-meaning covariance of the aspect of language under investigation as revealed by the naming units of the pertinent data, and (b) have bearing on the cognitive study of that aspect."[25]

Mathiot's use of cultural variables is limited to those cultural conditions that affect either the *number of sets that can be formed* with the linguistic variables or the *inventories of these sets*. I add a third set of conditions, the pragmatic ones that affect the use of items in each set by determining how much meaning references to a particular point in space can convey. All communication takes place in a specific time-space framework, and whenever we have evidence of *regular* features of meaning deriving from the time and place of communication, then we should consider those features as significant cultural variables affecting the meaning of the total communication. We have such evidence in prereservation Lakota culture, and we can demonstrate that the kinds of meaning conveyed through references to movements to and from particular spatial domains do structure the thematic components of many kinds of discourse.

As the discussion of prereservation spatial categories demonstrates, the particular place of any speech act had meaning potential that could affect the speech act. Important aspects of the Lakota system of interaction were once mapped out in the spatial plan of the camp circle. As a result, role functions could be communicated nonverbally, and the actual physical positions of participants in any communication situation could affect the structure and meaning of the verbal exchange. The importance of this point for an understanding of the relationship between Lakota language and culture cannot be overestimated. It links theoretical considerations to those features of actual communication that exhibit regularity. It also means that a specific designation of the cognitive features related to any verb of movement is dependent on specific analysis of texts with known performance conditions.[26]

Because we have some texts from prereservation times with carefully specified performance conditions, we can formalize the cognitive features of the verbs of movement in these texts and thereby show the structuring force of these verbs. Performance conditions related to specific spatial realms can affect the thematic structure of specific texts in ways that vary significantly from genre to genre. Demonstrating how generic distinctions affect the structuring force of verbs of movement would go beyond the scope of this paper, but since all explicit statements about the cognitive features of Lakota verbs of movement depend on the analysis of contextualized data, I will analyze one free-form text. Before analyzing that text, though, I will sketch the general cultural principles that enable the analyst to match semantic features of the verbs of movement to cognitive features. These general principles derive from the relationship of Lakota spatial categories to their potential symbolic significance for aspects of actual communication.

The semantic feature designated *direction* was generally related to specific spatial values in prereservation times. An example based on a common context can illustrate. If the performance context of a specific statement situates the speaker at the center of the camp circle and the direction feature of the verb of movement indicates that the subject of the verb is returning to the center of the camp circle, then all of the symbolic significance associated with the center of the circle as the place of ceremonial life and of leadership can become operative in the discourse. In that context, the cognitive significance of the verb of movement can be listed as a leadership feature. A model of the cognitive significance of the verbs of movement in any particular text would have to account for the various spheres of being within which action occurs and show their relationship to the total social structure.

The second regular semantic feature distinguishing verbs of movement has to do with the *stage of completion* of the action. Clearly this feature cannot always have a particular cognitive meaning in a given text, but within the prereservation social system it could imply various kinds of ambiguity. Incomplete action is quite obviously between points. To be in a constant state of existence between points or between spheres of being was the cultural definition of meaninglessness and ambiguity. Lakota life was given meaning through social custom, and the Lakota word for *custom* is *oũ*, a nominalization of a verb for localized being. Custom indicates how one lives in a specific place and moves between specific places.

The semantic feature of *location* had the cognitive potential in any given text of implying specific kinds of responsibility. The relationship between responsibility and location was made operative through the way that kinship roles structured responsibility. Raymond DeMallie has summed up the relationship between kinship, spatial values, and responsibility:

> At any level a social group was taken as a manifestation of a kinship group. The symbol of the circle represents the unity of the family group. . . . Most importantly, the *tiospaye* is a cultural model of a social group living in amicable cooperation according to the norms prescribed by the kinship system.[27]

Any coming and going to and from one's own immediate sphere of being was supposed to be in accord with one's particular kinship obligations, so reference to the sphere of being could also be a reference to one's role and its attendant responsibilities.

An understanding of the general principles determining the way one relates semantic features to cultural postulates of meaning does not in itself illustrate how cognitive features are operative in specific contexts. One brief text that I collected while doing fieldwork among the Yanktonais and the Hunkpapa Sioux on Standing Rock Reservation can illustrate how the cognitive features affect the style and the structure of one kind of free-form text. I collected the text from Lillian Fast Horse, a woman now in her seventies. She is a member of the Hunkpapa band of Lakotas, a niece of the famous Sitting Bull. Both she and her husband have retained traditional customs and modes of thought so that her text illustrates areas of cognitive meaning that have survived into current times only among the most traditional of the Lakota.

Lillian Fast Horse and her husband Harry arrived at my home one day just in time for the evening meal. By way of humorous explanation for their unexpected arrival, Lillian Fast Horse described the Sioux way of explaining an unexpected arrival. In her band, the custom was to claim that the unexpected guests had been in the presence of spirits and that the spirits had pushed them to the home of the host or hostess. Since Mrs. Fast Horse was teaching me the Lakota language and helping me to understand local customs, I felt at ease in asking her to write down what she had just told me while I prepared the meal. Her written statement is in both Lakota and English. She expands the single proverbial statement into a highly stylized and structured short statement of all the events leading up to her use of the proverb. Since Mrs. Fast Horse can speak idiomatic English, the nonidiomatic quality of the English cannot be the result of ignorance. Rather it is the result of direct translation from the Lakota. The text illustrates the spontaneous operation of traditional principles of text structure.

> [ã'petu kĩ le el a'tejapi o'ti kĩ he'tʃija wak'supi 'tipi kĩ hel wa[12] apiwaje, na wa'na 'opai a'juʃtãpi mi'tawa kĩ ma'hijohi tʃã'ke ũ'glitʃupi. ũ'kã he'pe, (solen) ek'ta le hãl om'nitʃije kta ʃke, tʃã'ke ũ'kupi na (solen) ek'ta ũ'hipi e'jaʃ e'tʃõpi ʃni tʃã'ke he'pe, (Elaine) e'wa jã'ke tʃa hel ũhipi. ũ'kan lol ũ'kin 'hãpi na wo'ũkipi. tʃã'ke he'pe, wa'naji te ũ'glilapi tʃa pa'jekjel ũa'kaupi. u'pija waũ'jutapi.]

> ("Today at the beadwork house at Our Father's House, I did beadwork. When the hour came to stop, my man came after me so we came. And so I said, 'At Solen all will gather.' So I said, 'We will go and see Elaine.' So we came to the place. She was sitting near a holy man's house. So she cooked for us and fed us. So I said, 'The ghosts loved us and so they pushed us here.' We ate nice.")

Lillian Fast Horse's entire text can be compared to a prereservation realistic line drawing that was first plotted out with points that were then connected with lines.[28] The points are the specific places mentioned in the text, and the lines are drawn through the use of the various verbs of movement. Even a glance at the English text can show the constant repetition of the word *came,* a word which has several distinctly different semantic and cognitive features in Lakota which simply do not translate directly into English.

Lillian begins by situating herself at the tribal office, the starting point which she characterizes in two different ways, as "the beadwork house" and as "Our Father's House," a conventional way of designating an important office connected with the tribal government. The redundant characterization of the starting point which is the center of tribal government, and therefore a power-filled place, is continued through her use of demonstratives. A translation of her first Lakota words reads as follows: "Today, there [at] the Our Father's House, at that place, the beadwork house, there, I repaired beadwork." Lillian not only delineates space clearly, but she also describes a particular point in time when the action central to her narrative begins. "And now, the hour for stopping, at that time. . . ." At that time her husband comes for her. The verb describing the husband's arrival is *hi,* meaning "arrival at a place not one's own." In this context the semantic feature of direction relates to the cognitive feature of spatial value so that the nature of the starting point colors the entire episode. The redundant characterization of the tribal office, the starting point, is a stylistic manifestation of the cognitive feature's significance.

The Fast Horses' presence at a place that is not their own is immediately contrasted with their beginning the trip to their own home. The verb used is *ũglitʃupi,* which means specifically "to start to come home" with the fact mentioned at home. This detail may well have particular significance. Another

(Lakota) woman whom I asked to comment on the text remarked that the verb should have been *ũkijaglapi* because Lillian was at my house rather than at home when presenting the text.[29] To quote the second informant, "*ũkijaglapi* would be more like it. She doesn't live where she is." Lillian Fast Horse may have been confused, but it is unlikely, because she took considerable time with the text and worked carefully with it in order to use it to teach me about the language. A plausible explanation for the verb is that when she wrote the text she was in a place where she *felt at home*. My second informant agreed that the verb could be a way of stating a compliment. If the explanation is correct, then the location feature of the verb has the cognitive significance suggesting a homelike quality to her presence in my house.

The text never does narrate arrival at the Fast Horses' own home. That action is interrupted by Lillian's suggestion that they go to Solen, a small town fifteen miles from their home, because she believes that there will be an important meeting there. Lillian's English version of traveling to Solen appears repetitive. "So we came and came to Solen." The Lakota version, though, has two different verbs, both of which translate into the English *came*. The first Lakota verb is general in reference (*u*), commenting only on the fact of movement. The next refers to their arrival at their chosen goal. The use of the first verb accents the process of coming, and possibly it also suggests some slight suspense, since there remains the possibility of a second change in plans. The verb has the cognitive feature of ambiguity. The thematic structure of the entire text could have guided this particular lexical choice, for Lillian's purpose is to show how their course of action was deflected by spirits who "pushed" or carried them to my house.

Upon arrival at Solen, the Fast Horses discover that they have been mistaken about the meeting date, so they decide to visit me. The act of moving to my place is the subject of an entire sentence: "So we came to the place" [Tʃãke ekta ũhipi]. The basic form of the verb is once again *hi* 'arrival at a place not one's own'. Like the first use of the verb, which initiated the action of the episode, this one also suggests that the nature of the space that is the point of arrival bestows a particular value on the action of coming to that place. This cognitive feature could help explain why the description of my house is more stylized in English than in Lakota. For some reason Mrs. Fast Horse felt compelled to add to the force of the English version, and part of the compulsion could be due to the weaker force of the English verb of movement so that in order to convey the importance of arrival she commented on the fact that I lived near a church: "She was sitting near a holy man's house." That entire sentence is absent in the Lakota version.

Only then, after carefully characterizing all of her specific points, does Lillian come to the folk saying which was all that I had asked her to write down in the first place: "Wanagi te ũglilapi tʃa pajekjel ũa'kaupi" ("The ghosts loved us so they pushed us here''). The Lakota verb for ''pushed'' has more the sense of being carried and implies even less human responsibility for the action than does the English verb. All of Lillian's careful structuring of movement was a gratuitous explanation of why people could believe that spirits would deflect them from one course of action and lead them to some unexpected and unplanned goal. The entire text shows the spontaneous operation of the structuring force and metaphoric potential that Lakota verbs of movement once possessed because of their intimate relation to the social order. Careful analysis of verbs of movement in traditional texts (analysis that takes into account all formalized performance conditions) shows that culturally related cognitive features manifest thematic structures in texts derived from the structure of relationships among performer, audience, and social structure.

The cognitive features noted in the example derive from knowledge attained within a framework of a specific kind of social action that is no longer consciously planned. Once that social action shared in the shaping of both external and internal reality, and various narrative genres could serve to functionalize the phenomenal qualities of the cosmology. The aura with which places were invested, the distinctions they conferred, were cultural conventions affecting both language and culture. Today these conventions deriving from the old social order and the functioning of these conventions can be observed and described in texts collected under the kinds of field-work conditions where all participants are behaving naturally and spontaneously and where all the performance conditions have been carefully noted.

The cognitive features related to the Lakota verbs of movement constitute what Melville Herskovits has called a ''cultural focus.''[30] A cultural focus encompasses values so central to the culture that they affect the direction of culture change. ''Where a culture is under pressure by a dominant group who seek to induce acceptance of its traditions, elements lying in the focal area will be retained longer than those outside it, though in this case retention will of necessity be manifested by syncretisms and in reinterpretations.'' Gradually, what were once reinterpretations of an older structure tend to become interpretations based on the current social order. Lakota people like the Fast Horses still maintain the older world view with its cultural focus of spatial categories and values. They express these categories and values, though, in modern terms. Their grandchildren tend to accept the modern terms and interpret them within a framework of contemporary American culture. This is not to say that the grandchildren reject their Indian identity. On the contrary, they are very articulate about what they perceive to be Indian values, but their cognitive framework differs from that of their grandparents.

The cognitive distinctive features of semantic fields that are central to the world view also form what contemporary scholars describe as a cultural deep structure that guides the direction of cultural change in various aspects of cultural life.[31] The cognitive distinctive features label what is particular about a culture and its world view. When these features change, the culture is significantly altered. The semantic distinctive features, on the other hand, label universal categories that are amenable to some kind of linguistic translation even though the features of one language do not reflect a direct match with those of the other.

The present social structure, formal educational system, and the mass media all militate against the continuation of the kinds of cognitive distinctive features that Lillian Fast Horse's tradition-oriented text illustrate. No doubt some people still attach particular cultural meanings to the verbs of movement, and these people are the most traditional of the Lakota. It seems unlikely, however, that the cultural meanings related to these verbs will persist in the contemporary world. If the verbs of movement lose all of the cognitive distinctive features that related them to the basic structures of Lakota culture, will the semantic distinctive features persist indefinitely? The history of languages would suggest that the Lakota way of marking direction, location, and stage of completion of movements will change in the direction of greater isomorphism with the English system. But such change has not yet occurred to any great extent. Part of the reason why it has not yet occurred is that the Lakota people perceive their language as their major tie to the past and as the emblem of their national identity. They take great care to continue to teach its major distinctions from English. Contemporary nationalism is a force that attempts to stall language change. How successful the attempt will be remains a task for future fieldworkers to examine.

For the present, the verbs of movement remain a semantic field that can serve to focus discussion about the directions of language change and of cultural change because the presence or absence of their cognitive distinctive features related to the traditional Lakota world view manifests the presence or the absence of one set of traditional interpretive structures.[32]

NOTES

1. See Florence and Charles Vogelin, "Genetic Classification of North American Indian Languages," *Indians of North America* (Chicago: University of Chicago Press, 1970), pp. 43–46.

2. This information is taken from an unpublished paper by David Rood, Linguistics Department, University of Colorado, Boulder, 1976.

3. The only book-length biography of Ella Deloria is Janette K. Murray, "Ella Deloria: A Biographical Sketch and Literary Analysis" (Ph.D. diss., University of North Dakota, 1974).

4. Alice Fletcher and Francis La Flesche, *The Omaha Tribe* (Lincoln: University

of Nebraska Press, 1972), p. 134 (originally published as U.S. Bureau of American Ethnology, *Twenty-Seventh Annual Report* [Washington, D.C.: Government Printing Office, 1911]).

5. Alice Fletcher, "Indian Ceremonies," *Peabody Museum of Ethnology and Archeology Report* 16 (1884): 276.

6. Ella Deloria, "Dakota Commentary on Walker's Texts," American Philosophical Society Library of Manuscripts, pp. 28–31.

7. In this context, spatial categories are not linguistic categories. Rather, they indicate emic cultural distinctions with each category distinguished by particular patterns and types of movement that make life in each category productive.

8. Personal interview with Joseph Flying By, a Standing Rock Sioux, in 1972.

9. J. R. Walker, "The Sun Dance and Other Ceremonies of the Oglala Division of the Teton Dakota," *Anthropological Papers of the American Museum of Natural History* 16 (1917): 61.

10. Almost every work on Sioux religion mentions directional symbolism. One reliable source is John G. Neihardt, *Black Elk Speaks* (Lincoln: University of Nebraska Press, 1961), p. 2. On ceremonial movement, see Joseph Brown, *The Sacred Pipe* (Norman: University of Oklahoma Press, 1953), p. 5.

11. See Raymond DeMallie, "Teton Dakota Kinship and Social Organization" (Ph.D. diss., University of Chicago, 1971).

12. Joseph Brown has elaborated on the importance of the tipi as a cosmos in miniature. "Since for every Sioux, every tipi is the world in an image, the fire at the center represents Wakan-Tanka within the world" (*The Sacred Pipe,* p. 23).

13. Neihardt, *Black Elk Speaks,* pp. 203–4.

14. Madeline Mathiot, *An Approach to the Cognitive Structure of Language* (Bloomington: Indiana University Press, 1968).

15. Ibid., pp. 5–6.

16. Franz Boas, "Some Traits of the Dakota Language," *Race, Language and Culture* (Toronto: Collier-Macmillan, 1940), p. 230.

17. Ella Deloria, "Notes on the Dakota, Teton Dialect," *International Journal of American Linguistics* 8 (1933): 97–121.

18. Eugene Buechel, *A Grammar of Lakota* (Rosebud, S. Dak.: Saint Francis Mission, 1936), pp. 165–67.

19. These data were taken from my own field work notes. The informants are Ann Keller, sixty years old, Rosebud Sioux, and Alfred Menard, approximately thirty years old, Rosebud Sioux.

20. Ella Deloria, "Teton Myths," American Philosophical Society Library of Manuscripts, pp. 10, 102–28. Ella Deloria, *Dakota Texts* (New York: G. E. Stechert, 1932), p. 100.

21. Deloria, "Teton Myths," p. 133.

22. Deloria, *Dakota Texts,* p. 203.

23. Boas, "Some Traits of the Dakota Language," p. 229.

24. Deloria, "Teton Myths," p. 1. See also Eugene Buechel, *Lakota-English Dictionary* (Pine Ridge, S. Dak.: Holy Rosary Mission, 1970).

25. Mathiot, *Approach to Cognitive Structure,* pp. 16, 62.

26. My emphasis on performance variables is a departure from Mathiot's specific focus. For a comparable approach, see Jurgen Habermas, "Towards a Theory of

Communicative Competence,'' *Inquiry* 13 (Winter 1970): 360–75. Habermas refers to dialogue-constitutive universals which establish the form of intersubjectivity between any competent speakers capable of mutual understanding. ''The classification of semantic fields is predetermined by the question of how far the net of intersubjectivity must be spread in order to stabilize the identity of the individuals as well as the social group in a given culture or subculture at a given time. The structural differences between the animistic, the mythical, the religious, the philosophical, and the scientistic views of life lie clearly in this dimension'' (p. 373).

See also the approach taken by Teunis A. Van Dijik, who says of the pragmatic component that it ''formulates the regularities underlying the relations between literary texts, structures, and their users. It is therefore concerned mainly with the general abstract conditions defining the appropriate use of literary texts or their elements in literary communication. Performance features form one component of the pragmatic branch of linguistics'' (*Some Aspects of Text Grammars: A Study in Theoretical Linguistics and Poetics* [The Hague: Mouton, 1972], p. 172).

27. DeMallie, ''Teton Dakota Kinship,'' p. 110.

28. Oscar Howe, a Sioux artist, has written about the point-to-point movement in Sioux art. ''Though the line visually dominates other characteristics in a painting, its function and movement depend entirely on aesthetic points. 'Owa' not only means drawing-painting, but also means writing with a point-to-point movement always aesthetic or kinesthetic'' (''Theories and Beliefs—Dakota,'' *The American Indian Speaks,* ed. John Milton [Vermillion: University of South Dakota Press, 1969], p. 69).

29. The woman is Mrs. Anne Keller, a Rosebud Sioux, currently living in Lincoln, Nebraska.

30. Melville J. Herskovits, ''Problem Method and Theory in Afro-American Studies,'' *The New World Negro: Selected Papers in Afroamerican Studies,* ed. Frances S. Herskovits (Bloomington: Indiana University Press, 1966), p. 59.

31. Because myth dramatizes the cognitive distinctive features of semantic fields with particular clarity, most studies of cultural deep structure concentrate on myth as the major genre. Pierre Maranda's comments on the way myths manifest a culture's deep structure correspond with my views of how genres other than myths can also describe the structure if the genre's performance conditions are correctly related to the formal characteristics of the text. ''Myths display the structured, predominantly culture-specific and shared semantic systems which enable the members of a culture area to understand each other and to cope with the unknown. More strictly, myths are stylistically definable discourses that express the strong components of semantic systems'' (*Mythology* [New York: Penguin Books, 1972], pp. 12–13).

Dell Hymes's approach to genre classification and interpretation also corresponds to mine. ''One assumes that persons growing up in the community in question acquire a grasp of the structures and functions of the genre, such that they are able to judge instances as appropriate or inappropriate not only in terms of overt formal features ('surface structure'), but also in terms of underlying relations ('deep structure')'' (''The 'Wife' Who 'Goes Out' Like a Man: Reinterpretation of a Clackamas Chinook Myth,'' *Social Science Information,* 7 no. 3 (1967): 173–99.

32. The entire approach suggested in this paper tests the Sapir-Whorf hypothesis, but I do not presume to comment on the nature of any determinism between language and culture. My data suggest that the relationship is a dialectical one.

Language Attitudes of Mexican-American Adolescents in Two Midwestern Cities

EILEEN M. BRENNAN, MIGUEL A. CARRANZA,
AND ELLEN B. RYAN

Both indirect and direct measurement methods have been profitably used within the field of sociolinguistics to investigate language attitudes. Generally researchers have employed the methods to compare attitudes toward different languages or varieties of the same language. By means of direct measures, the present study investigated relationships between the language background, language attitudes, and other cultural attitudes of Mexican-American adolescents.

W. E. Lambert reported several pioneering studies using indirect measurement in which persons were asked to react to tape recordings of readings in different languages or language varieties.[1] Unknown to the subjects, the recordings were prepared by the same reader who produced the "matched guise" stimuli. By the use of the matched guise and similar procedures, investigators were able to elicit biased attitudes toward French-Canadian speech compared with English-Canadian speech, Black English with standard American English, French-accented Canadian English with standard Canadian English, and regional dialects of British English with received pronunciation.[2] In all cases, the standard language variety was accorded more favorable reactions.

In an extension of Giles' technique, M. A. Carranza and E. B. Ryan employed tape recordings produced by a variety of readers and also obtained more favorable reactions to readers using English (which was the standard in the geographical area of the study population) than to readers using Spanish. In a follow-up study by the same investigators, persons speaking Mexican-American accented English were rated less favorably on status than those speaking standard English.[3]

Following Ryan and Carranza's line of inquiry, E. M. and J. S. Brennan found that the degree of downgrading of a Mexican-American speaker's status was dependent on the level of accentedness present in his speech. In order to determine the level of accent of the readers, a panel of linguists made detailed analyses of the speech produced by each.[4] It should be noted that the linguists' assessments of accent significantly agreed with ratings given by linguistically naïve adolescents tested in the same study.

In contrast with the number of studies employing indirect methods to explore language attitudes, very few investigations have utilized direct methods, which involve questioning subjects about their attitudes toward different speech varieties. R. L. Cooper and Joshua A. Fishman, and William Labov are among the few researchers who have successfully employed direct methods in combination with other methods to investigate language attitudes.[5]

Ryan and Carranza have employed direct attitude measurements with Mexican-American adolescents in order to assess their attitudes toward speech varieties and some associated values.[6] The investigators argued that language prestige and language loyalty were both heavily influenced by value systems. In fact Ryan and Carranza asserted that if speakers were to maintain a language variety less prestigious than the standard, they must associate that variety with values that its speakers feel are useful and with which they identify.

Therefore, they developed an instrument to delve into the language background, language attitudes, and other cultural attitudes of Mexican-American adolescents. Young Mexican Americans are at a particularly critical point in their development of attitudes toward language since they are exposed to conflicting sets of norms and values in the home and educational settings and are preparing to enter the world of work.

Ryan and Carranza employed thirty-six female and twenty-two male subjects from a large Catholic high school in Chicago. The students completed a questionnaire dealing with language background (family language and language dominance), language attitudes (language preference, attitude toward bilingualism, and accentedness as a handicap), and other cultural attitudes (cultural allegiance, anomie, and authoritarianism).[7] Additionally, respondents were taped reading an English passage. The readings were rated for accentedness on a seven-point scale by twenty-eight college students who were native speakers of English.

Results of the investigation revealed that the subjects had Spanish as their family language, were positively disposed toward bilingualism, and had a cultural allegiance to Mexico over the United States but were nevertheless English-dominant and slightly preferred English to Spanish. Accentedness and the other language background measures were found to be significantly intercorrelated, but few relationships were found among the attitudinal measures. The only measure significantly related to language background measures was language preference, which correlated positively with accentedness, language dominance, and family language.

As an extension of the Ryan and Carranza investigation, the present study attempted to examine the relationships between accentedness, language background, language attitudes, and other cultural attitudes for adolescents in a different speech community. Specifically, another midwestern site, Kansas City, Kansas, was chosen in order to study the relationships in a setting with a far smaller Mexican-American population and with far fewer people of foreign stock in general in the population.[8] Additionally, the relationship of language fluency to the other variables was investigated, since it was expected that dysfluent speakers would have different language backgrounds and hold different attitudes from fluent speakers.

For the present investigation, twenty-seven males of Mexican descent served as paid subjects. The adolescents all attended the same Catholic high school in Kansas City and reported some knowledge of Spanish. While all of the subjects were born in the United States, twenty-three had both parents of Mexican origin. The median level of education for both parents was slightly higher than eighth grade. Considering both parents' education and the father's occupation, the median socioeconomic status of the students was lower middle class. Average grade level of the students was 10.2, and their average age was 15.7 years.

An English passage of 570 words was prepared to be read and tape-recorded by each student in order to obtain data about his accentedness. The test passage included ten or more repetitions of each of eighteen English phonemes known to elicit accented pronunciations from Mexican-American speakers.[9]

Based on the work of Ryan and Carranza, a three-part questionnaire, including 108 items, was also prepared. The first section of the questionnaire included 15 items designed to produce a demographic description of each student in terms of his age, education, nationality, and parents' education and occupation. In the second part of the instrument, language background items were used to investigate family language and language dominance. The final section of the instrument included several attitudinal scales. One set of scales was constructed to examine language attitudes and investigated language preference, view of accentedness as a handicap, and attitude toward bilingualism. The other set of attitude scales included items on other cultural attitudes, namely cultural allegiance, anomie, and authoritarianism.

Each of the twenty-seven readers was tape-recorded in an individual session as he read the standard passage. Next, each student completed the questionnaire immediately following the taping. The experimenter gave oral instructions about the purpose of the questionnaire and answered questions about the content and directions. The students were given as much time as they wished (usually half an hour) to complete the instrument and were free to ask any further questions as they arose.

Following the recording sessions the taped readings were played for three expert linguists who were trained in both Spanish and American-English phonology. The linguists listened to a recording of each student reading the same 162-word excerpt of the 570-word test passage. The excerpt contained at least three opportunities for each of the eighteen accented pronunciations to occur.

Ratings of overall judgments of accentedness and of fluency were made independently by each linguist and were recorded on separate seven-point scales for each reader. The accentedness scale ranged from 1 = no Spanish accent to 7 = Spanish accent. The twenty-seven readers were found to be moderately accented, since they obtained a mean accentedness score of 3.05 on the seven-point scale. The seven-point fluency scale ranged from 1 = fluent to 7 = dysfluent. In regard to fluency, the linguists rated the readers as moderately fluent, giving them a mean fluency rating of 2.99. The rating task was followed by several other judgment tasks which yielded data for another study.

Overall mean scores on the remaining language background variables and attitudinal measures were also obtained. For each variable, scores were based on a scale from 1 to 5, and *t* tests were calculated to analyze differences between observed means and expected population means.

On six of the eight measures, obtained scores were significantly different from the neutral score of 3.0, with probability levels of 0.05 or less.[10] The language background of the students was found to be English-dominant, although the mean score on family language was midway between Spanish and English. On language attitudes, the students showed a marked preference for English and tended to view accentedness as a handicap, while showing a highly favorable attitude toward bilingualism. As a group, the adolescents maintained cultural allegiance to Mexico and tended to be authoritarian, while not exhibiting significant anomie.

Because of the high level of comparability between the Kansas City subjects and the twenty-two Mexican-American male students tested by Ryan and Carranza in Chicago, a joint analysis was performed on scores obtained from the two groups.[11] *T* tests completed on language background measurements revealed that the Kansas City group was significantly more English-dominant than the Chicago group and that the Chicago subjects were found to have Spanish as a family language more frequently than the Kansas City subjects. Also, the Chicago subjects were rated as more accented than the Kansas City group. On all measurements of attitudes, there were found to be no significant differences between the groups.

Pearson product-moment correlations (*r*) were computed on the scores of the highly English-dominant Kansas City subjects in order to assess the relationship between language background measures and measures of attitude. Language preference was significantly related to three measures of language background, accentedness, language dominance, and family language.[12] Students who tended to have a higher preference for English than Spanish also exhibited lower accentedness, greater English dominance, and more frequently had English as their family language. On the other hand, students who tended to agree that accentedness is a handicap also reported more Spanish dominance and more often had Spanish as their family language.

In testing for relationships between cultural attitudes and language background variables, it as found that anomie was related to degree of accent, with students rated as less accented reporting less anomie. Authoritarianism was found to be related to both level of accentedness and reported family language. Students with a low degree of accent tended to be less authoritarian in their attitudes, and students reporting greater use of English as their family language were also found to be less authoritarian.

Using Pearson's r, intercorrelations were also computed for the six measures of attitude.[13] It was determined that language preference was significantly related to accentedness being viewed as a handicap. Persons tending to prefer English also did not perceive accentedness as a handicap. Cultural allegiance was also significantly related to accentedness being viewed as a handicap. Those students with a greater degree of cultural allegiance to the United States tended not to perceive accentedness as a handicap. Anomie was found to be negatively correlated with cultural allegiance, implying that persons with cultural allegiance to Mexico tended to be less anomic. Finally, authoritarianism and anomie were positively correlated.

To complete the analysis, Pearson's correlations were calculated among the four measures of language background. Language dominance and family language were found to be significantly related ($r = 0.54, p < 0.01$), with students reporting greater English dominance also tending to report greater use of English at home. Fluency and accentedness were moderately correlated ($r = 0.43, p < 0.05$), indicating more highly accented readers were rated as less fluent. All other language background relationships were nonsignificant.

The present investigation provided information about the language background, language attitudes, and other cultural attitudes of a group of Mexican-American adolescent males in Kansas City. The English speech of the subjects was rated by linguists as relatively unaccented and fluent. Analysis of questionnaire responses found the students to be English-dominant, with family language about equally divided between Spanish and English. The students as a group tended to prefer English over Spanish, viewed accentedness as a handicap, and regarded bilingualism as highly favorable. As a whole, the students reported more cultural allegiance to Mexico than to the United States and tended to be authoritarian.

The high level of comparability between the male subjects in Ryan and Carranza's Chicago study and the present sample has been demonstrated. Important demographic characteristics (age, ethnicity, level of education, type of school, and socioeconomic status) have been found to be highly similar. When overall questionnaire responses were compared, the Chicago and Kansas City groups had no significant differences on any of the attitude measures. However, the groups were found to be significantly different on three language background measures. The Kansas City group was more English-dominant, had more use of English as a family language, and was less accented than the Chicago subjects.

Several important relationships found for the Chicago subjects were replicated within the Kansas City group. For both sets of students language preference was found to be related to language dominance and to accentedness. A preference for English, therefore, was connected both to English dominance and to a lower degree of accentedness. Both groups also had significantly related language dominance and family language measures, showing that prevalence of a language at home is related to the dominance of that language for the adolescent.

The differences between relationships found within the Kansas City and within the Chicago groups are perhaps even more provocative than the similarities.

Several relationships between language background and attitudes were found only within the Kansas City group. First, family language was moderately correlated with language preference, suggesting that the use of a language in the home environment may have affected language loyalty in the adolescents.

In a second finding, both language dominance and family language were highly significantly related to level of agreement by the students that accentedness is a handicap. Less English-dominant students and subjects with Spanish as a family language tended to agree that accent handicapped speakers. Additionally, it was found that students who had greater degrees of cultural allegiance to Mexico also tended to have greater agreement that accentedness is a handicap. The finding suggests that in a milieu such as Kansas City, which has less foreign stock than Chicago and presumably less diversity in spoken English, persons with accents are quite noticeable and may face discrimination. Indeed, the Brennans found that both Anglo- and Mexican-American adolescents in Kansas City rated more highly accented speakers as lower in status than persons with less accent. However, it is entirely possible that subjects need to be aware of their own accent, as less English-dominant students with a Spanish home language and greater allegiance to Mexico might be, in order to recognize it as a target for biased evaluations. Unfortunately, the present questionnaire did not include items requiring subjects to rate their own accentedness.

A third major difference between the Kansas City and Chicago groups was that moderate relationships were detected in the former group between accentedness and both anomie and authoritarianism. This indicates that less highly accented subjects felt less isolated and held less rigid standards. Indeed, the less highly accented subjects may face less discrimination from the mainstream society and therefore feel less isolated and less discouraged with their place in society than more accented speakers. Also, as the recipients of less biased evaluations, the less accented students may have developed more flexible and democratic ideologies themselves.

Finally, only within the Kansas City group was family language significantly related to authoritarianism. Students with greater use of English as a family language tended to be less authoritarian. Perhaps the greater openness to diversity exhibited by those with English as a family language is affected by their wider access to opportunity within the Kansas City community. In any case, a more intensive study of language attitudes, language usage, and access to opportunity at various midwestern sites seems warranted.

The next set of comparisons of patterns of intercorrelations within the two subject groups dealt with attitude measures. Only the Kansas City group had a significant correlation between language preference and view of accentedness as handicap. That is, the more the subjects preferred English, the more they did not perceive accentedness as being a handicap. Anomie was found to be related both to authoritarianism and to cultural allegiance for the Kansas City students. Therefore, the greater their feeling of isolation, the greater the rigidity of their standards. On the other hand the greater their cultural allegiance to Mexico, the less their anomie. This relationship suggests that those subjects with greater awareness of their cultural roots felt less isolated and normless.

The Chicago students held two sets of attitude relationships not found in Kansas City: cultural allegiance was related to attitude toward bilingualism, and language preference was linked with authoritarianism. The Chicago students with greater cultural allegiance to Mexico favored bilingualism more highly. Also, the students who preferred Spanish had high authoritarianism scores.

Finally, the Chicago group differed from the Kansas City subjects on only one relationship among language background measures: within the Chicago group language dominance was highly correlated with accentedness. However, the Kansas City subjects had significantly less accent and were much more English-dominant than the Chicago subjects, restricting the range of variability.

Counter to the investigators' speculation, fluency was related to only one other measure, accentedness. One interpretation of the finding is that an additional variable, the degree of familiarity with a language, influences both accentedness and fluency. Future research may enable researchers to clarify the relationship among the three variables.

As a whole, the findings of the present investigation have demonstrated the usefulness of Ryan and Carranza's questionnaire for uncovering relationships among language background, language attitudes, and cultural attitudes.[14] The instrument, especially with additional questions probing the components of preference (affective, communicative, instrumental, and integrative) suggested by Carranza may be most valuable for assessing the attitudinal impact of bilingual-bicultural education and of human relations programs.[15]

NOTES

The present study was supported by a grant from the National Institute of Health, NICHD-06921. This paper is a revised version of one presented at the annual meeting of the Midwest Sociological Society, Minneapolis, April 1979.

1. W. E. Lambert, "The Social Psychology of Bilingualism," *Journal of Social Issues* 23 (1967): 91–109.

2. On French-Canadian: W. E. Lambert, R. C. Hodgson, R. C. Gardner, and Samuel Fillenbaum, "Evaluational Reactions to Spoken Languages," *Journal of Abnormal and Social Psychology* 60 (1960): 44–51; on Black English: G. R. Tucker and W. E. Lambert, "White and Negro Listeners' Reactions to Various American-English Dialects," *Social Forces* 47 (1969): 463–68; on French-accented Canadian English: Alison d'Anglejan and G. R. Tucker, "Sociolinguistic Correlates of Speech Style in Quebec," in *Language Attitudes: Current Trends and Prospects,* ed. Roger W. Shuy and Roger W. Fasold (Washington, D.C.: Georgetown University Press, 1973), pp. 1–27.

3. Miguel A. Carranza and Ellen B. Ryan, "Evaluative Reactions of Bilingual Anglo- and Mexican-American Adolescents toward Speakers of English and Spanish," *International Journal of the Sociology of Language* 6 (1975): 83–104; Ellen B. Ryan and Miguel A. Carranza, "Evaluative Reactions of Adolescents toward Speakers of Standard English and Mexican-American Accented English," *Journal of Personality and Social Psychology* 31 (1975): 855–63.

4. Eileen M. Brennan and J. S. Brennan, "Language Attitudes Toward Mexican-American Speech" (Paper presented at Midwest Sociological Society, Omaha, April 1978); "Measurements of Accent and Attitude Toward Mexican-American Speech" (Paper presented at the Ninth World Congress of Sociology, Uppsala, Sweden, August 1978).

5. Robert L. Cooper and Joshua A. Fishman, "A Study of Language Attitudes," in *The Spread of English,* ed. Joshua A. Fishman, R. L. Cooper, and A. W. Conrad (Rowley, Mass.: Newbury House, 1977), pp. 239–76; William Labov, *The Social Stratification of English in New York City* (Arlington, Va.: Center for Applied Linguistics, 1966).

6. Ellen B. Ryan and Miguel A. Carranza, "Language Attitudes and Other Cultural Attitudes of Bilingual Mexican American Adolescents," *Ethnicity,* forthcoming.

7. Items addressing anomie (feelings of isolation and personal dissatisfaction) and authoritarianism (rigidity, antidemocratic ideology) were included to extend to Mexican-American subjects from the work begun by R. C. Gardner and W. E. Lambert (*Attitudes and Motivation in Second Language Acquisition* [Rowley, Mass.: Newbury House, 1972]). In their study of second-language learning, Gardner and Lambert employed an anomie scale to detect whether knowing two languages produces a feeling of being lost between two cultures. They also investigated authoritarianism, since it was argued that bilingualism may provide a liberalizing influence.

8. U.S. Bureau of the Census, *County and City Data Book* (1977), pp. 548, 558, 648, 660, 696.

9. Jacob Ornstein, "Sociolinguistic Research on Language Diversity in the American Southwest and its Educational Implications," *Modern Language Journal* 55 (1971): 223–29.

10. A probability level of 0.05 or less can be interpreted to mean that the result obtained would appear by chance alone less than 5 times in 100 such studies. Similarly for $p < 0.01$, the result would appear by chance less than 1 time in 100; for $p < 0.001$, less than 1 time in 1,000.

The specific tables dealing with the analysis referred to in this chapter have not been included. Those wishing to obtain copies of these tables may write to Miguel A. Carranza, Department of Sociology, University of Nebraska, Lincoln, Nebraska 68588.

11. The table is available from Miguel A. Carranza; see note 10 above.

12. The table is available from M. A. Carranza; see note 10 above.

13. The table is available from M. A. Carranza; see note 10 above.

14. See note 6.

15. Miguel A. Carranza, "Language Attitudes and Other Cultural Attitudes of Mexican-American Adults: Some Sociolinguistic Implications" (Ph.D. diss., University of Notre Dame, 1977).

The English Spoken by German Americans in Central Texas

JOSEPH WILSON

In previous articles, I have written about the German spoken in the German communities in Texas around the cities of La Grange (Fayette County) and Giddings (Lee County).[1] This area is the more easterly of the two major focal points of the large German population of Texas; the other is in the west-central part of the state around New Braunfels and Fredericksburg.[2] The Lee-Fayette settlements are especially interesting because they are composed to a great extent of German Wends (Sorbs)—indeed, they are the only Wendish-German immigrant colonies in the Western Hemisphere. The area has thus been basically trilingual in Wendish (a conservative Slavic tongue still spoken by about one hundred thousand people in East Germany), German, and English.[3] A generation ago there were many older people living who were natively fluent in all three of these relatively different languages, but these people have now nearly all died out.

From the beginnings of these settlements (in the 1850s), the Wends merged with the other Germans and gradually gave up Wendish in favor of the dominant German language. In a sense they became the most German of them all and then clung tenaciously to German in the inevitably doomed struggle against English. Today German is still spoken by thousands of people in this area, but it is no longer the language of the schools and newspapers. Therefore the children are now being raised in English, making it only a question of time until the use of German will be completely gone (approximately six churches in the area still have services in German, but no longer every Sunday). The German spoken is a modified High German, much like other forms of American German (with reduction of cases, unrounding of umlauts [that is, *ö* and *ü* pronounced as *e* and *i*, respectively], and many anglicisms), but it does have its own few regional peculiarities, such as a slight East Middle German (Saxon-Silesian) coloration, since the Wends and most of the other Germans of this area came from Saxony.

The purpose of this paper is to discuss the English currently spoken by these German Americans, who are now three or four generations removed from the original immigrants (but only one generation removed from the predominance of the German language).[4] It should be stressed at the outset that these people pride themselves on being Americans and Texans. They probably would object to being called "German Americans"; they call themselves alternately Americans and Germans, that is, "Americans of German ancestry." They take their German background rather for granted, not boastful of it but certainly not ashamed of it. Very few of them have ever been to Germany or know anything about their ancestral homeland, and very few have any correspondence with relatives there. Even as long ago as the First World War, there was never any question of their allegiance to America. Their English is comparatively quite excellent, especially considering that only thirty or forty years ago their world—church life, weddings, newspapers, school, and plays—was predominantly German.[5] Obviously there are generational and individual differences, depending on the extent of usage of German and, conversely, on the length and degree of exposure to standard English. Many older people (over approximately sixty years of age) speak with a general German accent (with distinct chopping of the words), the most noticeable single feature of which is usually the trilled *r* (or perhaps, glaring by its omission, the lack of a Texas drawl).[6] The younger people usually do not have a German accent, but they still use many of the germanized constructions listed here, unaware that these are not standard English. Because these German Americans have very strong family and religious bonds, they tend to intermarry, continue in the same church groups and church-affiliated social organizations, and send their children to church-run schools, so that their slightly germanized English tends to perpetuate itself.[7] Since the teachers in the schools are also from the same stock, even the English instruction given—although in general very good—is nonnative and passes on the same minor flaws.

Most of the pronunciation influences, such as the trilled *r,* are typical of the accent many German speakers have, but some are peculiar to this particular area. The most striking of the latter type is the use of *w* where English has *v,* as in *wery* (for *very*), *wegetables, Welma,* and elsewhere, quite the opposite of the usual German substitution of *v* for *w.*[8] The reason for this is that in this area the German *w* (as in *wissen* and *wohnen*) is pronounced much like English *w,* evidently a Middle German regionalism. The English short *u* [ʌ] apparently was difficult, so that *putty, lucky, pulse,* and *rosebud* were pronounced with the vowel of *put* and *look.* Some people had trouble with initial English *ch* and pronounced it as *sh* (*shicken, shair*). Like most Germans, they had a tendency to unvoice final *b, d,* and *g* (that is, to *p, t, k*), but this never seemed very noticeable to me, except in a few individual words, such as *kits* for *kids.* The omission of *g* in words like *single* and *finger* (that is, pronouncing the latter to rhyme with *singer*) is also shared with other Germans. The lack of phonetic consistency in English spelling (for example, *finger* versus *singer, put* versus *putty*) certainly doesn't make it any easier for the nonnative to learn the spoken distinctions. The misleading spelling is doubtlessly a major factor in such mispronunciations as *worms* with the vowel of *forest,* and *wonder* (at times) as *wander* (the latter mistake is reinforced by the occurrence of the impure rhyme of *ponder* and *yonder* with *wonder* in well-known hymns). Similarly, unaccented vowels which are indistinct (schwa) in English, as in *beautiful, bountiful* (common words in hymns, sermons, and prayers) and *uniform* are given a hypercorrect fullness (like *byoo-tee-full*). Along the same line of overpronunciation because of the spelling is the sounding of the *l* in *salve* and of the *th* in *months* and *clothes,* where it normally is silent, and in *Thompson,* where it is normally pronounced as *t*.

Perhaps the most commonly and tenaciously overpronounced word is *aunt,* which was (and is) regularly spoken as if written *ahnt,* as many dictionaries and schoolteachers prefer, but which is as completely out of place in colloquial Texas surroundings as *tomahtoes* would be. Another hypercorrect pronunciation is *manor* as *mayner;* undoubtedly a desire to avoid confusion with *manner* is involved here. The tendency toward hypercorrect pronunciation is naturally increased upon ascension into the pulpit to deliver a sermon, but the only word I have noticed in widespread use with its own special pulpit pronunciation is *Gawd* for *God* (and this is probably not limited to German Americans). The younger ministers nowadays, with their more natural speaking style, seem happily to have given that pronunciation up.

Other mispronunciations I have noticed, but which are probably not so common, are *pedal* as *paddle, nests* as *nestes, Edith's* as *Edithes, food* rhyming with *good,* and *aluminum* as *alunium*.

Some place-names have a Germanized pronunciation in German (*Austin* as *Owsteen, Smithville* as *Schmidtville, San Antonio* as *Sankt Anton*[*io*], and others), but these—being obviously German—generally don't carry over into English. It does happen in a few cases where the germanization has gone unnoticed, as in *-burg* (as in *Schulenburg*) as *-boork* and *Beaumont* with the accent on the second syllable.

Passing from pronunciation to constructions (morphology and syntax), hypercorrectness again plays a large role, especially since the hypercorrect usage in English often agrees with the normal construction in German, so that the two major influences towards unidiomatic English coincide, as when the German-American says *Whom did you see?* and *With whom are you going?* And, as in the case of many other Americans trying to talk correctly, sometimes things as bad as *just like I* and *nobody but we* come out.

Most unidiomatic English constructions are naturally a direct reflection of the German usage, as in the case of the very common indirect discourse imperative construction, as in *She said I should be quiet* for "She told me to be quiet."[9] The lack of German distinction between *either* and *any* and between *neither* and *none* naturally influences the English usage, so that in answer to the question *Which one of those (five) dresses do you want?* a person may be startled to hear *Neither one of them* or *I don't want either one of them*. A similar lack of distinction yields the common phrase *Everyone wants something else* meaning "Everyone wants something different."

The German employment of the present tense for a currently continuing situation begun in the past (where English uses the present perfect) results in the frequently heard type *How long are you in Houston now?* or *They are married twenty years*. A similar German employment of the present gives sentences like *This is the first time I'm seeing you* (or *I see you*) *for a long time,* and *This is the first time I'm eating Greek food.* The most noticeable tense discrepancy, however, is the very common *didn't yet* construction, as in *Did you do what I told you? / No, I didn't yet, but I will,* and sentences like *Did she have her baby yet?* (In all fairness, I have to admit that it seems that many native speakers of English are making these same mistakes more and more frequently, apparently often no longer feeling the antithesis between the English simple past verb form and verbs of continuation into the present.)

As in German *by* (*bei*) with the verbal noun means "while" or "during" the activity, as in *I'll sew on that button by driving,* meaning "while driving" or "while we drive."

Another direct Germanism, which is still very much alive today, is the usage such as *We were three* for "There were three of us." Similarly, one hears *How many are we?* for "How many are there of us?" and the answer *We are twelve,* as well as *We were thirteen ladies at the shower*. In these constructions, contrary to the general brevity of English, the English idiom is more cumbersome than the German, so the germanized forms are very widely used. Another abbreviated English construction borrowed from the German is the omission of the expletive *There* when not initial, as in *Next Friday is a wedding at our church*.

Germanisms in the sequence of tenses in indirect speech are very common, as in *She told me she's coming* (for *she was coming*) *to the party, but she wasn't there; He came over and said his wife is* (for *was*) *very sick*. Another problem of verb usage is the idiomatic English distinction between the past subjunctive and the conditional, which are essentially synonymous in German, as in the distinction between *if I knew that* and *if I would know that*. The German speaker tends to use the conditional for both, yielding such unidiomatic sentences as *If she would be any fatter, she couldn't get through the door,* and *if I wouldn't know you so well, I would think you're serious.*

German prepositional usage is reflected in the common phrases *What are you laughing?* (that is, *at*); *He didn't have anything to talk* (that is, *about*); *She was operated* (that is, *on*), which can be extended to *She was operated on cancer,* meaning "operated on for cancer," and similarly, *She died on* (for *of*) *cancer. At the meeting, at the wedding,* are commonly *on the meeting, on the wedding. Come by daddy* means "Come to daddy." *She stayed* (or *went*) *herself* is used for "by herself," that is, "alone." *She's a sister to Mrs. Fehrle* means "a sister of Mrs. Fehrle" or "Mrs. Fehrle's sister" (reflecting the local German *eine Schwester zu Frau Fehrle*). Another germanism of filial relationship is *He doesn't have a mother,* meaning "His mother is no longer living."

The elliptical usage of proper names (given names or surnames) usually differs slightly from normal English (and is again sometimes actually handier): *We're going to Kriegels* means "to the Kriegels'" ("to the [house of the] Kriegel family"); *We're going with Kriegels* means "with the Kriegels." Similarly, *Alfred's* (used only with the man's name) means "Alfred and his wife" or "Alfred and his family" (*We're going to* [or *with*] *Alfred's; Alfred's are coming, too*). Conversely, where English says *to Alfred's* or *at Alfred's,* meaning to or at his house, the German American says *to Alfred* or *at Alfred* (the two types obviously often merging in meaning).[10] Another common construction is the type *Alfred's Esther,* meaning "Esther, the wife of Alfred" (as opposed to *William's Esther*).

Reflections of the German relative pronoun or adverb usage are seen in such phrases as *That's all what's to it,* meaning "That's all there is to it, that's final"; *That's all what I know* for "That's all I know"; *the one what I saw; everywhere where (for that) we went.*

The German spoken in the area has a strong propensity to drop the definite and indefinite articles in many phrases, especially prepositional phrases, and a similar omission occurs in certain English usages, as in *That was long time ago; They're coming end of August; at quarter to nine; It costs dollar twenty-five.* This dropping is, however, not used nearly so much in their English as in their German; thus the very common regional omission of the article in the German phrases of location *in Küche, auf Gallery, in Esszimmer* ("in [the] kitchen, on [the] porch, in [the] dining room") is not extended into English.

Since German regularly considers it superfluous to specify ownership in such structures as *He put the* (for *his*) *hand in the* (for *his*) *pocket,* we are not surprised to hear such things in the people's English, as in *She walked out with the baby on the arm.*

It's stopping to rain means, of course, "It's stopping raining" (or, as would probably normally be said in standard English, in order to avoid the double *-ing* "The rain is stopping"), again a direct translation of the German. A combination of two synonymous English phrases seems to be the basis for such statements as *We'll be there in a week from today,* instead of *in a week* or *a week from today.* A confusion of two equivalent phrases can also occur, as in *He does that kind of work on the sideline* from *on the side* and *as a sideline.*

The only influence of the German gender system (which confers masculine or feminine gender on such things as chairs and carrots) on this English is that animals of indistinct sex, which would be referred to as *it* in English, are often given the *he* or *she* they would receive in German: thus a cat is normally referred to as *she* (*She's hungry, give her something to eat*) and a dog as *he,* unless very specifically a male cat or a female dog is meant. This perspective on dogs and cats is not so strange from the English point of view, but it is surprising to hear wasps, snakes, and squirrels referred to as *she* (the local German term for *squirrel* being *Eichkatze,* feminine, as opposed to the more standard German word *Eichhörnchen,* which is neuter). My father-in-law tells a story about being with a non-German acquaintance when they came upon a snake; my father-in-law struck the snake with a stick and said, "I killed her," whereupon the other man asked, "How can you tell that snake is a *her?*" Such humorous misunderstandings must have been very common.

In a number of everyday words the divergent singular or plural usage of German has become affixed to the English word (even though a conflict of forms then comes about in English), so that one commonly hears *a scissors, a pliers, that grapes* (German *Wein*), *that weeds* (*Unkraut*), and even, evidently as an extension of the same usage, *that peas,* although the German word here would be plural, like the English (however, the German word, *Erbsen,* is not used, even when speaking German). Conversely, hair is often referred to as if plural (like German *Haare*): *those hair,* and similarly sometimes *those spaghetti. Those cotton* is a special case, diverging from both English and standard German (which would use *Baumwolle,* singular, which is understood but not commonly used in this area); the reason is that the English word *cotton* sounded like a German plural of a singular *Cotte* or *Kotte* (like *Bitte / Bitten*), so in the local German *eine Kotte* came to mean a single boll of cotton and *die Cotton* (*Kotten*) for cotton in general was felt to be a plural (like *weeds* and *peas* and *grapes* in English).[11] Only the latter usage, that is, of cotton as plural, (*Those cotton look good*) has carried over into English. Naturally enough, number divergence from English usage is also sometimes heard when English employs a grammatical plural as a logical singular or vice versa, as in *those* (for *that*) *ten dollars,* and *Ten years are a long time.*

Most of these constructional peculiarities are still very much in use, even among younger people. Since for many of the germanisms there is a very similar English construction (as in *to Alfred's*), which, however, has a slightly different meaning, these influences of German structure are often much more elusive and difficult to eradicate (whether consciously or unconsciously) than the more easily pinpointed peculiarities of pronunciation or vocabulary.

Besides matters of pronunciation and grammatical construction, there are naturally a number of individual vocabulary items whose usage deviates from normal Texas English. I will simply list some of the more common ones with brief comments.

After while for "afterwards" (*First we'll go to church and after while we'll go to the picnic*). Extension of the English range.
All the time or *always* for "already" (*Go on all the time, we'll come in a few minutes*). Germanism for *immer* in sense of *schon* (*geht immer*).
Anything for "any" (adverbially; *That doesn't hurt anything,* meaning "that doesn't hurt [or "matter"] at all"). Germanism (*Das schadet nichts*).
To become for "to do good, agree with" (*That stuff we ate didn't become me*). Germanism (*bekommen*).
To have birthday (*She has birthday today; When does she have birthday?*) Germanism (*Sie hat heute Geburtstag*).
Blackeye peas for "black-eyed peas." Evidently hypercorrect.
A blue eye for "a black eye." (*He hit him and gave him a blue eye*). Germanism (*ein blaues Auge*).
Bluffed for "surprised, astounded, started" (*When he saw the sheriff, he was so bluffed he dropped his gun*). Germanism (*verblüfft*) plus confusion of similar English words.
To borry (the normal regional pronunciation of *borrow*) is used also in the sense of "to lend" (*I'll borry you the money*). Germanism (*borgen,* used for both senses).
Brogue for "accent" (*Those Bohemians talk with a brogue*). Range extension of English word.
Bungalow does not have the usual "cozy" connotation of English, but is used for any low building (even any old shack) with a *bungalow roof* (roof without gables). Evidently an English regionalism.[12]
To butcher is used also for small animals like chickens and fish. A natural extension of the English range of usage, combined with the influence of the German (*schlachten*).
Butterfly also for "moth." Germanism (*Schmetterling* in both senses).
Chicken bone for "chicken leg, drumstick." Germanism (*Bein* 'leg').
Chips for "kindling wood." English regionalism.
To chop off (a tree) for " to chop down." Germanism (*abhauen*).
Cluck (pronounced *clook* [like *look*]) for "setting hen." Germanism (*Klucke*) plus obsolete English. *Dumb cluck* is used as in English, except for the slight difference in pronounciation and that it is taken to mean "dumb setting hen."
Coffee can for "coffee pot." Germanism (*Kaffeekanne*).
To cook for "to boil" (*The pot is cooking*) or "to make" (*to cook coffee*). Germanism (*kochen*).
A couple for "a few" (the two are often not distinguished). Germanism (*ein paar*).
To dig up for "to bury" (*Dig up these potato peelings in garden*).
Dozen(s) of for "dozen" (*a dozen of eggs, two dozens of eggs*). Evidently hypercorrect, archaic, or an extension of phrases like *dozens of eggs,*

since the German usage is the same as normal English (*ein Dutzend Eier, zwei Dutzend Eier.*).

Drummer for "traveling salesman." Correct but obsolete.

Except for "unless" (*We won't be able to go except he gets the car fixed*). Germanism (*ausser*).

-ever often omitted as in *what* for *whatever, when* for *whenever,* and so forth (*a rifle or shotgun or what it was*). Germanism (*was, wo,* and so forth).

To express oneself frequently for "to say" (*He expressed himself that it had been a very nice sermon*). Hypercorrect.

Extra for "special (ly)" (*We don't have to extra go back for that now*). Germanism (*extra*).

Featherbed for "feather quilt." Germanism (*Federbett*).

First for "only," "not until" (*She's coming first tomorrow* or *tomorrow first; We first got there at ten o'clock*). Germanism (*erst*).

To freeze for "to be cold" or "to make cold" (*My hands are freezing* [without the drastic literal meaning of the English]; *The cold glass is freezing my fingers*). Germanism (*frieren,* in such as *mich friert*).

From sometimes for "of" (*a picture from the whole family*). Germanism (*von* in both senses).

To greet for "to say hello" (*Whenever I see her, she never greets me.*) Germanism plus hypercorrect.

Greeting for "greeting card, Christmas card," and others (*I got a greeting from her*). Germanism (*Gruss*).

To come handy for "to come in handy." Evidently merely a shortened form of the English, perhaps influenced by such German constructions as *zustatten kommen*.

To put one's head (or *neck*) *through* for "to get one's way." Germanism (*seinen Dickkopf durschsetzen*).

Highgear for "hegari" (a widely used fodder grain). Evidently English regionalism.

Hollow for "cave" or "hole in a hollow tree" (*The squirrel ran into a hollow of the tree*). Germanism (*Höhle*) plus confusion of English terms.

To lighten for "to lightning" (*It just lightened in the west; Did you see it lighten just then?*). Obsolescent plus hypercorrect plus desire to keep verb distinct from noun.

And the like more for "and other such things" (especially in sermons: *drunkenness, adultery, and the like more*). Germanism (*und dergleichen mehr*).

From little on (or *from small on*) for "since childhood." Germanism (*von klein auf* or *an*).

Littler avoided as improper (*smaller* used instead). Hypercorrect.

To go lost for "to get lost" (*A lot of money goes lost* ["is wasted"]; *The child was in the woods and went lost*). Germanism (*verloren gehen;* the second example would, of course, be *sich verlaufen* in German).

Love to (for "of") *someone* (especially in sermons: *to do good works out of love to God*). Germanism (*Liebe zu Gott*).

Lunch for "snack, light meal, Sunday supper" (*We'll eat a little lunch about four o'clock before we leave*). Range extension of English word.

To meet for "to pass" (going in opposite direction; *We met him on the highway yesterday*). Germanism (*begegnen*) plus hypercorrect (compare *to overtake*).

To mix (cards, dominoes, and other things) for "to shuffle." Germanism (*mischen*).

Neck for "head" in *to cut an animal's neck off* (*She cut the chicken's neck off*). Germanism (*den Hals abschneiden*).

Nightmare for "sleepwalking" (*He had a nightmare last night* for "He walked in his sleep last night"). Origin unclear.

Not? for "not true, isn't that right, didn't he" and so forth (*They're coming tonight, not?*). Germanism (*nicht*).

On the car for "in the car," *off the car* for "out of the car" (*She's sitting on* [for "in] *the car; Take those eggs off* [that is, "out of"] *the car*). Evidently from older German and English usage with *wagon*.

Once, one time, used where no equivalent expression is stated in English (*Come here once; Let me look at that one time*). Germanism (*einmal, mal*).

Onliest often for "only" (*That one rabbit was the onliest one I saw*). Evidently a widespread English and German colloquialism.

Over for "around" and vice versa (*Turn the package around* [that is, "over"]. Germanism (*um* in both senses).

The other Saturday (or *week*) for "the next" (or "the previous") "Saturday" (*Next Saturday is a wedding and the other Saturday is another wedding and the other Saturday is the reunion*).

To overtake for "to pass" (going in the same direction: *He overtook us going real fast*). Germanism (*überholen*) plus hypercorrect (compare *to meet*).

Past or *by* for "missing the mark" (*Don't pour it by* for "Don't miss the cup"; *The garbage men always throw some of it past*). Germanism (*vorbei, daneben*).

Peeling, shell, and related words confused (*to peel pecans; cook beans in the shells*). Germanism (*Schale, schälen*).

Pickles for "small cucumbers." Possibly English regionalism and/or influence of German (*Gurken* for both "pickles" and "cucumbers"), but large cucumbers are not called pickles.

A piece of soap for "a bar of soap." Germanism (*ein Stück Seife*).

Pinery for "pine forest" (*down where the road goes through the pinery*). Correct but obsolete.

To pull a face for "to make a face" (*He pulled a face when I said that*).

Germanism (*ein Gesicht ziehen*).

The whole push for "the whole bunch" (*The mother and father and the whole push came to visit*). Origin unclear.

Rainworm for "earthworm." Germanism (*Regenwurm*).

To rest off for "to rest" or "rest up" (*We'll have to rest off a while*). Germanism (for the local idiom *sich abruhen*).

Sand for "dirt" (*You have to put some more sand* [that is, "dirt, loam, soil"] *around that plant*). Evidently hypercorrect, influenced by Germanism, since German *Schmutz* means "dirt," but only in the sense of "filth."

To say for "to tell" (a lie, the truth) (*She said a lie; Always say the truth*). Germanism (*sagen*).

That's not said for "That's not necessarily so." Germanism (*Das ist nicht gesagt*).

To scare oneself for "to be frightened, startled" (*When she saw the snake she scared herself so bad she almost fainted*). Germanism (*sich fürchten*).

Second Easter, Second Christmas, and other for "the day after Easter, Christmas" (*There's no school on Second Easter*). Germanism (*am zweiten Weihnachten*).

To smell after (for "like") *something* (*It smells after gasoline in here*). Germanism (*Es riecht nach etwas*).

Sprinkler for "sprinkle, rain shower." (*Yesterday we had a few little sprinklers*). Evidently confusion of *sprinkle* and *sprinkler*.

Steak formerly meant "ground meat, hamburger meat" (steaks in the current normal sense were unknown). Origin unclear.

Steeple also in sense of "staple" (U-shaped nail). Evidently simply a confusion of the two similar English words.

Stem for "trunk" (of tree). Germanism (*Stamm*).

To step in (for "on") *a sharp object* (*She stepped in a nail*). Germanism (*in einen Nagel treten, sich einen Nagel eintreten*).

To stick for "to be somewhere, in something" (*She left the keys sticking* [that is, "inserted"]). Germanism (*stecken*).

To swallow oneself for "to choke" (*I swallowed myself* for "I choked," or "I got water in my windpipe"). Germanism (*sich verschlucken*).

To swim for "to float" (*The cork is still swimming in the water*). Germanism (*schwimmen* in both senses).

To taste for "to taste good" (*Does it taste?; This stuff just doesn't taste*). Germanism (*schmecken*).

To tear for "to break" ropes, thread and other things (*The rope tore* for "broke"). Germanism (*reissen, abreissen*).

That time for "in those days" (*That time we didn't know about air conditioning*). Germanism (*damals*) plus English *at that time*.

That too yet! for "That had to happen now, too, on top of it all." Germanism (*das auch noch!*).

That way for "That's the way it is," "So that's what you mean"). Evidently abbreviated English, influenced by the local German idiom (*den Weg*).

To thaw up for "to thaw" or "thaw out" (*You have to thaw it up before you can cook it; If you're cold, come over by the fire and thaw up*). Germanism (*auftauen*).

Underthrough for "under (and away)" (*The calf went underthrough the fence and got onto the road*). Germanism (*unter/unten durch*). Felt to be a necessary distinction from *under* since *went under the fence* is considered to connote *and stayed under it*.

Whole for "all" (*He painted the whole walls* [for "all the walls"]; *The whole traffic was stopped*). Germanism (as in the colloquial *die ganzen Wände*).

Wine for "grapes" (*We picked some wine; wine jelly*). Germanism (*Wein*).

Those people who actively speak (or formerly spoke) German naturally insert German words, phrases and sayings into their English when talking among themselves.[13] Even younger people who speak little German but have been exposed to their relatives' German and germanized English will use certain of the more common phrases, such as *Wie geht's, Danke schön, Gute Nacht*. The fluently biligual ones also use German frequently as a secret language, as in a store when they want to say something without being understood by others. They also often switch immediately to German when addressing an old (German) person. The German items inserted into otherwise English utterances fall to a certain extent into natural groups, the most common category being that of greetings like those just mentioned. It is very common to begin a conversation with *Wie geht's?* 'How goes it, how are you?' and a suitable German reply, often humorous (for example, *Es muss gehen* 'It has to go', (that is, "You have to get along somehow"); or *Auf zwei Beinen* ('On two legs') and then switch into the English that has become the more comfortable language. Similarly, on taking leave, one of many stock German phrases may be used, such as *Kommt gut nach Haus* 'Have a safe trip home'; the humorous *Schmeisst nicht um* 'Don't turn over' ("Don't have a wreck"); *Halt* (that is, *Haltet*) *euch munter* 'Stay happy'; *Nächstes Mal wieder so* 'Next time this way again' (that is, "We'll have a good time together again, as we did today"). On arriving at one's destination the phrase is usually *Glücklich angelangt*! 'Safely arrived!'

German nouns of relationship, like *Tante* 'aunt,' which have become practically a part of the proper name, are naturally often carried over into English (*Let's go visit Tante Minna*).

Some items of daily life were so common in German and so patently German (even to the extent of having the German word printed in large letters on them), that it was only natural to refer to them by the German term even when speaking English, as in *Taufschein* 'baptismal certificate,' *Trauschein* 'marriage certificate' (such certificates were usually framed and displayed on the wall), *Gesangbuch* 'hymnboook,' *Liederperlen* (literally "pearls of song") a popular songbook (*Get out the old Liederperlen and we'll sing*).

Since a few German foods were not known in English or easily equatable to English terms, the German words continued to be used in English. For example, the kinds of coffeecake the Germans made were unique and therefore the German designations were carried over into English. The most common type was known by the most general word: *Kaffeekuchen,* which meant a flat "sheetcake" kind of coffeecake, topped with the sugar-cinnamon mixture called *Streusel* (which latter word seems lately to have become an accepted part of the standard English vocabulary, quite independently of the Texas Germans). Another variety of this type of coffeecake is *Quarkkuchen* ("cottage cheese cake"), made with a delicious sweetened cottage cheese topping instead of *Streusel*. Nowadays the English terms *coffeecake* and *cheesecake* are more commonly used for these when speaking English. On the other hand, *Striezel* is a sort of raisin coffee cake, for which no English word has yet been found, so the German word is still actively in use (at least among those people who still know how to make the pastry, of course). *Kochkäse* was a special kind of homemade soft cheese. *Kochwurst* is the kind of sausage (still made) which is misleadingly designated as "headcheese" in English. *Biersuppe* ("beer soup") was unknown in English, but popular among the Germans, and *Zwiebelsosse* is a special kind of "onion gravy."

Certain home remedies and the plants they were made from were known only in German. *Schreckkräutig,* literally "fright greens," was a wild plant used (to this day by some people) to prepare *Schrecktee* ("fright tea"), a remedy for nervousness. Another such remedy is *Kamillentee* (literally, "camomile tea") which term again is unknown in these people's (or my own) English. Other plants and animals were generally known bilingually or in some cases only by the English terms, since they were not known (or so distinguished, like *fryers*) in Germany. I have heard other German plant and animal designations used at times in English, such as *Mücke* 'gnat', *Kolibri* 'humming bird', and *Engerling* 'grubworm,' but the English words for these are (at least nowadays) well known, and there is no necessity to use German.

Items of household furniture and tools were known bilingually, with few exceptions. One term for which no English word has been found (although one surely must exist), is the *Wirbel*, a pivotable piece of wood which can be turned to keep a door shut or to hold a window open. The word *Flaschenzug* was often used in English, possibly because it is less cumbersome than "block and tackle." Similarly, although *chifferobe* was later learned, the term *Kleiderschrank* was (and is) often used instead (as a matter of fact, in my wife's family a *chifferobe* was purchased later, and was so called [in German and in English] to distinguish it from the old *Kleiderschrank*). A small low bucket is called a *Fusswanne* ("foot tub"). The German card games *Skat* and *Schafskopf* have no English equivalents; especially *Skat* is still very popular in the area, and announcements of *Skat-Tournaments* can be seen in the local newspapers. Naturally the people who play these games frequently use the special German vocabulary relating to them. (When my brother-in-law taught me to play *Schafskopf* many years ago, there were German terms he could not avoid using, such as *Die schwarze Dame sticht alles* [literally, "The black lady stabs everything"], which I naturally didn't understand, but which were so self-evident to him that he had great difficulty in explaining them to me; the example just given means, "The queen of clubs or spades beats any other card.")

The names of certain German customs were retained for a long time, and again some, like *Federschleissen,* have no English translation. *Federschleissen,* literally "feather stripping," was a kind of work party (like a quilting party), at which feathers (saved up for a long time) were stripped from their quills, to be used for making featherbeds and pillows. *Katzenmusik* ("cat music") was a humorous term for what was usually called (in English and German) "shivaree." As in Germany, Christmas presents were said to be brought by the *Christkind* ("Christ Child"), but there was also a Santa Claus type figure called *Ruprecht* (or *Rumplicht* or *Rumpricht*, all varieties of the name *Rupert*); since these figures did not equate very well to the English, the German terms were frequently used. Nowadays, of course, the two German figures have merged into the English Santa Claus, but the German tradition is still followed to the extent that Santa Claus comes on Christmas Eve (while the children are in church).

German epithets and expletives are frequently used in English, the emotional value of such things naturally being great. Examples are: *dummer Junge* 'dumb boy'; *Dummlak* 'dumb person, dummy'; *dumme Gans* or *dumme Liese* ("dumb goose," "dumb Lisa") for "stupid girl"; *Gescheeche* ("ghost, scarecrow") for "strange looking person"; *Panschgans* ("spilling goose") for a clumsy person who spills something. Common expletives are *Ach was!* 'Oh, come on!' or 'Really?'; *Du liebe Zeit!* ("You dear time!") for "My goodness!" and the exact equivalent of the latter: *Meine Güte!* The expletives are usually tame because the people, being very church-oriented, avoid strong language. *Landsmann* 'fellow countryman' is a common form of address, as in *Wie geht's, Landsmann!* or *Hello, Landsmann!* More pejorative terms are *Schweinerei* 'mess', *Quatsch* 'nonsense', *Dreck* 'excrement' (*We found rat-Dreck in the house,* similarly *roach-Dreck,* and others, and *Gejukele,* a dialect word meaning "poking along, driving too slowly" (*What kind of a Gejukele is that!*).

A few items of baby talk were retained for a long time, again because of the emotional attachment to the terms and the frequent difficulty of close translation. *Pat the kitty* seems bland when one is used to *Make kitty ei,* from the saying (spoken to the cat) *Ei, kitty, ei,* which is about like the English ''nice kitty.'' The prayer *Abba, lieber Vater* (pronounced by the child in rhyming fashion *lieba Vata*), *amen,* meaning simply ''Abba, dear Father, amen,'' was and still is widely used as the table prayer of very small children.

The regular German table prayer before meals and giving of thanks after meals were also frequently preserved long after the switch to English had been made: *Komm, Herr Jesus, sei unser Gast, und segne, was Du uns bescheret hast;* and *Danket dem Herrn, denn Er ist freundlich, und seine Güte währet ewiglich.* For these the English translations are now normally used: ''Come, Lord Jesus, be our guest, and let these [or ''thy''] gifts to us be blest''; and ''Oh, give thanks unto the Lord, for He is good, and His mercy endureth forever.'' Prayers, Bible verses, and hymns which were learned in German naturally possess an emotional and nostalgic impact in that language which English can never replace. Also, the rigorous German confirmation instruction of a generation ago required the memorizing of hundreds of Bible verses, Luther's explanations of the commandments, and other matter, with the result that a person who went through the instruction will probably always know these things better in German than in English and will often quote them in German even though otherwise speaking English. A striking example of this is the beautiful new church marker at the old Lutheran church in the little community of Fedor (north of Giddings), which is basically in English, but of which the most prominent words are the bold proclamation *Gottes Wort und Luthers Lehr vergehet nun und nimmermehr* (''God's word and Luther's teaching will never perish, now or ever,'' the motto of the Lutheran Church of the Missouri Synod).

Sayings and proverbs are, of course, also remembered in the mother tongue and will be so reproduced if the hearer will understand; otherwise a direct translation will be made, as in *One crow doesn't chop the other's eyes out;* and *Little children, little worries, big children, big worries.*

Many other words and phrases are more difficult to categorize, but their retention is understandable because they seem handier or more expressive than the English (or in some cases because no comparable English is available or known). Examples in typical contexts are *She's always jammering* (''wailing, moaning'') *around about something; That's just Aberglaube* (''superstition''); *She's sitting there so andächtig* (''piously, pensively''); *I feel so matt* (''weak, hungry, exhausted''); *I feel really übel* (''sick at my stomach''); *Those salesmen are so aufdringlich* (''pesky, importunate''); *He has gotten so pucklig* (That is, *bucklig* 'humpbacked, stooped') *in his old age; When I changed lanes, there was such an Absatz* (''offset, difference of level'') *that I almost lost control of the car; She complained to the teacher, but his attitude was just kümmere dich* (literally ''you worry,'' that is, ''about yourself,'' meaning ''that's your own worry, don't bother me''); *Where are you going so aufgedonnert* (literally, ''thundered up,'' that is, ''dressed up fine, overdressed''); *By now the burglars are über alle Berge* (''over all the mountains,'' that is, ''far away, long gone''); *You're staying home and fertig damit* (''finished with it,'' that is, ''That's the end of that''); *It's so dumpfig* (''stuffy, dank'') *in here; He nailed a little Dreieck* (''triangle, triangular piece of wood or metal'') *over the hole; What is that old Gerippe* (''skeleton'', that is, ''framework'') *in the garage?; The table is pretty wacklig* (''wobbly''); *The paint is all klebrig* (''sticky''). The original German *Das auch noch!* of the phrase ''That too yet!'' (mentioned above) is still very frequently heard (*First car trouble and now it's starting to rain—das auch noch!*).

Although, as was mentioned, some of these and similar German words and phrases are used even by people who speak little German, the insertion of such German items into English speech is naturally rapidly vanishing in cadence with the disappearance of German in general. The more subtle influences on English usage, as discussed above, will last longer.

The Wendish once spoken by many of these people has left almost no obvious traces on either their German or their English, although it may have strengthened some of the divergences from standard English described above as germanisms (for example, in regard to the pronunciation of *r* and *w*). The only Wendish word that one can still hear sometimes employed in English (or German) is *der Braschka,* meaning the man in charge of the food at a wedding—evidently used because of a lack of German or English equivalent. People who spoke Wendish (or who were exposed to it) will sometimes use the Wendish greeting *Kak chodźi?* (''How are you?'' pronounced like *kahk-káwdgy*), even when speaking English, and then may throw in a Wendish saying, as with the inserted German phrases mentioned above (like, on taking leave, the humorous rhyming saying *Doma jeć, piwo pić* [''Go home, drink beer''], pronounced *dáwma yitch, péewa pitch*).

Now that the German language is nearly dead in this area, the region is rediscovering its German (and Wendish) heritage, and here and there a German word will be consciously fostered, as in the newspapers. Thus, the annual city fair in Giddings in now officially called the *Giddings Geburstag* (''birthday''); this term is a fairly recent innovation (dating from the one-hundredth birthday of the town in 1971) rather than an old tradition. Some of the other towns (like Brenham) call their May fete a *Mai-Fest,* and in some of these cases the usage of the German term undoubtedly represents genuine tradition. Of course, it is laudable that this pride in the local heritage is being fostered at all—it's just a pity that it is happening too late and is now rather artificial, thus one of the local newspapers, attempting to say ''happy birthday'' in regard to the *Giddings Geburtstag*, printed *froehlich Geburtstag,* omitting the ending *en* on the adjective. a mistake no Texas German would ever make.

NOTES

1. See Joseph Wilson, "The German Language in Central Texas Today," in *Texas and Germany: Crosscurrents*, ed. Joseph Wilson, *Rice University Studies* 63, no. 3 (1977), pp. 47–58. As in all my studies of the Texas Germans, I am indebted to my wife and her family and my many German friends and relatives for serving as my informants.

2. See Terry G. Jordan, *German Seed in Texas Soil* (Austin: University of Texas Press, 1966) passim (and especially the maps on pp. 42, 46, and 56); Glenn G. Gilbert, *Linguistic Atlas of Texas German* (Austin: University of Texas Press, 1974).

3. See George C. Engerrand, *The So-called Wends of Germany and their Colonies in Texas and Australia*, University of Texas Bulletin no. 3417 (Austin, 1934); and Reinhold Olesch "The West Slavic Languages in Texas with Special Regard to Sorbian [Wendish] in Serbin, Lee County," in *Texas Studies in Bilingualism: Spanish, French, German, Czech, Polish, Sorbian, and Norwegian in the Southwest, with a Concluding Chapter on Code-switching and Modes of Speaking in American Swedish*, ed. Glenn G. Gilbert, Studia Linguistica Germanica no. 3 (Berlin: Walter de Gruyter, 1970), pp. 151–62.

4. To my knowledge, there have been no studies made of the English of any of the Texas Germans, although the subject is given limited treatment in certain more general articles, for example, Gilbert Jordan, "The Texas German Language of the Western Hill Country," in *Texas and Germany: Crosscurrents*, ed. Wilson, pp. 59–71. There have been a number of articles dealing with the English of other American-German groups, especially of the Pennsylvania Germans. For references, see Wolfgang Viereck, "German Dialects Spoken in the United States and Canada and Problems of German-English Language Contact Especially in North America: A Bibliography," *Orbis* 16 (1967): 549–68, and 17 (1968): 532–35; and Jürgen Eichhoff, "Bibliography of German Dialects Spoken in the United States and Canada and Problems of German-English Language Contact Especially in North America, 1968–1976, with pre-1968 Supplements, "*Monatshefte* 68 (1976): 196–208. It has been pointed out that the nonstandard English of German Americans can be traced to the following factors: standard German and dialect German usage, English provincialisms, common American errors, errors natural to any foreigner, and the preservation of English archaisms. To this list should be added hypercorrectness and, for the area of Texas considered here, the influence of Wendish.

5. The rapid transition to standard English stands in contrast to the Pennsylvania Germans, whose centuries-old mixture of the languages produced a more germanized English.

6. Else Hünert-Hofmann, "Interferenzerscheinungen in der Idiomatik einer zweisprachigen Gruppe," *Zeitschrift für Dialektologie und Linguistik*, Beiheft, supplement, n.s. 13 (1975): 106–13, notes this same feature in the English of the Texas Germans of the New Braunfels area and asserts that the speakers are aware of it and consciously strive for more standard English. I do not believe that this assertion is true for the group here described, which does indeed endeavor to speak correctly (and therefore often falls into hypercorrectness), but not more correctly than the neighboring natives. As a matter of fact, when one (tactfully, of course) mentions to them that such

and such a usage is not standard English, they—like anyone else—immediately defend their usage by one means or another (calling on logic and other means). They are comfortable with their language, consider it to be correct (or correct enough), and are not looking for ways to improve it; thus they consider the use of the article in such phrases as *the Kriegels* (discussed below) to be an unnecessary bother.

7. Most of the Texas Germans in this area are Lutherans of the conservative Missouri Synod.

8. This reverse substitution of *w* for *v* seems, however, to be widespread; it is noted, for example, by George C. Struble, "The English of the Pennsylvania Germans," *American Speech* 10 (1935): 165: and by R. S. Graham, "The Transition from German to English in the German Settlements of Saskatchewan," *Journal of the Canadian Linguistic Association* 3 (1957): 11.

9. Since nearly all of the types given in this section stem from general German usage, not restricted to this area, it is surprising that only a few of them have been attested for other areas; I am confident that practically all the types would be found in any area of German influence. On the other hand, many of the idioms frequently cited for other areas (especially for the Pennsylvania Germans), such as *fress* 'to eat sloppily' and *tut* 'paper bag' are not used in this region because they are too obviously un-English. It will be noted that most of the types listed here are not so obvious, for which reason they continue to be used even after long contact with standard English.

10. The more direct translation of the German *bei Alfred* and *bei Kriegels* (meaning "at Alfred's" "at the Kriegels") as *by Alfred* and *by Kriegels* used to be common but has now generally been corrected to *at*, as in the examples given.

11. Such restrictions of number are not unusual in language history: thus in English *peas(e)* was originally singular and collective (like *corn*), but later was taken to be plural and a new singular *pea* derived from it. One might, indeed, be tempted to see an English archaism preserved by the Texas Germans in the case of *that peas*, but the switch to *pea / peas* long antedates their immigration. It will be seen, later, however, that in a few instances obsolescent English has been retained. Pennsylvania German naturally did this to a much greater extent: cf. Carroll E. Reed, "English Archaisms in Pennsylvania German," *Publications of the American Dialect Society*, 1953.

12. *Bungalow*, meaning originally "Bengal (house)," was first used for the low, veranda-enclosed buildings used by the Europeans in India. The word came in America to denote the cozy, small, inexpensive one-family dwellings popular in the early decades of this century; see, for example, Marcus Whiffen, *American Architecture since 1780: A Guide to the Styles* (Cambridge, Mass.: M.I.T. Press, 1969), pp. 217 ff. (and literature cited). The word evidently took on differing regional meanings, for this Texas usage is quite at odds with the description by G. A. Stokes, "The Bungalow in Louisiana," *Louisiana Studies*, no. 41 (1965), pp. 78 f., which depicts a rather country-store type of building with gables at front and back, and with a lean-to porch roof built onto the front gable.

13. Of course, when the old settlers were first learning English, German words could always slip in inadvertently, often with amusing results, as when my wife's grandfather would say *It's getting hell in the east* (that is, German *hell* 'bright, light').

Conclusion

PAUL SCHACH

Einar Haugen's contribution to this volume is a discussion of two of the first Norwegian texts he ever recorded. These texts are two versions of the same story, related by the same individual. As Haugen points out, the language of the first version is stilted, since the speaker—a man of only modest formal education—was trying to transcend his dialect and speak what he perceived to be a "higher" form of language. Although informants frequently respond to questionnaires with hypercorrect forms, it is unusual for an individual to maintain a sort of elevated style for an entire narrative. Perhaps the effort required to speak in such an unnatural manner accounts for the greater degree of English interference in this version of the story. In any event, we find here an illustration of two typical forms of linguistic conflict among speakers of non-English immigrant tongues—conflict between native dialect and a perceived higher form of the language and conflict between the imported language and the dominant one.

Around the turn of the century Swedish was spoken almost as widely in the midwestern and Great Plains states as German, although the Swedes were less numerous than the Germans. Both Folke Hedblom, who carried out five extensive expeditions to record Swedish speech in America, and Nils Hasselmo, whose *Amerikasvenska* is the standard work in the field, comment on some of the reasons Swedish Americans had for abandoning their native language. Hedblom stresses dialect incompatibility, the inability of many Swedish Americans to speak standard Swedish, and the role of high and low prestige dialects. This kind of intralingual, interdialectal conflict has always fascinated me. Although I have not heard *Sächsisch* spoken for years, I recall that we used to think this German dialect was excruciatingly funny to listen to.

While doing research work at the Sprachatlas in Marburg in 1957 I recorded a local anecdote about a gentleman from Leipzig who wished to purchase some rum for medicinal purposes. His question to the pharmacist was "Kann ich hier Rum kriegen?" ("Can I get some rum here?"), but the pharmacist thought he had asked, "Kann ich hier 'rumkriechen?" ("Can I crawl around [on the floor] here?"). His reply was appropriate: "Es ist zwar ein bißchen eng—aber meinetwegen," which means something like "Well, it's a bit crowded—but it's OK with me." Among some of the Russian Germans of Nebraska the dialect of Norka is said to enjoy low prestige: I have had relatively little success in recording it. And just recently some Swedish-American acquaintances of mine refused to join Swedish visitors at a table in a restaurant because they were speaking the dialect of Skåne.

Hasselmo stresses other aspects of the language shift. In addition to the social and economic mobility in American society and a readiness on the part of the immigrants to become americanized, he emphasizes the manner in which Swedish Americans perceived themselves while speaking their native dialects and while speaking English. Their native speech branded them as peasants; when they spoke English, however, they were the peers of the native speakers of that language. Hasselmo's observations on the petrifaction of written Swedish because of loss of contact with the mother country are noteworthy. Similar observations have been made for German, Latvian, Icelandic, and other languages. An extreme case of this among the Amish has been reported on by Heinz Kloss.[1] Whereas isolation from a dominant foreign language helps preserve immigrant dialects, isolation from the mother country leads to the petrifaction of literary languages. With the disappearance of the American-Swedish written language, the complexity of linguistic conflict was simplified, and with the passing of the third generation of Swedish Americans, American Swedish will be a thing of the past.

The Danes seem to have resisted linguistic acculturation less stubbornly than the other ethnic groups discussed in this book. Even though Danish-American intellectual leaders vigorously advocated *danskhed* 'Danishness', they found few followers among farmers and laborers, for whom English had a higher utilitarian value when it came to making a living. Furthermore, the very aggressiveness of the well-educated proponents of *danskhed* may have increased the tension between "high" and "low," between themselves and farmers, craftsmen, and laborers. Another factor that emerges from Donald K. Watkins's well-documented sociolinguistic study is the apparent ineffectiveness of the church to inspire language loyalty among the Danes.

The Norwegians, on the other hand, are generally regarded as having been more tenacious in the retention of their ancestral dialects than other Scandinavians. These general impressions are borne out by some of the statistics quoted by Watkins for 1970. Of Americans claiming Danish as their mother tongue, 30 percent were foreign-born, and only 15 percent belonged to the third and fourth generations. A somewhat higher rate of retention is characteristic of Swedish speakers, with 21 percent of them being foreign-born and 18 percent belonging to generations later than the second. By contrast, the statistics for Americans with Norwegian as their native language show only 15 percent foreign-born and 33 percent belonging to the third and fourth generation. Thus twice as many Norwegians as Danes retained their ancestral tongue after the second generation. The time span for the retention of Norwegian, however, does not seem to have been appreciably longer than for the retention of most immigrant tongues; for when Einar Haugen recently visited the city of his birth, he heard no Norwegian spoken there.

Of the non-English immigrant tongues spoken on the Great Plains, German is represented by both the largest number of speakers and by the greatest variety of dialects. East Frisian Low German and Hutterite are not mutually understandable. Indeed, the language distance between them is as great as that between English and standard German, and it would be more realistic to speak in such a case of two related languages rather than of two dialects of the same language. A speaker of the American Mucsi-Fulda dialect could understand Volhynian Palatine reasonably well, but would have considerable difficulty making himself understood to Palatine speakers.

The first paper on German dialects presents a concise but comprehensive description of the acculturation of an East Frisian Low German dialect that has been spoken in southeastern Nebraska for the past century. Jan E. Bender is thoroughly acquainted with this dialect and its speakers. His doctoral dissertation, "Die getrennte Entwicklung gleichen niederdeutschen Sprachgutes in Deutschland und Nebraska," is a diachronic analysis of the divergent development of two Low-German dialects—under the influence of standard German on the one hand, and under the influence of American English on the other. Bender's Nebraska informants were third-generation dialect speakers; his European informants were relatives of the Nebraska Low-German speakers. Bender has spoken both of these dialects—a form of East Frisian and a form of Eastphalian—since childhood. His paper is based on field work conducted during the summers of 1966–73.

By contrast, the speakers of the American Mucsi-Fulda dialect are recent immigrants, most of whom came to the United States from Hungary by way of West Germany shortly after World War II. It is striking to note that, whereas relatively few Hungarian words had crept into the dialect in Mucsi in a century and a half, the diffusion of English words and phrases after only a few decades in America is quite strong. The reasons are obvious. Mucsi was an isolated rural speech enclave; in America the dialect speakers live in urban areas such as Omaha, Aurora (Illinois), and Milwaukee. Although most of these people cannot speak standard German, many of them have become bidialectal, especially in Milwaukee. In conversing with persons who do not know their dialect, they resort to a West Middle German lingua franca that has been described to me as being similar to Pennsylvania German in its salient linguistic features. Gommermann's paper is based partly on his doctoral thesis, written under the direction of Professor Dieter Karch, but in larger measure on subsequent research and fieldwork. Gommermann is a native speaker of Mucsi-Fulda German.

Kurt Rein did his field work on the Hutterite, Volhynian ("Swiss") Mennonite, and Amana German dialects (the latter not included here) during his guest professorships at the University of Chicago and the University of Nebraska (1963–65). While at Nebraska Rein codirected a master's thesis with me on the phonology and morphology of the dialect of Volhynian Mennonite German spoken around Freeman, South Dakota. In this thesis Cora Miller (now Mrs. Maurice Conner), a third-generation speaker of "Swiss," states that the dialect "is in retreat." As a major cause of the "rapid loss" she mentions intermarriage with speakers of incompatible dialects or with spouses who know only English.

This, of course, is true as far as it goes, but the death blow was probably struck by the repressive laws passed in the Great Plains states forbidding the use of non-English languages in public (1919–23). Not long afterwards there was a major shift in church policy from the introversive identification of religion with the German language to the extroversive promotion of English for the purpose of extending the boundaries of Mennonite influence. Had standard German been retained as the lingua sacra, the moribund "Swiss" dialect might still be thriving today in the two Volhynian Mennonite colonies on the Great Plains, just as Pennsylvania German has remained the language of everyday interaction among the Old Order Amish, for whom standard German is the language of worship and English the language of the school and technology. Having exchanged their native Swiss Alemannic for a Palatine tongue, these Mennonites remained remarkably loyal to their adopted language for two centuries, first in speech enclaves in a Slavic linguistic environment and then in two settlements surrounded by English as well as by other German dialects. As Rein has pointed out, the only non-Palatine Alemannic feature to survive is the use of /ai/ < Middle High German *ei* instead of Palatine /e:/ in the South Dakota variety of the dialect. Mrs. Conner modeled her master's thesis on Carroll E. Reed's monograph, *The Pennsylvania German Dialect Spoken in the Counties of Lehigh and Berks: Phonology and Morphology,* thus facilitating a comparison of these two Palatine tongues.

Whereas Bender and Gommermann investigated forms of interference between English and German, Rein focused on the forces and strategies of linguistic survival, especially in the case of Hutterite. After skillfully tracing the exceedingly complex history of this highly stratified language, which has experienced diffusion from disparate sources, he states his reasons for being optimistic about the future of Hutterite in a hostile environment. A major factor in the preservation of minority tongues is isolation from the dominant language and culture; in their *Bruderhöfe* the Hutterites enjoy a higher degree of isolation than any other German-speaking groups in America. Although the coexistence of three strata, or subcodes, of Hutterite plus English and standard German might seem to be a weakening factor, the opposite seems to be true; for, to use the oft-quoted observation of Joshua Fishman, the ''differential use'' of languages in a bilingual society serves both ''to integrate the society as well as to preserve its bilingualism.'' Even after English, the language of education, has supplanted standard German as the written medium, it may be possible for the Hutterites to preserve their language on the firm bases of religious separatism and social isolation.

Nebraska Czech differs basically from American German and Swedish. Unlike these languages, which exhibit sharp cleavages in dialect, Nebraska Czech is quite homogeneous, partly because the dialectal differences of the earliest settlers were relatively small to begin with and partly because of the strong influence of the literary language. The high rate of literacy among Czech immigrants must have played an important role in leveling what dialectal differences there were in their speech. The lack of dialectal splintering, the greater linguistic distance between Czech and English, and the more striking contrast between Czech and American culture would all seem to favor retention of the ancestral language. Yet Czech does not seem to be in a stronger position than Swedish or German. Only rarely do we encounter a member of the fourth generation who has a good command of the transplanted language. Most of Bruce Kochis's informants belong to the second and third generation of Czech speakers.

The two Lakota communities discussed by Elizabeth S. Grobsmith represent two stages in the acculturation of that language. In both communities we find bilingualism, with differential use of both languages. In one community the situation seems to be stable—primarily because of isolation and the presence of monolingual speakers of Lakota. In the other community, however, English has made such inroads that survival of Lakota except as a cult language seems unlikely unless bilingual education is introduced soon. Ironically, the very parents who neglected to teach their children Lakota are now the ones who are most concerned about having the language taught in school, since they realize that the disappearance of their ancestral tongue will mean the loss of group identity.

Elaine Jahner has examined a different form of linguistic acculturation. All of us would prefer filet mignon to a chunk of dead cow, to use one of Hayakawa's illustrations of how our choice of words influences our perception of reality. Changing the symbol does not change the referent, but it can change our attitude toward it. But what happens if the referent is changed and the symbol remains the same—or, to use a different semantic metaphor, what happens if we use the old map for a new terrain? To a certain degree, of course, this happens in all languages, bringing about semantic extension or semantic shift. In Lakota, however, we find a very close relationship between certain aspects of language and the areas of culture that they reflect. The verbs of movement, and especially the highly complex system of verbs of going and coming, are predicated upon the traditional Lakota view of existence as a configuration of ever-widening concentric circles, beginning with the tipi and the circular camp or village and extending ultimately to the world and the universe. This world view no longer corresponds to external reality—at least as far as the circular tipi and camp are concerned. To what extent will it be possible to preserve the traditional cultural meanings of the verbs of movement now that the old culture has been so fundamentally changed? Many Lakota speakers emphasize the major distinctions between their language and English and consciously resist the convergence of the two languages, but the pressures of the dominant language and culture are incessant and inexorable. The Lakota admit that "the old words are dying." As Jahner stated, it will remain for future studies to determine the success of the Lakota speakers in the preservation of their language, which to many is "their major tie to the past and the emblem of their national identity."

In all the papers in this collection the importance of attitude toward one's native language or dialect is touched on in one way or another. This question is the central concern in the contribution by Eileen M. Brennan, Miguel A. Carranza, and Ellen B. Ryan. They report a surprisingly positive attitude on the part of Mexican-American adolescents toward their ancestral language and culture in Chicago, Illinois. This healthy attitude toward bilingualism no doubt results in large measure from the fact that "these students are in an educational environment that is tolerant of language and cultural diversity." Surprisingly, the adolescents in Kansas City, Kansas revealed an equally strong loyalty to their Mexican heritage despite the fact that Spanish is no longer their dominant language. In the less cosmopolitan milieu of Kansas City, however, they perceive a Mexican-Spanish accent to be a social handicap, and, perhaps for this reason, there is a stronger feeling of isolation among those who speak English with a marked Mexican accent.

At the Tenth Germanic Languages Symposium held at the University of Texas at Austin (18–20 November 1971) Don Yoder of the University of Pennsylvania asserted that "too little attention has been paid to the English spoken in areas of the United States populated by the descendants of Germans and other non-English language groups."[2] One of the participants of that symposium, Joseph B. Wilson, has been studying this aspect of linguistic acculturation in Texas for a number of years. Some of the data he has collected are discussed in his contribution to this volume. Many of his examples of loans and loanshifts are similar to those I collected in Pennsylvania; many are quite different.[3] Although not so urgent as the preservation of the rapidly disappearing non-English languages and language fragments, the collection and study of such substratum diffusion in English is extremely important—partly for practical pedagogical reasons, partly for purposes of linguistic analysis, and partly because this is all part of our linguistic and therefore our cultural heritage.

The atmosphere in America toward non-English-speaking immigrants was often hostile. The degree and the forms of hostility varied from time to time and from place to place. Many immigrants escaped the hostility by settling among colinguals and remaining isolated from people of other language and culture. But difference can easily be confused with deviance. Recently I overheard two young men in South Dakota order a tourist not to speak German "because we don't know what you're talking about." In Colorado in recent years I have often observed that Spanish Americans speak more softly in public when they speak Spanish than when they speak English. As an adolescent in that state I occasionally went swimming in a municipal swimming pool despite the sign over the entrance that proclaimed ANGLO-SAXONS ONLY. I recall that as a child in Philadelphia I was once sitting beside my mother on a streetcar in front of two women who were conversing in Italian. My mother became more and more agitated and finally blurted out to me in a loud whisper, "Diese Ausländer!" ("These foreigners!"). People of foreign speech are to be feared and suspected and, under certain circumstances, to be hated and punished.

How irrational and irresponsible such hostility could become is shown by Frederick C. Luebke in his carefully documented essay on legal and extralegal restrictions on the use of foreign languages on the Great Plains, especially from 1917 until 1923. Although this hysterical hatred was directed primarily at German speakers, there was enough of it left over to make life miserable for speakers of other non-English tongues. As Luebke points out, in Nebraska the prohibition of the use of foreign languages specifically included Czech, Danish, and Swedish, as well as the hated German.

In 1923 the Supreme Court of the United States declared the Nebraska Siman Act of 1919 to be unconstitutional, and subsequently all similar state prohibitions against foreign languages became null and void. To quote Luebke: "Ethnic churches, whose interests were most directly and most adversely affected by the movement [to restrict the use of foreign languages], immediately turned to the courts for redress. Although state tribunals were unresponsive to their constitutional arguments, the federal judiciary ruled in their favor and thereby clarified and enlarged American freedom."

In conclusion we should ask ourselves (as I suggested in the Introduction) what approaches to the further study of ethnic languages on the Great Plains will be most productive for the linguist, the humanist, and the social scientist. Obviously the most urgent task is to salvage the still abundant but rapidly disappearing material by recording as many of the native and immigrant languages and dialects as possible. This can be done most efficiently with the aid of carefully prepared questionnaires like those devised by Haugen for Norwegian and by Carroll E. Reed and Lester W. Seifert for Pennsylvania German and Wisconsin German, respectively, supplemented by personal accounts, anecdotes, proverbs, poems, and other freely related forms.[4]

During personal interviews the field worker should seek to ascertain attitudes of the informants toward their dialects, toward other dialects, and toward English. The importance of such subjective information was demonstrated in the essays by Hedblom, Hasselmo, and Watkins, as well as by a study made in Europe by Haugen.[5] Of the informants who participated in this investigation "only two percent of the Norwegians and not a single Swede preferred Danish to their own language, while forty-one percent of the Danes preferred Norwegian and forty-two percent preferred Swedish to their own language." Would it be unreasonable to suggest that the relatively rapid demise of Danish in America was due in considerable measure to lack of pride in the native tongue, which has been characterized by other Scandinavians as "not a language, but a throat disease"? As suggested in the Introduction, the use of sociolinguistic studies on language attitudes like the one reported on by Brennan, Ryan, and Carranza could yield information of use to educators as well as to linguists and sociologists.

Opinions regarding the appropriateness of various languages and dialects for religious services should also be solicited. There is much evidence—for example, the Old Order Amish and the Hutterites—that "faith preserves language and language preserves faith."[6] But the bitter conflict that preceded and accompanied the transition from the ethnic tongues to English in various denominations on the Great Plains suggests that the opposite can also be true. We have many data about this language conflict, but the statistical skeleton needs to be fleshed out with personal opinion from those who actually experienced what for many was a traumatic experience.

Sophisticated word-association and sentence-completion tests have been devised to elicit associations from bilinguals, such as the one Rein used with the Hutterites. There is still abundant opportunity on the Great Plains for psychologists and psycholinguists to use such tests—for example, to distinguish various kinds or degrees of bilingualism (compound, coordinate, and convergent) or to explore problems of semantics or the question of the dominance or salience of the two languages in given social situations. Another interesting experiment in the area of bilingualism is to have informants relate their life histories in the ethnic language and, after a lapse of several weeks, in

English. Bilinguals have two retrieval systems, and just as each language enables (or causes) them to perceive external reality differently, so their two retrieval systems enable (or cause) them to recall differently.

The linguistic raw material gathered in the manner described above can be analyzed and utilized in many ways. Many of the Russian-German dialects are compromise dialects. Some of these can be analyzed diachronically with methods such as the one Rein employed for Hutterite or the one I devised for the diachronic reconstruction of Palatine dialects.[7] Other dialects will be more amenable to the method employed by Reed and Seifert for Pennsylvania German. All of them will yield invaluable material—phonological, morphological, syntactic, lexical—that will broaden and deepen our understanding of the processes of linguistic change and linguistic acculturation. The insights thus obtained from the observation of living speech can be applied to the solution of linguistic phenomena far from us in time and space.

The life histories, folk tales, religious and secular verse, and other forms will be a gold mine to the ethnohistorian, the folklorist, and the student of oral literature as well as to the linguist. By having the informants relate some of their stories in English as well as in the native dialect, the field worker can simultaneously collect examples of substratum diffusion, and this will help him test the relative dominance of the two languages.

Most of what has been said about immigrant dialects applies also to the badly neglected Indian languages, all of which need further study. It will be interesting and informative to compare Indian folk tales and historical accounts recorded a generation or two ago with their present-day versions.

In highly condensed form the results of this research can be organized into a comprehensive sociolinguistic speech atlas on historical principles, which will be both a record of human experience on the Great Plains during the past century and a valuable research tool for coming generations who, linguistically homogenized, will otherwise be cut off from their cultural roots and their spiritual heritage.

NOTES

1. See "German Folklore in America: A Discussion," in *The German Language in America: A Symposium,* ed. and introd. Glenn G. Gilbert (Austin: University of Texas Press, 1971), p. 159.

2. Ibid.

3. See note 2 to the Introduction.

4. Einar Haugen, *The Norwegian Language in America,* 2d ed. (Bloomington: Indiana University Press, 1969) pp.644–53; Carroll E. Reed, *The Pennsylvania German Dialect in the Counties of Lehigh and Berks: Phonology and Morphology* (Seattle:

University of Washington Press, 1949), pp. 12–19; Lester W. Seifert, ''Wisconsin German Questionnaire,'' typescript (Madison: University of Wisconsin, 1946).

5. Einar Haugen, ''Semicommunication: The Language Gap in Scandinavia,'' in *The Ecology of Language: Essays by Einar Haugen,* sel. and introd. Anwar S. Dil (Stanford, California: Stanford University Press, 1972), p. 229; reprinted from *Social Inquiry* 36 (1966): 280–97.

6. The statement, made by Marc-Adeland Tremblay (''The Acadians of Portsmouth: A Study in Culture Change'' [Ph.D. diss., Cornell University, 1954]) is quoted here from Einar Haugen, *Bilingualism in the Americas: A Bibliography and Research Guide,* Publication of the American Dialect Society no. 26 (1956), p. 75.

7. Paul Schach, ''Zum Lautwandel im Rheinpfälzischen: die Senkung vom kurzem Vokal zu *a* vor *r*-Verbindung,'' *Zeitschrift für Mundartforschung* 26 (1958): 200–222 (plus six maps).

List of Contributors

Jan E. Bender is an assistant professor of German at Lewis and Clark College. He is affiliated with the Institut für Niederdeutsche Sprache (Bremen) and is continuing his study of the history, culture, and dialects of Low German speakers on the Great Plains.

Eileen M. Brennan is an assistant professor in the School of Social Welfare at the University of Kansas. Her major areas of interest include psycholinguistics and language attitudes, and she has published papers in these fields in *Anthropological Linguistics* and the *Journal of Psycholinguistic Research*.

Miguel A. Carranza is an assistant professor of sociology and ethnic studies at the University of Nebraska–Lincoln. His areas of specialization include sociolinguistics and Chicano studies. He has published papers in these fields in *The Bilingual Review/La Revista Bilingue* and in *Language and Speech*.

Andreas Gommermann is an associate professor of German at Creighton University. His publications deal with his ongoing study of linguistic and cultural-historical aspects of the Danube Swabians in the Midwest.

Elizabeth S. Grobsmith is an assistant professor of anthropology at the University of Nebraska–Lincoln. Her fields of specialization include bilingualism and sociolinguistics, and she has published papers in the *Plains Anthropologist* and the *Transactions of the Nebraska Academy of Sciences*.

Nils Hasselmo is a professor of Scandinavian languages and literature at the University of Minnesota. He is the author of *Amerikasvenska: En bok om språkutvecklingen i Svensk-Amerika* (1974) and *Swedish America: An Introduction* (1976) and the editor of *Perspectives of Swedish Immigration* (1978).

Einar Haugen is emeritus Victor S. Thomas Professor of Scandinavian and Linguistics at Harvard University. His publications include *The Norwegian Language in America: A Study in Bilingual Behavior* (1953; rpt. 1969), *Bilingualism in the Americas: A Bibliography and Research Guide* (1956; reprint, 1964), and *The Ecology of Language* (1972).

Folke Hedblom is emeritus assistant professor of the Royal University of Uppsala and emeritus director of the Institute of Dialect and Folklore Research. He is former ediitor of *Svenska Landsmål / Swedish Dialects and Folk Traditions* and present editor of *Saga och Sed*. His recent publications include *The Tape Recording of Dialects for Linguistic Sound Archives* (1961) and *En hälsingedialekt i Amerika: Hanebomål från Bishop Hill, Illinois* (1978), which is based on fieldwork in the United States (1962–76).

Elaine Jahner is an associate professor of English and ethnic studies at the University of Nebraska–Lincoln. Her publications are in the field of cross-cultural poetics. She is coeditor and editor, respectively, of the James R. Walker papers in two volumes, *Lakota Belief and Ritual* and *Lakota Myth* (forthcoming).

Bruce Kochis is an assistant professor of modern languages at the University of Nebraska–Lincoln. His fields of specialization are sociolinguistics, literary theory, and Russian literature. Professor Kochis is currently studying the semiotics of Czech culture in Nebraska.

Frederick C. Luebke is a professor of history at the University of Nebraska–Lincoln. He is the author of *Immigrants and Politics: The Germans of Nebraska 1880–1900* (1969) and *Bonds of Loyalty: German Americans in World War I* (1974), editor of *Ethnicity on the Great Plains* (1980), and coeditor of *The Great Plains: Environment and Culture* (1979).

Kurt Rein holds the chair of linguistics and didactics of German at the University of Munich. His publications include *Siebenbürgisch-Deutscher Sprachatlas* (1961–64) and *Religiöse Minoritätsgruppen als Sprachgemeinschaftsmodelle: Deutsche Sprachinseln täuferischen Ursprungs im Mittelwesten der Vereinigten Staaten von Amerika* (1977).

Ellen B. Ryan is chairperson and associate professor in the department of psychology at the University of Notre Dame. Her major research interests include bilingualism and psycholinguistics. She has published articles in the *Journal of Experimental Child Psychology* and the *British Journal of Social and Clinical Psychology*.

Paul Schach is Charles J. Mach Professor of Germanic Languages at the University of Nebraska–Lincoln and editor of *Scandinavian Studies*. He has published papers on German-American dialects in the United States and Germany. His research interests include bilingualism, German and Scandinavian dialectology, and the literature of medieval Germany and Scandinavia.

Donald K. Watkins is an associate professor of Germanic languages at the University of Kansas. His fields of specialization are Germanic linguistics and Scandinavian-American studies, and he has published articles on these topics in American and Scandinavian journals.

Joseph B. Wilson is an associate professor of German at Rice University. His research interests include Germanic philology, computerized lexicography, and Paleo-Indian archeology. He has published articles in *Rice University Studies, Texas Studies in Bilingualism,* and *Literatur- und Datenverarbeitung*.